Rebuilding The Reichstag

First published in the United States in 2000 by The Overlook Press, Peter Mayer Publishers, Inc. Lewis Hollow Road, Woodstock, New York 12498
www.overlookpress.com

Foster. Norman, 1935-
    Rebuiding the Reichstag / Norman Foster.
        p.   cm.
    Includes index.
    ISBN 0-87951-715-8 (hardcover)
    1. Reichstagsgebaude (Berlin, Germany) 2. Public buildings-Remodeling--Germany--Berlin. 3. Foster, Norman, 1935--Contributions in architectural remodeling. 4. Berlin (Germany)-- Buildings, structures, etc. 1. Title.
NA4415, G3B44 1999   99-33579
725'.11 '0943155--dc21   CIP

ISBN 0-87951-715-8
Designed by Mark Vernon-Jones
Typeset in Rotis Semisans
Printed and bound in Italy

Page 10-11: Norman Foster looks out onto Christo and Jeanne-Claude's 'Wrapped Reichstag' from the balcony of the former Reichstag President's Palace, July 1995.

Page 246-247: Riggers on the pediment of the Reichstag cloak the building in silver fabric, June 1995.

Author's Acknowledgement

I would like to thank my colleagues who worked with me on the Reichstag and all those people who have contributed to this book and made its realisation possible, both in the foreground and behind the scenes.

Frederick Baker, Peter Buchanan, Helmut Engel, Martin Pawley and Wilhelm Vossenkuhl have each contributed pieces of extraordinary insight and fluency, bringing to light issues and material that I could not have hoped to cover myself. The book is immeasurably richer for their input.

The photographers Rudi Meisel, Richard Bryant, Dennis Gilbert, Michael Westmoreland and Nigel Young have each added their own special interpretations of the building. Rudi especially has followed the project faithfully from the beginning and his is a unique record.

Editorially, my wife Elena has been a dedicated proof-reader and supportive critic, while David Jenkins, the book's editor, and Kenneth Powell have each spent many hours patiently reviewing manuscripts, facilitating revisions, writing captions and cross-checking documents for the record.

The book's designer, Mark Vernon-Jones, has made elegant sense of all these ingredients and we are all grateful to him.

Finally I would like to thank my publisher and friend, George Weidenfeld, for suggesting that I record the story of the project, though neither of us knew at the time that it would become such a Herculean undertaking.

Rebuilding

Norman Foster

The

Reichstag

Contributors

Martin Pawley

Helmut Engel

Peter Buchanan

Frederick Baker

Wilhelm Vossenkuhl

Editor

David Jenkins

The Overlook Press

Woodstock • New York

Contents

On 20 June 1991, after a memorable debate, the MPs of the German Bundestag voted that Berlin should once again become the capital of Germany and the seat of its reunited Parliament. On 30 October 1991 the Council of Elders decided that the new Parliament should be housed in the historical Reichstag building, which would be refurbished for the purpose. A competition for this conversion was announced in April 1992 and during an international colloquium in July 1992 various aspects of the project and specifications for the redesign were examined. After a second stage, Norman Foster won the competition in June 1993.

Over the following years, the cost of the move to Berlin and the refurbishment of the Reichstag was the subject of heated debate. Never before have architecture and art been so frequently discussed by politicians and the public. In 1995 the Reichstag disappeared beneath Christo and Jeanne-Claude's 'wrapping' and when it re-emerged two weeks later the building was seen with fresh eyes. All those who came to the city at that time, from all over the world, experienced a new, more relaxed Berlin.

Work on the Reichstag progressed rapidly under the close scrutiny of an initially sceptical but increasingly approving public and on 19 April 1999 the refurbished building became the seat of the Bundestag, the heart of our parliamentary democracy. The fact that hundreds of thousands of Berliners, as well as visitors from all over Germany, Europe and the world, have since visited the Reichstag with its impressive dome shows how attractive the architecture is to the public.

Foreword

Wolfgang Thierse
President of the German Bundestag

The symbolic value of our Parliament building has also been intensely and heatedly discussed over the last decade. To many, the building still embodies the spirit of the imperial era in its mixture of styles, from Italian Renaissance to Neo-Baroque. But art historical analysis and political comment bring one no closer to understanding the historical importance of the building. Nor do these views take into account the innovations and implications of the recent refurbishment. It is significant that the refurbishment was undertaken by a non-German who was invited, along with other leading architects, to enter the competition. The decision to choose Norman Foster demonstrates that Germany is serious in its attempts to unite Europe and its people, and sends out a signal against narrow-mindedness. The embodiment of this attitude in the refurbished Reichstag building is an encouraging sign for the future work of the German Bundestag in a united Europe.

Norman Foster has successfully connected old and new, past and present so that the new interiors of the Reichstag meet our expectations of this epic building, but are at the same time welcoming rather than forbidding. His concept of integrating a new dome and parliamentary chamber into the historic shell has created a powerful synthesis, which reflects architecturally the building's history, its present and future. Not only has Norman Foster made history visible: he has also created fitting spaces for parliamentary activity and the workings of democracy. We owe him our gratitude for his excellent work.

It is a pleasure and an honour for me to write this foreword. This book is about our Parliament, about our future and our past. It celebrates one of the most important tasks undertaken by the Bundestag during my tenure as its President; a task that stands as a tribute to a great architect and his team. In my capacity as a client of many years, I would like to express my admiration for this magnificent new building and my esteem for an individual and his creativity.

The Reichstag building has a chequered past. It has both shaped history and become history itself. It is a landmark that has suffered and survived the course of time. It was in flames at the beginning and the end of Germany's darkest years. It was marked by these flames, by wounds and distortions. It was a victim of domestic and foreign power politics. It was hated and misunderstood, and for more than four decades — nearly half its existence — it was almost forgotten. It no longer seemed important; it was simply a relic of a lost era. Time passed and attitudes changed, but because of the border hard against the building's eastern flank, a border that divided the world into two power zones, all efforts to revive the Reichstag building seemed futile.

Few people expected the Reichstag to have a future, but those who did were vindicated. Nine years ago, the collapse of the border between East and West Germany at precisely its most tangible point — close to the Reichstag and the Brandenburg Gate — suddenly brought the building back

8

Foreword

Rita Süssmuth
Former President of the German Bundestag

into the public eye, and into the hearts and minds of the people. It became important again, a symbol of central significance. Who now could be surprised that the Reichstag was chosen to be the seat of the most important institution of our community — the German Parliament?

In a world shaped less and less by national borders and more and more by internationalism, it was understandable that we should seek the very best architects from Germany and abroad to carry out the Reichstag's refurbishment. The competition organisers and jury — architects, experts, politicians — were all in agreement that art and culture have never been constrained by national frontiers. To many people the outcome of the competition must, nonetheless, have been a surprise. No one could have expected proposals from three architects from outside Germany to be joint winners. But this was exactly the right message for the building to transmit. It exemplified a spirit of openness, freedom from national boundaries, and above all the pursuit of peaceful coexistence and cooperation between nations: we and our neighbours are Europeans above all.

Jumping ahead, it seemed only logical that we should finally realise Christo and Jeanne-Claude's twenty-year quest to 'wrap' the Reichstag. The project aroused controversy among public and politicians alike but the commitment paid off. That event, I believe, made the building's transformation apparent. It was a powerful signal to Germany and the world at large.

Two years earlier the decision had been taken to commission Norman Foster to undertake the Reichstag's refurbishment. As so often with great architectural ideas, both past and present, the architect's vision at the competition stage could not be fulfilled. As a client accountable to our own rulers — the people — we were not at liberty to give the project free rein. We had to accept limitations. We also had to consider issues that were sensitive both within Germany and beyond, relating to previous abuses of the state's authority and its self-portrayal in grandiose architectural statements.

Perhaps this is not the place to record how crucial the architect's patience and willingness to listen were in achieving and implementing the final design. That is evident from the published minutes and documentation of the project's development. Many will remember the deliberations associated with the design of the cupola alone. The discussion and controversy about its shape were both logical and necessary, however, for the dome has historically been a device for the portrayal of power over people and nations. Thus it carried the risk of misinterpretation, something that had to be avoided.

Norman Foster has found a way to give this intended crown a form that has an appropriate stateliness but, by virtue of its functionality, also has a certain modesty. To allow people to climb its heights — their elected Parliament beneath them — and to encourage in them a feeling of belonging and indeed ownership, is something completely original, possibly unique. It transcends the public's conventional, regulated participation in parliamentary proceedings via the public gallery or the television screen. As a Parliament we welcome this idea and want to restrict it as little as possible, whether or not the Bundestag is in session. Never since the words *Dem Deutschen Volke* — 'To the German People' — were inscribed above the Reichstag's west portal, have they been taken so literally, although the achievement may have been hard won.

The new parliamentary chamber — its form set in spatial harmony with the cupola above, which fills it with light — is perhaps Norman Foster's greatest creative achievement within the building. It offers a new vision of democracy, the impact of which is felt both within the Reichstag and without. It has countered the chilling effect of the Reichstag's enormous mass, which was yet more forbidding than its historical associations. The architecture of power has been replaced with an architecture of openness and freedom, appropriate to our vision of Germany as a truly democratic society.

Another sensitive and illuminating idea — a *leitmotiv* which will catch the reader's attention — is the way in which previously hidden traces of the building's history have been revealed. The few surviving decorative forms from Paul Wallot's original Reichstag of a century ago have been brought to light and preserved, becoming living parts of the building. So too have the wounds that history has inflicted upon it, including the victorious inscriptions made by Soviet soldiers at the end of World War II. To read these traces of history is to unfold an important chapter in Europe's tumultuous past.

This book considers all these issues, and its illustrations speak many languages. It is both enjoyable and interesting to read and I thoroughly recommend it. Finally, I would like to thank Norman Foster for the great landmark that he has created for our reunified country.

9

Our work to transform the Reichstag into the new seat of the German Parliament is rooted in four interconnected issues: the significance of the Bundestag as one of the world's great democratic forums; a commitment to making the process of government publicly accessible; an understanding of history as a force which shapes buildings as well as the life of nations; and a passionate adherence to the low-energy, environment-friendly agenda which is fundamental to the architecture of the future.

When, in April 1992, I received the letter from the President of the German Bundestag that invited us — alongside thirteen other architects from around the world — to enter an open Reichstag competition, I was honoured but sceptical. Could a foreign architect really be given the responsibility for a task of such significance — not only national but European and international? The answer to that question was not long in coming. The first round of the competition produced three joint winners of which we were one. A second round concluded with our appointment as architects in June 1993.

Rebuilding the Reichstag became an all-consuming experience for those of us involved. It was a great privilege for my colleagues and myself to have been entrusted with that task and to have helped the Reichstag to its rebirth. That this process was followed through from start to finish with complete openness, fairness and resolution speaks more about the qualities of German society than anything that I could say on the subject.

12

Preface

Norman Foster

The building that has evolved from that process is metaphorically like the tip of an iceberg. What you cannot see is the extent of debate, the many hours in which directly or indirectly every German MP was counselled on every issue, on every decision. The former President of the Bundestag, Rita Süssmuth, played a very significant role in this process and I would like to express my gratitude to her. My special thanks must also go to Dietmar Kansy, Chairman of the Building Committee, and to Peter Conradi, a leading Committee member, whose support throughout the project was greatly appreciated.

The project is also the outcome of collaboration on an immense scale. I would like to pay tribute to the many other professionals — the young architects, the consultants, the engineers and technicians, and the 1100 workmen who assembled on site the many products from factories in Germany and elsewhere around the world.

I have described the results of our transformation as radical; where else in the world could everyone — citizens and visitors — walk through the main ceremonial entrance of their national Parliament building together with the politicians, rise to a public plaza on the roof, continue by ramps to a viewing platform, look down into the main chamber of Parliament below, or meet for a coffee or a meal?

The new cupola results from a quest for transparency and lightness as well as democracy. I believed it essential that Parliament should be open, accessible and inviting to the society that it serves. The public's access to the roof terrace and the cupola are the outcome of that philosophy, as is the fact that — light conditions permitting — you can look down into the main chamber, both from the roof and from the press lobby, and see proceedings unfolding below. All of these elements result from our quest to 'lighten' the spirit and mass of the old Reichstag. This was echoed by the architect Pi de Bruijn — a fellow finalist in the Reichstag competition — who very generously wrote to me after the opening. He said: 'I can surely appreciate the constraints that the old granite monster laid upon the design process. Yet clarity, transparency and light have come about in the corridors, the staircases, the patios ... '

The cupola is symbolic of this lightening, but it is also a physical source of daylight, a key part of our strategy for energy efficiency in the building. We have relied on natural sources of lighting and ventilation and eschewed the use of fossil fuels in our new services installations in favour of clean and renewable sources of energy: refined vegetable oils from plants that can be regrown. Not so long ago the Reichstag — like so many buildings of its age — was a vast consumer of energy, discharging 7000 tonnes of carbon dioxide, a greenhouse gas, into the atmosphere. Today, that figure has been reduced to less than 400 tonnes — a 94 per cent improvement — and the building's energy demands are so modest that it has become a net producer of energy, able to perform as a power station for the new government quarter.

Equally progressive is the attitude to history and culture that we have pursued in relation to the fabric of the building. In 1994, when we began to investigate it in earnest, the interior of the building was entirely of the 1960s. I did not know what we would find when it was stripped away. What we discovered were visible memories of the building's past — nineteenth-century mouldings, mason's marks, graffiti and the scars of war. I argued that all of these should be retained, and that the new work should be of the present, not historical pastiche. In that sense the Reichstag can be read as a city in miniature, richer because it contains layers of intervention from different ages. It is also enriched by contributions from major German and foreign artists. I have characterised the Reichstag as a 'museum of memories', but it is also an extraordinary gallery of art, a repository of works that celebrate the contemporary creative spirit, the majority of them commissioned specifically for the building. Together they represent another layer in the Reichstag's history.

Today the Reichstag functions as the democratic forum for a new nation of 80 million people. Standing in front of the Reichstag at the opening ceremony, on 19 April 1999, it was with affection, with some sadness but with delight in sharing in its symbolic process of renewal that I handed over to the new President of the Bundestag, Wolfgang Thierse, a key to the rebuilt Parliament building. This book is the outcome of that personal experience. It explores in detail the themes I have outlined above, but importantly it includes other voices and different viewpoints from my own: Frederick Baker, Peter Buchanan, Helmut Engel, Martin Pawley and Wilhelm Vossenkuhl have each contributed pieces that form 'interludes' punctuating the main narrative. Their perspectives add immensely to an understanding of the Reichstag, its place in social and architectural history, the social upheavals and personal histories to which it has formed a backdrop and the metamorphosis that it has undergone.

Alongside these contributions is the work of the photographers — Richard Bryant, Dennis Gilbert, Rudi Meisel, Michael Westmoreland, Nigel Young and others — who between them have recorded the project's progress from building site to functioning Parliament. Rudi especially has tracked the project from the beginning; his is an invaluable record, as the 'picture stories' which punctuate the book attest. All of them have my thanks and appreciation. Finally I would like to pay tribute to David Jenkins. He has been much more than an editor, guiding and shaping the book from its first concept through to final realisation with an inspired hand and a critical eye. I am deeply grateful to him.

13

The Reichstag

Almost from the beginning of its history the Reichstag has provided a popular focus — a world stage — for

as World

public events, from political demonstrations to pop concerts. The first competition scheme built

Stage

upon that tradition, placing the building at the heart of a new public forum.

Norman Foster

14   Looking at the Reichstag today, transformed and functioning as the new home of the Bundestag, it is easy to forget the process that made its realisation possible. It is tempting to imagine that as architects we summon up all our powers of analysis and persuasion and somehow, as if by magic, spirit fully formed solutions out of the air. The truth is of course quite different. Aside from the processes of consultation and patient negoti- ation that underlie any project, every new building is nourished by the fruit of past experience and the body of learning that the design team collectively carries with it. The Reichstag is no exception. Many of the ideas we progressed there — democracy and public access, an approach to historical context, attitudes towards energy and ecology, and the use of natural light — echo themes that we have explored in earlier projects and in other situations. This chapter charts that process from initial ideas to the end of the first Reichstag competition.

The first competition scheme placed the Reichstag beneath a broad oversailing roof and envisaged the building as the centre-piece of a new city quarter where social activity would have complemented the political life within.

When Germany was reunited, on 3 October 1990, the accord between the Federal Republic and the GDR agreed Berlin as the capital. There was a popular expectation that Berlin would once again become the centre of government, but the matter still had to be decided by Parliament. Less than a year later a reunited German Parliament opened the twelfth session of the Bundestag and on 20 June 1991 voted, albeit by a slender majority – 338 for Berlin, versus 320 for Bonn – that Berlin should be the seat of Parliament and government. It required a tremendous act of faith to take that step. In a further vote it was decided that the Bundestag would return to the Reichstag, the historical seat of the German Parliament.

Throughout the 1990s Berlin has been the largest building site in Europe – its skyline a riot of construction cranes and contractors' signs. It is a city that still seems to alter almost daily. I have lost count of the visits I made over the seven-year course of the Reichstag project, but I have registered the changes to the city, trip after trip, and the pace is astonishing.

Now I fly in and out of Berlin at will, but I remember flying into Tempelhof Airport in the early 1980s at the controls of a Piper Navaho, and having to ensure that I had an extra crew member on board who was familiar with the route through the narrow approach corridor. In theory at least, unidentified aircraft that strayed into GDR airspace could be summarily shot down. That was at the height of the Cold War when Germany was still divided and the city's future far from certain. Now, as

16

3

4

1
2

the capital of a reunited nation, Berlin is taking on a new significance within Europe and the Reichstag building is once again centre stage.

My first trip to Berlin, in spring 1974, was prompted by a commission from Sir Robert and Lady Sainsbury to design a building to house the extraordinary collection of art and sculpture they had donated to the University of East Anglia in Norwich. As part of our research, the Sainsburys and I visited many of the great twentieth-century museums. Our destination in Berlin was Ludwig Mies van der Rohe's magnificent New National Gallery. When one of our early presentations on the Reichstag project took place in Mies's building I recalled that first visit and the Sainsbury Centre. As with the Reichstag, openness, transparency and lightness are all fundamental to the Sainsbury Centre's design.

The Sainsbury Centre for Visual Arts was completed in 1978. The following year, we won the competition for the Hongkong and Shanghai Banking Corporation Headquarters tower in Hong Kong and for seven years that city became almost a second home. The practice's first major project, in the late 1960s, was for the Norwegian shipping line, Fred Olsen, and we had maintained an office in Oslo for several years. But it was really the Hongkong Bank that established ours as an international practice, which it has been ever since. By the time we were invited to enter the Reichstag competition, in April 1992, more than three-quarters of our work was located outside Britain.

The city and architecture of Berlin have been influential from the earliest days of the practice. 1, 2: Flying into Tempelhof Airport. 3: Mies van der Rohe's New National Gallery in Berlin was the subject of a research trip in 1974 in preparation for the design of the Sainsbury Centre for Visual Arts. 4, 5: The Sainsbury Centre for Visual Arts, completed in 1978; the themes of transparency and natural light which were central to its design are continued in the new Reichstag.

Today in our London studio you can hear perhaps 35 languages spoken. It is so cosmopolitan that I sometimes joke that it is another country. You do not need a passport to visit us but we do have our own currency — the 'Foster dollars' that we exchange at our long bar. It is also a very young office — the average age is around 30 — and there is an extraordinarily high level of motivation. The studio is open 24 hours a day, seven days a week, and you will find people working there at all hours. Two crucial characteristics of the studio and the way that we work are the democracy and freedom of communication that we enjoy. The studio has no partitions or separate rooms and meetings tend to take place informally, often around the drawing board or computer screen. And every member of the office, whatever his or her role, has an identical workspace at one of the long benches that span the width of the room.

You might describe that as 'democracy in the workplace'. It is an idea that we pioneered in many of our buildings, beginning with the Reliance Controls Factory in Swindon, which spanned the break-up of Team 4 and the formation of Foster Associates in 1967. Thirty years ago factories in Britain had a front door for the management and a back door for the shop-floor workers; the 'them and us' mentality extended into the provision of segregated canteens and the like. Reliance Controls challenged those conventions, providing integrated facilities — to unprecedented standards — for all the company's employees. We went on to work with other enlightened clients — IBM, Willis Faber & Dumas, HSBC and the

5

6

7

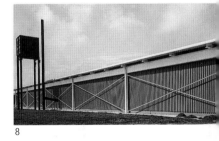
8

Commerzbank among them — who saw the irrelevance to modern business of the old ways and shared a belief that every member of staff was to be valued equally. If a factory can be a symbol of democracy, how much more significant is a parliament building? It is symptomatic of the differences between Britain and Germany that at Westminster the public queues to be let in by a side door, whereas in the Reichstag the people enter the building through the same front door as their elected representatives.

Before the Reichstag, our strongest contextual challenge came perhaps from the Carré d'Art in Nîmes, a competition we won, in 1984, to build a complex containing a museum of contemporary art and a *médiathèque*, or public library. The site faces the ancient Maison Carrée, a perfectly preserved Roman building and the source of Thomas Jefferson's inspiration as an architect. Such was the architectural power of this exquisite temple that one of our competitors proposed to place the new arts centre below ground. We chose instead to confront history head on, as we have at the Reichstag, and to design a modern building which was contextual yet declined any attempt at historicism. Significantly, one of the key themes in the Carré d'Art was the public use of the roof level. There we placed a café and terrace, which quickly became a popular vantage point with marvellous views across the old city. The same thing is happening now in Berlin, where, at the time of writing, thousands of people every day go up to the roof of the Reichstag to climb to the top of the dome or pause for coffee in the restaurant with its terrace overlooking the Brandenburg Gate.

Other early Foster projects have provided formative themes that are re-explored in the Reichstag. 6: The headquarters tower for the Hongkong and Shanghai Bank, 1979-85, opened up the ground level to provide a much used civic space. 7: The Willis Faber & Dumas building, 1970-75, pioneered the provision of workplace amenities including a roof garden on the scale of a small public park. 8: Reliance Controls, a factory project completed in 1967, abandoned traditional conventions of management versus workforce in favour of integrated, democratic facilities for all.

The design of the Sackler Galleries at the Royal Academy in London, completed in 1991, also confronted history, this time far more directly. The new galleries replaced the undistinguished nineteenth-century Diploma Galleries on the top floor of the seventeenth-century Burlington House. The scheme was not just an addition to a historical structure, but a rediscovery of the potential of Burlington House and the Victorian building behind it, much of which had become inaccessible. The solution was to peel away the redundant historical accretions and to insert a lift and staircase in the reclaimed space between the two buildings, leading to the new galleries. In the process, the Palladian facade of Burlington House was revealed to view for the first time in over a century. Cleaned and repaired it contrasts strikingly with the new insertions and the Victorian structure. Our work in the Sackler Galleries is demonstratively of its own time, using modern materials for modern ends. For me it demonstrates that contemporary interventions can enhance the old if they rely on sensitive juxtaposition rather than pastiche. In retrospect, the Royal Academy was almost a dress rehearsal for the Reichstag. It was also the first in a line of projects to demonstrate a clear philosophy about contemporary interventions in historical structures — establishing a meaningful relationship between old and new — which continues with the Great Court at the British Museum.

Contemporary with the Royal Academy was the completion of our new terminal building at Stansted, London's Third Airport. Just as we have done at the Reichstag, we used natural

9

10

11

12

light consciously as an architectural device. Our intention was to create a transparent, luminous space far removed from the strip-lit claustrophobia of many modern air terminals, and to evoke the thrill and drama of early air travel, which has become blunted in the age of the jumbo jet. Stansted's concourse is entirely daylit, illuminated from above by a system of roof-lights and reflectors. This arrangement is so effective that only on the gloomiest of days is supplementary artificial lighting required. That we could create a building that was able to reduce a reliance on artificial lighting and cut energy consumption while capturing the popular imagination was a particular satisfaction.

The year that Stansted opened to the public, 1991, also saw our success in the competition for the Commerzbank Headquarters in Frankfurt, which is now the tallest tower in Europe. It is a building in which commercial imperatives are married to strong environmental concerns. The latter have always been implicit in our architecture. They are rooted in a conviction, partly formed through my association with the late Richard Buckminster Fuller — a great friend and mentor — that the beneficial, sustainable use of technology is the only way ahead for the world. At the Commerzbank we were able to cut energy consumption to half that of a conventional building by maximising the use of daylighting and relying on systems of natural ventilation rather than wasteful air-conditioning. These ecological lessons were channelled directly into the Reichstag.

Confronting history. 9, 10: The Carré d'Art in Nîmes, 1984-93, is placed in the context of the Roman Maison Carrée. Its roof-level café — another Reichstag theme — offers spectacular views of the city. 11, 12: Two London projects, the Sackler Galleries at the Royal Academy of Arts, 1985–91 (11) and the Great Court of the British Museum, 1994-2000 (12) make contemporary interventions in historical buildings, unlocking hitherto inaccessible spaces in the process. 13: The Design Centre, Essen, Germany, 1992-94, gives new life to a redundant powerhouse.

We enjoy working in Germany, not least because of the enlightened attitudes that prevail there towards issues such as energy conservation and urban regeneration. By the early 1990s, the practice had a strong track record in Germany and a growing group of valued friends and collaborators there. At the time of the Reichstag competition we had several German construction projects, including those in Duisburg, where we formulated a regenerative masterplan and designed a series of low-energy buildings, and Essen, where we had been commissioned to convert a magnificent early twentieth-century powerhouse into a centre for industrial design. We had been successful in a number of competitions in Berlin, such as the World Trade Centre, but we had yet to realise a project there. I wanted to build in the city because it seemed to encapsulate so many of the issues that were coming to the fore in our work, not least the vital one of confronting and working with the past.

In 1991, two years after the Wall came down, we submitted an entry to the competition for a masterplan for the Potsdamer Platz-Leipziger Platz area, a key location in the reunified city. The site was a desolate no-man's-land where East and West had been held apart. We proposed a dense scheme which balanced the pressure for commercial development with the provision of new public buildings and civic spaces that responded to Berlin's future aspirations. In a way, the project underlined the need for a masterplan for the whole city, which had become so fragmented after the war.

13

14

15

16

That same year, following the removal of the Wall, we were one of a number of international firms invited by the German Architecture Museum and the *Frankfurter Allgemeine Zeitung* to submit ideas for a strategic masterplan — 'Berlin Tomorrow' — which would unify the two sectors of the city whilst respecting such issues as identity and history. In our proposals the zone occupied by the Wall became a sequence of landscaped open spaces — a linear park. The old street patterns of the two sectors were knitted together through the park to repair the original framework, while the park's edges created prime sites and frontages for redevelopment. Thus it offered a gentle reminder of the past, but also an optimistic symbol for the future. The dark history of the Berlin Wall had to be remembered, but not celebrated. It was a dilemma we were to face again at the Reichstag.

The Reichstag competition details were published on 26 June 1992 and the deadline for submissions was five months later, on 23 October. That summer I still seriously doubted whether a non-German architect could possibly get the job. Many of my colleagues were also highly sceptical. However, I felt strongly that the invitation had to be taken up. It was an opportunity to be involved with a building the transformation of which would become symbolic of the new Germany and a new Europe; and there was the possibility that our architecture could be the catalyst in that process. I began to assemble a team.

Energy and ecology have been constant concerns in the practice's work. 14: Stansted, London's Third Airport, 1981-91; the building's services are located below concourse level, freeing the roof as a transparent canopy and thus reducing reliance on artificial lighting. 15: The Commerzbank in Frankfurt, Germany, 1991-97, uses natural ventilation as part of a controlled internal climate. 16: The Business Promotion Centre, Duisburg, 1988-93; it was planned to mount photovoltaic cells on the roof to convert the sun's energy into electrical power.

Much of what the practice has achieved over the years has been the result of really first-rate teamwork and I am a firm believer in the strength of small teams. I gathered together a tight-knit group of people based in our London studio, chief amongst whom were my partner (and colleague of 23 years) David Nelson; Mark Braun, a brilliant young German architect, then only 30, who grew up in Berlin and would return there as project director to oversee construction; and Stefan Behling, another German architect, with an expertise in energy matters, who was to become the youngest Professor of Architecture at Stuttgart University. Other valued collaborators from outside the practice included Norbert Kaiser, an inspired energy specialist and our client on the early Duisburg projects; the American lighting consultants Claude and Danielle Engle; the German architect and world-famous illustrator, Helmut Jacoby; and Wilhelm Vossenkuhl, Professor of Philosophy at Munich University and a good friend of many years.

My doubts about whether or not we should enter the competition were dispelled by a meeting I had with a small group of German parliamentarians at the Press Club in Bonn in June 1992, shortly before the summer recess. The meeting had been organised by Norbert Kaiser through his contacts in EuroSolar — the European Parliamentary Committee on Energy — and its President, the German MP Hermann Scheer. I met Barbara Jakubeit, President of the *Bundesbaudirektion* (BBD), the Federal Authority which was organising the competition and was to act as the agent for the Bundestag in Berlin. (The BBD was

17

18

19

20

in fact replaced by a new agency a little more than a year later.) And I was also introduced to the SPD member, Peter Conradi, who had trained as an architect and planner and was a prominent member of the Bundestag's Building Committee. We went on to have a number of informal conversations with him as the competition progressed. He remained extremely supportive throughout the project even though he would rightly challenge us on some occasions.

I questioned this group about the Reichstag and what they thought were the key issues in rehabilitating it for the future. I asked: 'What is your new Germany going to be like? How do you feel about moving to Berlin? How should Parliament be seen in Berlin?' The strongest issue that emerged was that the building should become truly open and transparent. We were obviously thinking along similar lines. Then I asked Conradi: 'Why are you inviting foreigners to enter the competition: is it just for show, or do we have a real chance of winning? And if we win, will we get to build our scheme?' He said, 'No, it is not for show; and yes, if you win you get the job.' Seven years later, on the day of the Reichstag's opening ceremony, Conradi reminded me that at that time I had replied: 'Then we are going to win!'

I came back to London convinced that we should follow our instincts, and that if we did, we stood a very good chance. The politicians, I concluded, were genuinely searching for the right solution to rebuilding the Reichstag. The challenge of the project was now irresistible.

The Reichstag as it existed in 1992 was a forlorn relic, but it carried powerful memories of past events. 17: Berliners picnic in the Platz der Republik, 1986. 18: German reunification is celebrated in and around the Reichstag on 3 October 1990. 19: In July 1992, before work on the competition began, the Foster team explored the building for the first time. 20: Seen from the north the scars left by the Berlin Wall are still apparent. 21: Berliners gather in readiness for a firework concert given by André Heller in 1984.

We began to consider the principles that defined the project. As architects we had no preconceptions. As non-Germans — as outsiders — our job was to learn first, then to add that knowledge to the experience we had gained from previous commissions where history and modernity confront each other. To those dichotomies we added public versus private, and access versus security. The brief requested that the design should 'express the joy of communicating and a closeness to the citizen'. From the outset we were convinced that the assembly chamber should be at the heart of the rebuilt Reichstag, that it should be flooded with natural light, and be visually and physically accessible. Bringing the public into the building became our guiding principle.

Intensive research underpins almost every project we do. Our first step was to discover how the Bundestag works as an institution. Following that first meeting in Bonn, my colleagues and I flew again to Germany at the invitation of Peter Conradi and Barbara Jakubeit. We were given a detailed tour of Günter Behnisch's impressive new Bundestag building in Bonn, which was then in the process of completion, nearly twenty years after the project's inception.

The more we explored the history of the Reichstag, the more the links between architecture, politics and history became clear. In the 1920s, during the Weimar Republic, when Parliament was at last freed from imperial direction, there were suggestions that Paul Wallot's building should

be modified, stripped of its elaborate Wilhelmine decoration, or even pulled down as an unhappy relic of a past age; but the accession of the Nazis, and the infamous fire of 27 February 1933, closed that debate abruptly. It would be another 20 years before discussion of its future resumed.

After the war the Reichstag became symbolic of very different values, of West German democratic defiance in the face of a belligerent and Communist East. The battle-scarred building was reconstructed by Paul Baumgarten. Much of its fabric survived but it was inexplicably robbed of its elaborate interiors and the remaining effects of war damage were concealed beneath the lining of its new decor. Externally, its dome already gone, it was stripped of most of its ornament in an exercise that inadvertently rendered it all the more forbidding. The Reichstag nonetheless became a landmark for Berliners in both West and East, a masonry fortress on the frontier. The Wall was erected within feet of its eastern flank, and the Reichstag's survival seemed to epitomise the resilience of Berlin itself. In fact one corner of the Reichstag's eastern facade was technically on East German soil and access from the ground at that point was impossible.

For younger Berliners — in both East and West — the Reichstag was equally significant as a backdrop for rock concerts and other popular festivals. The park in front of the building has witnessed almost every major public event in post-war Berlin from protest rallies against the Soviet Blockade to the reunification celebrations and the fall of the Wall. When we embarked on the

22

23   24   25

22

competition, few Germans had any love for the Reichstag. It was a building with very mixed historical and emotional associations. For many it was a sinister presence, an isolated monument, and its rebuilding was naturally a matter of some controversy.

On 14 February 1992, the first Reichstag colloquium was held in the old building to launch the process of democratic consultation that would characterise the project. It was a lively forum, attended by some 300 people, including politicians, members of the press, historians, philosophers, and a small number of architects. It brought many issues and tensions out into the open. There were some architects present who had worked with Baumgarten and wanted the Reichstag to be preserved as it had been rebuilt in the 1960s. There was another energetic camp, led by Oscar Schneider, former Conservative (CSU) Minister of Housing and Urban Development, that argued for the Reichstag's restoration in facsimile to its pre-war condition, including Wallot's historical dome. Peter Conradi, who took part in that meeting, recalls: 'Schneider's argument was that you might alter the interior, but from outside the building should look the way it had always been. I said that was a very Conservative attitude — to have the facades right, no matter what was behind — and there was laughter of course.'

Although it drew derision, the historicist camp remained a vociferous minority. The view of the great majority, however, was that the Reichstag as it stood was unusable and its

Life in the Foster and Partners studio at Riverside Three, beside the River Thames in London. 22: Everybody in the studio works at one of the long benches that span the room. 23: The Riverside building seen from Albert Bridge. 24: The partners meet for a regular Monday morning session; from left: Spencer de Grey, Norman Foster, Barry Cooke, Ken Shuttleworth, David Nelson, partner in charge of the Reichstag project, and Graham Phillips. 25: Stefan Behling and Mark Braun (right), key members of the competition team. Mark Braun would later run the project on site in Berlin.

26

services installations were obsolete; it had to be transformed through architecture and art, so that the Bundestag could claim it as its own. It could not shed the weight of its past associations but it had to be lightened symbolically. As the competition brief put it, we had to engage with '... the changing historical fortunes of the building, its symbolic significance and future function'. Appropriately the brief went on to quote Rodin's dictum: 'An art that has life in it does not restore the works of the past: it continues them'.

I saw that the building had, metaphorically at least, to be 'blown apart' in a very novel way. Mark Braun relayed a conversation he had at the time with one of our German clients, an industrialist for whom we were building a house. He said three things about the Reichstag: 'Sell, sell, sell ... You have to work a miracle. It has to be the eighth wonder of the world'. Yet in order to achieve that we had to come to terms with the Reichstag's history.

At the heart of our thinking were four related issues: the significance of the Bundestag as one of the world's great democratic assemblies; a commitment to opening up the process of government to the public; an understanding of history as a force which shapes buildings as well as the life of nations; and a passionate adherence to the low-energy, environment-friendly agenda which is fundamental to the architecture of the future. We also took inspiration from the idea of the Reichstag as a 'world stage', a place at once both a platform and a backdrop for international political and social events.

The Foster studio in London is a place of informality and openness where discussions are as likely to focus around the drawing board or a sketchbook as they are around a formal meeting table.
26: From left, Mark Braun, David Nelson, Norman Foster and Graham Phillips.

In our first competition scheme we envisaged the old building as the centre-piece of a raised public forum which took its cue from the great popular gatherings of the recent past. This forum was sheltered beneath a broad, oversailing roof 'umbrella' which had a symbolic importance, tying together the historical and the new. We placed the Reichstag asymmetrically as just one element in a much larger urban composition in which Parliament became the generator of a new city quarter. The Reichstag's chamber would have coexisted with theatres, cinemas, galleries, bookshops, riverside cafés, nursery schools and playgroups for children, together with vast underground parking facilities, all extensive enough to serve the people of Berlin. In this way the old fabric of the Reichstag was both demystified and exalted and it became a heroic symbol — not only architecturally — of an enlightened democratic society, without any resort to historicism.

The initial brief was for 33,000 square metres of accommodation, twice the area that could reasonably be contained within the shell of the old building. There was no presumption in the competition brief that the Reichstag's interiors should be retained. Its existing spaces had little relevance to the Bundestag's requirements and so we proposed to reconstruct the building totally within its walls — creating a 'house within a house' — and to locate most of the committee rooms, restaurants, administrative and other functions of Parliament in a new podium wrapped around its base. The podium rose two

27

28

29

30

storeys to the top of the ground floor in the old building. A moat-like lightwell between the shell of the Reichstag and the podium allowed daylight into the new and the existing buildings. The lower-podium level was for cars and the upper floor was devoted to offices, with cafés and restaurants lining the river's edge. Externally it was approached by gentle ramps or the long grassy inclines which extended into the park.

The assembly chamber was located in the heart of the building, dug deep into the plinth. We retained the Reichstag's original cloister but gave it a new democratic focus to form a daylit, public ambulatory around the chamber at the upper-podium level. This route connected the main public spaces, both inside and out, and extended through to the riverside cafés and galleries. The public also had access to the roof of the Reichstag, allowing them to see down into the chamber and symbolically elevating them above their democratic representatives seated below.

The building's vast translucent canopy — 250 metres long and 160 metres wide — was as light and ethereal as the podium was heavy. It would be the new symbol of Parliament on the skyline, tying together past and present. It was also a vital element in our ecological strategy for the building, in which we aimed for energy self-sufficiency. Its photovoltaic cells harvested energy in the form of sunlight to generate electricity and it created a benign climatic zone, protecting public gatherings from the weather, while deflecting diffused natural light into the Reichstag's interiors and aiding a system of natural

In his 1960s rebuilding Paul Baumgarten created a building at odds with the logic of the original. 27: New office floors had been added; corridors were arbitrarily built across the courtyards. 28: A sketch made by Norman Foster on his first site visit in July 1992. 29: As a prelude to the competition, in June 1992 the Foster team visited Günter Behnisch's Bundestag building in Bonn, then nearly complete, where they met a group of parliamentarians. 30: President of the *Bundesbaudirektion* (BBD) Barbara Jakubeit, Peter Conradi and Etienne Borgos with Norman Foster in Bonn.

ventilation. Structurally the canopy was supported on twenty slender stainless steel columns, 50 metres high, one of which dipped its toes in the River Spree, the former border between East and West, thus acknowledging the reconciliation that had made the project possible. It was a first step in bringing the river frontage alive, creating a place where people might picnic or embark on a trip on a pleasure boat.

       This first project was as much about the public realm and the city as it was about Parliament. Even at this stage the roof level was envisaged as a public plaza with views of Parliament below and the city on the horizon. The old Reichstag assumed a subordinate role, but it was also given a new importance and a grandeur that it had previously lacked. I remember first seeing the building as it stood. It was an enormous anticlimax. It had a dramatic history, yet seemed to me a sterile hulk. The post-war reconstruction had so homogenised what survived of its original structure that you had little sense of the past. In retrospect, however, our approach then was perhaps too radical. Later, as we got to know the building better and looked beneath the lining of the 1960s interiors, we grew to understand that history still resonated through its fabric and should not be swept away. Nonetheless, our proposals, submitted in autumn 1992, touched a lot of emotions; we were aware that they were controversial, and they were certainly deeply felt.

       For three days in late January 1993, the international jury met behind closed doors in the Reichstag building. At its first meeting earlier in the month it had selected an initial 25 of the 80

31: Norman Foster and Mark Braun visit the Reichstag in spring 1995.

32

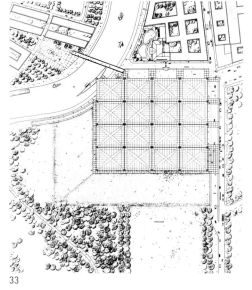

33

34

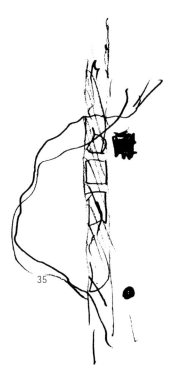

35

26

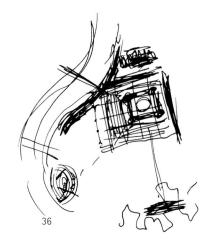

36

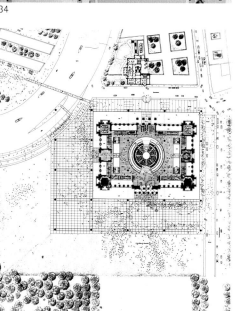

37

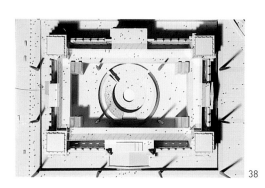

38

The first competition scheme encapsulated the Reichstag within a broad urban vision. A great oversailing roof united the composition and provided shelter for a new public forum. 32, 36: Concept sketches by Norman Foster. 33: Site plan. 34: Plan view of a model made of the first revised scheme following the announcement of the Schultes-Frank Spreebogen masterplan; the northernmost sections of the roof and podium were removed to accommodate the masterplan buildings. 35: Concept sketch of the revised arrangement. 37, 38: Plan and plan-view model of the competition scheme.

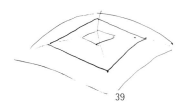

39

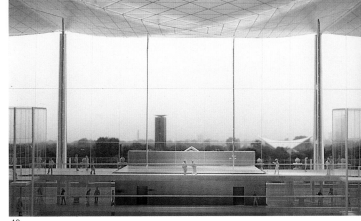

40

42

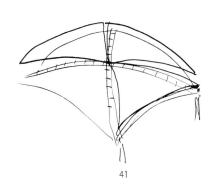

41

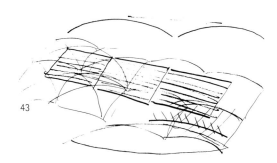

43

44

entries received. Rumours abounded as to who or what would win. On the eve of the decision Mark Braun had a call in Berlin from Michael Cullen, the Reichstag historian and a competition juror, who said, 'It looks good, it looks good'. The next morning we were given another clue, when a journalist from the *Berliner Zeitung* called to offer congratulations. Nonetheless, the *Berliner Morgenpost* of 28 January confidently reported that '... some of the more abstruse ideas, such as a Reichstag without a dome, are out of the running'.

It was not until 19 February that we finally learned that we had been awarded joint first prize in the competition, together with Pi de Bruijn from the Netherlands and Santiago Calatrava, a Spanish architect whose practice is based in Switzerland. The presumption that a non-German architect could not succeed had been turned on its head. Our scheme had won strong support from the competition jury — three-quarters of the votes cast — but the competition organisers had decided at the outset that the vote should be unanimous, hence the decision to name three winners. We had won, but the future of our project remained far from certain.

To complicate matters, while the Reichstag competition was taking place, there had been another major competition, for a masterplan for the whole of the government quarter of Berlin, located in the Spreebogen, the area formed by the bulge in the course of the River Spree north of the Reichstag. The result was announced simultaneously with that of the Reichstag competition. The winners

A public viewing platform was proposed at the roof level of the old Reichstag building, symbolically elevating the public above the heads of their elected representatives. This idea was a constant in the development of the project and would later inform the design of the cupola with its public viewing platform. 40, 42, 44: Views of the competition model. 39, 41, 43: Norman Foster's design sketches of the 'pillow' roof elements.

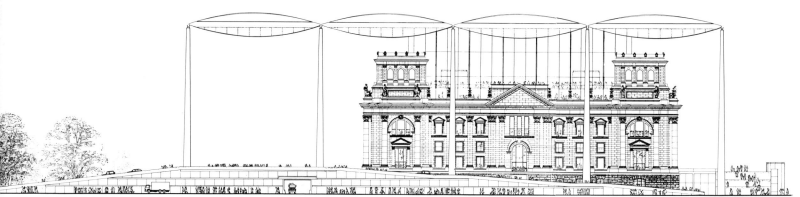

45

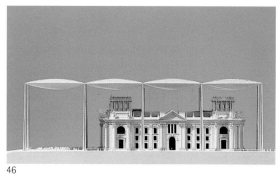 

28   A new podium was established around the walls of the old Reichstag, creating an open forum for public gatherings and setting a new datum for the principal activities within the building. 45: The south elevation. 46, 47: Two views of the model seen from the south and north. 48: East–west section through the building.

46   47

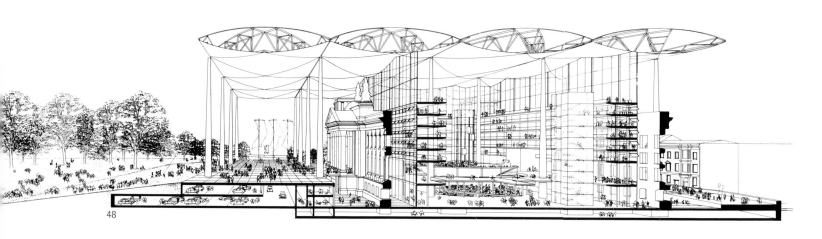

48

49

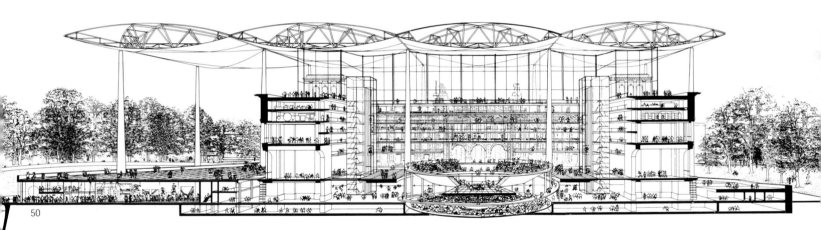

50

The 'big roof' unified the
historical and the new, and
announced the Reichstag's
transformation. 49: A view
of the sectional model looking
north into the chamber. 50: The
corresponding view in sectional
perspective. 51: Galleries and
cafés lined the river bank;
sketch by Norman Foster.

51

Reichstag

The riverside walk
galleries cafés museums bookshops
fishing pleasure boats ferries paving outdoor cafés

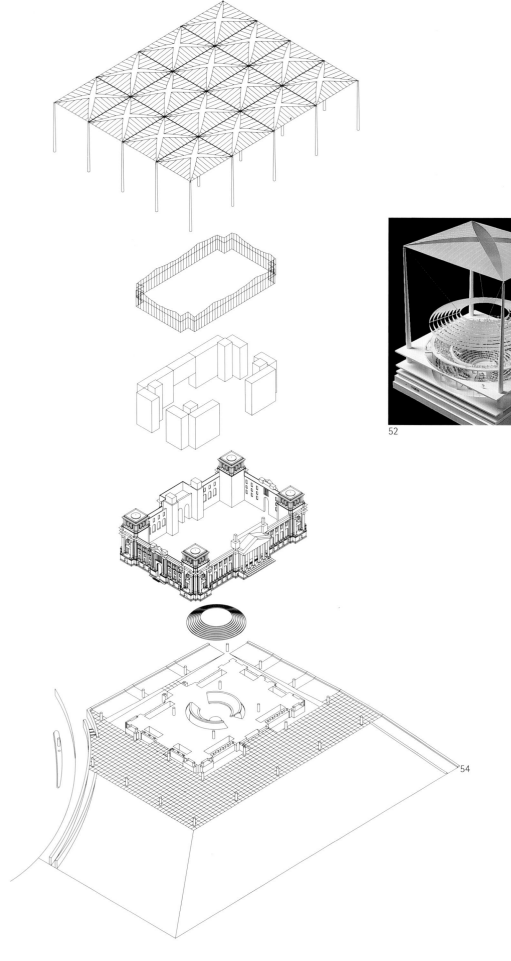

30

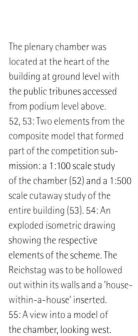

52

53

54

The plenary chamber was located at the heart of the building at ground level with the public tribunes accessed from podium level above. 52, 53: Two elements from the composite model that formed part of the competition submission: a 1:100 scale study of the chamber (52) and a 1:500 scale cutaway study of the entire building (53). 54: An exploded isometric drawing showing the respective elements of the scheme. The Reichstag was to be hollowed out within its walls and a 'house-within-a-house' inserted. 55: A view into a model of the chamber, looking west.

were the Berlin-based architects, Axel Schultes and Charlotte Frank, who proposed a linear complex of buildings which twice spanned the river, creating a 'bridge between East and West'. It was envisaged that these buildings would contain the new Chancellery and garden, and a Bundesforum open to the public, together with a library, MPs' offices and committee rooms for the political parties, and a station linking the complex to Berlin's main transport network. The most significant implication of Schultes' masterplan, from our point of view, was that much of the accommodation originally intended for the Reichstag would now be located elsewhere. It was immediately clear that when the run-off between the three finalists came it would have to be on the basis of a rewritten brief.

We discovered much later that the jury was well aware of the problem with the brief. As Peter Conradi put it, 'we had overfilled the rucksack'. The Building Committee had decided, therefore, even before the result of the competition was announced, that none of the three winning schemes would be built. What they were looking for was not a definitive proposal but the architect with the most sympathetic approach, with whom they could enter a dialogue. The three schemes were also used politically as a method of testing public reaction and there was much lobbying behind the scenes.

The economic climate in Germany was also changing for the worse and budgets were being cut. When the brief for the second round of the competition was issued, we discovered

56

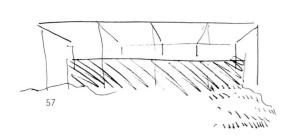

57

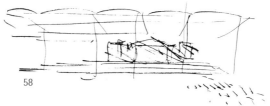

58

59

that the rules had changed dramatically. It was as if the client had originally said, 'Design me a bus for 40 people', and then found that they had to ask: 'Would you please modify your bus? Because what we actually need now is a small but very important car'. Rather than try to adapt our scheme or trim it to meet changed circumstances, however, I knew that we would have to start again, from a new beginning.

All of us involved in that scheme felt passionately about it. To abandon it seemed like an impossible decision. I could hardly contemplate a scheme that simply built within the Reichstag's existing walls. But I could feel the political pulse and I knew that the honeymoon of reunification was over. I sensed that our scheme, which might have been appropriate a year ago, might now be judged too majestic and too costly. I believed also that there was no reason why the new brief should not produce an equally compelling architectural response even if it was appropriately more modest from the outside.

My instincts were confirmed in Bonn, on 9 March 1993, when we met the President of the Bundestag, Rita Süssmuth, together with Peter Conradi and Dietmar Kansy, Chairman of the Building Committee. Their message was clear: much as they loved our scheme, Parliament required something more modest, more pragmatic, in keeping with the political mood. It was apparent that if collectively we failed, political support for the project might ebb away. It was a setback. But setbacks can be stimulating as well as frustrating, and I relished the next stage of the competition.

The 'big roof' would have become a Berlin landmark. Economic realities ruled it out, but the idea of providing a marker on the skyline informed the design of the cupola that followed. 56: Helmut Jacoby's perspective of the Reichstag. 57, 58: Designed at the same time as a house for a German client, the Reichstag's 'big roof' found an echo in its smaller counterpart. 59: The model viewed from the south-west. 60: A Norman Foster concept sketch. 61: The west elevation. 62: The Reichstag as seen from the north bank of the Spree: perhaps the most romantic image the practice has produced.

60

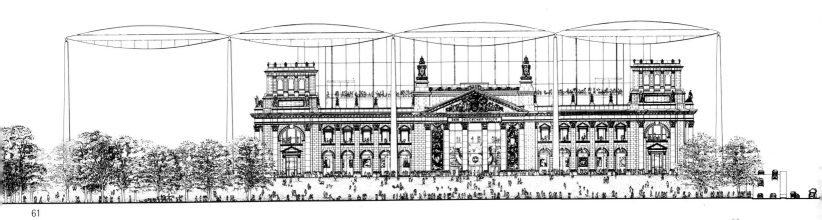

61

62

The Day Before

Rudi Meisel and Wolfgang Volz

34

Christo and Jeanne-Claude's 'Wrapped Reichstag' was the catalyst for a two-week long festival focused around the building in late June and early July 1995. From all over Germany and across Europe people came to see the Reichstag sparkling in its silver shroud. The wrapping represents a powerful catharsis in the life of the Reichstag. It seemed to rid the building of its grim historical associations and to cleanse it symbolically in readiness for the next phase of its career. At the end of the event, on 7 July, the wraps came off and the demolition men moved in. The transformation had begun.

The Rise and Fall of the Reichstag

Twice destroyed and twice restored, the Reichstag has a notorious past. But it has been dogged by misconceptions: Kaiser Wilhelm held it in contempt; Hitler never spoke there; and the Red Army mistakenly targeted it as the bastion of Nazi power. This is the secret history of the Reichstag.

Martin Pawley

36   There can be few buildings that have compressed more history or more changes of fortune into a hundred years than the Reichstag in Berlin. From its birth in a nineteenth-century architectural competition that took ten years to declare a winner, to its nadir as a bombed and burnt-out shell at the end of World War II, the image of this building symbolised German aggression in Europe. Now it has been transformed from a grim relic of those former days into a symbol of the unification not merely of Germany, but of all Europe into a democratic community of nations. Because the Reichstag is — and always has been — a symbol, its story is more than that of a building. It is also the story of democracy in Germany, a country that began the nineteenth century as a collection of 39 separate kingdoms, grand duchies, duchies and principalities, and ended it as the most powerful nation in continental Europe.

On the night of 27 February 1933, a month after Hitler became Chancellor, a fire mysteriously destroyed the Reichstag chamber and surrounding rooms. Hitler used the disaster as a pretext to attack his enemies. The Nazis have always been suspected of conspiring in the burning of the Reichstag building, but no evidence has been found to support this assumption.

The project for the construction of a German Parliament building in Berlin began with an architectural competition, announced on 16 December 1871. Democracy had come hesitantly to the former German archipelago of mini-states. Its driving force was the largest state of all, the Kingdom of Prussia, where an upper and lower house (the Herrenhaus and Abgordnetenhaus, predecessors of today's Bundesrat and Bundestag) came into being as a royal concession to the political unrest that swept through Europe in 1848 – 'the year of revolutions'. A quarter of a century later, this Prussian Parliament became the model for the Parliament of the unified states of Imperial Germany following the defeat of France in the Franco-Prussian War of 1870-71.

Inevitably the triumphalist associations of war and empire influenced the conduct of the competition and the decisions of its judges – a panel of six architects and one sculptor, heavily outnumbered by twelve Members of Parliament. While some parliamentarians called publicly for a simple, modest building, the majority saw it as an opportunity to erect a monument to German unification.

The latter sentiment certainly held sway in the press. Considerable hostility was levelled at foreign entries and a strong stylistic preference was expressed for powerful, Neo-Classical schemes redolent of Prussian assertiveness. The stylistic range of the 101 submissions ran from the Gothic Revival of George Gilbert Scott and Wilhelm Cremer to the Neo-Classical vision of the winner Ludwig

38

1

2

3

Bohnstedt. Yet even Bohnstedt fell foul of the newspapers. No sooner was the result announced, in June 1872, than the press began to attack him on the grounds that he was half Russian. This unedifying controversy ran head on into a major mishap that was to delay the building of the Reichstag for over a decade.

No doubt as a consequence of the haste with which the Imperial Parliament had been cobbled together out of the assemblies of Prussia and the smaller German states, an important detail had been neglected. The site for the new Reichstag – the Raczynski Palace and grounds at the eastern end of the Königsplatz near the Brandenburg Gate – had been selected at the very outset, when it was assumed that the owner would gladly allow it to be purchased. However, no one had told Count Raczynski of this assumption, and he only found out about it from the newspapers. Shocked at being treated in such a fashion, he announced that Parliament should not have his property until he was dead.

With the Riechstag Building Commission ready to start work, Count Raczynski's intransigence was referred to Kaiser Wilhelm I, who insisted on respecting the Count's wishes. Thus, through a scarcely credible error, the project came to a halt and the German Parliament continued to meet in its temporary home, the former Royal Prussian Porcelain Manufactory in the Leipzigerstrasse.

Count Raczynski died in 1874, but it was not until 1881 that the Kaiser was able to make an agreement with his son transferring the site to the state. By then the passions of 1872 had

Even before it was built, Germany's new Parliament was beset by a series of blunders. A competition in 1871 produced a suitable scheme, but the owner of the proposed site, Count Raczynski, refused to relinquish his property. 1: The winning scheme by Ludwig Bohnstedt. 2: George Gilbert Scott's submission, which won second prize. 3: The proposed site of the new Parliament, to the east of the Königsplatz in the Spreebogen – the bulge formed by the River Spree.

waned and support for Bohnstedt's design had evaporated. As a result the Parliamentary Committee resolved to hold a new competition, with new judges, and entry confined to German-speaking architects. With a new and simpler brief, the second Reichstag contest was announced on 2 February 1882 and closed six months later with just under 200 entries. The majority of schemes were designed in the Beaux Arts style.

This time the assessors — seven architects, one painter and thirteen Members of Parliament — operated in a less contentious atmosphere. After due deliberation they declared two first prizewinners: Paul Wallot, a little-known 41-year-old architect from Frankfurt, whose scheme would be built, and Friedrich Thiersch, a Munich-based architect whose scheme was not developed. Wallot had been a pupil of Martin Gropius — the architect responsible for adapting the Royal Prussian Porcelain Manufactory for parliamentary use and great-uncle of the celebrated Modernist. Coincidentally Wallot had also been an employee of Heinrich Strack, architect of the doomed Raczynski Palace.

Despite the embarrassment of a shared first prize, Wallot's appointment raised few objections, but his task was destined to be lengthy and onerous. The demolition of the Raczynski Palace began promptly enough in 1883 and the Reichstag's foundation stone was laid in the following year. As work progressed, however, Wallot's design began increasingly to be altered by the Kaiser and the Reichstag Building Commission until only his four corner towers remained unchanged. Aside from the loss

4

5

6

of two lightwells and the addition of a Corinthian portico facing the Königsplatz, the most contentious item was the dome, the shape and location of which were to remain bones of contention for several years.

In Wallot's original design the dome had been of stone construction, with few windows, placed towards the rear of the building above the assembly chamber. However, as a result of interference by the Building Commission and the Kaiser himself, it was moved forward to a position above the octagonal entrance hall. Wallot strenuously resisted this change, even protesting to the Kaiser in person, but to no avail. He dared not protest again until, in 1888 — the so-called 'year of three kaisers' — Wilhelm I died and his son Friedrich III, who reigned for only three months, was succeeded by the young Wilhelm II.

At the end of this episode, having bowed to the Building Commission's suggestion that the dome be made smaller and lighter in the style of a glass house, Wallot finally obtained Kaiser Wilhelm II's agreement to return the dome to its original position over the assembly. This necessitated new foundation work and left a large amount of redundant stone and brickwork behind. After this expensive change of direction, work continued until the building was officially opened in 1894, although it was to take until the end of the century to complete the interior decoration. By this time, worn out by eighteen years of interference and argument, Wallot had resigned and retreated to academic life, where he remained until his death in 1912.

With the dispute over its site unresolved, Parliament was forced to meet in a temporary home at the Royal Prussian Porcelain Manufactory. The chosen site remained unavailable for ten years, after which a new competition was launched. The winner was the Frankfurt-based architect, Paul Wallot. 4: The Royal Prussian Porcelain Manufactory on the Leipzigerstrasse. 5, 6: Wallot's drawings for the second competition in 1882 showing the east facade and a view from the south-east.

Wallot did, however, leave one legacy. He had proposed the dedication *Dem Deutschen Volke* – 'To the German People' – in huge letters beneath the west pediment. The Kaiser disdained such egalitarian sentiments, however, and it was not until 1916, in the middle of World War I, that it was belatedly inscribed as a patriotic gesture. The bronze letters themselves constituted a gesture within a gesture, cast as they were from Napoleonic cannon captured at the Battle of Leipzig a century earlier.

Between 1894 and 1914 the Reichstag served as the Imperial Parliament, a body subservient to the Kaiser but admired throughout Europe for its enlightened social legislation, initiated by Otto von Bismarck, Chancellor of Germany from the formation of the empire until 1890. However, this legislative programme itself brought to light a problem with the building that was destined to get worse. Like many public buildings subject to delays in completion, the Reichstag was already too small for its expanded functions by the time it was finished. In 1912 work began on the extension of the roof structure to form a second floor of offices, accommodating around 100 Members of Parliament.

Time, though, was running out for all the empires of Europe. The assassination of Austrian Archduke Franz Ferdinand in Sarajevo in the summer of 1914 was the spark that ignited war between the Central Powers (Germany and Austria-Hungary) and the Allied Powers (France, Russia and Britain). In Berlin, as in Paris, London and St Petersburg, the call to arms was answered with popular enthusi-

40

7

8

9

10

asm. In the Reichstag the deputies unanimously voted credits to pay for the war and granted the upper house (the Bundesrat) extraordinary wartime powers to mobilise the economy. Within a year, political power fell into the hands of the military and all consideration of the enlargement of the Reichstag ceased.

Despite the joy that greeted its declaration, World War I proved catastrophic for Germany. Its early dynamic phase soon crumbled into a struggle of attrition that lasted more than four years and destroyed all the continental empires. The Russian Empire was the first to crack, collapsing into revolution in 1917. By October 1918 Germany too was exhausted and sought peace, but the Allies refused to negotiate with the military government. Then, while the generals argued, the German High Seas Fleet mutinied and a general breakdown of military discipline began. The tremors soon reached Berlin.

On the morning of 9 November 1918 the Kaiser abdicated and fled, and the military government dissolved itself, formally surrendering its powers to the Social Democrats in the Reichstag so that talks to end the war could begin. By now the domestic situation was as bad as the military. With the Kaiser gone and the Imperial Constitution in tatters, only the Reichstag deputies stood between Germany and revolution. By midday there was a total vacuum of power. An ever-growing crowd of soldiers and armed workers gathered in the Königsplatz, blocking the main entrance to the Reichstag and demanding an immediate end to the war.

The completed Reichstag was scorned by the Kaiser as the 'Imperial ape house'. The building was intended to embody the might and unity of the new German Empire. It was loosely Italianate in style, but jumbled together elements from a wide variety of sources, including Gothic, Romanesque, Baroque and Germanic. 7: A detail of the east facade. 8: The north courtyard with a staircase inspired by a Loire chateau. 9: A detail of the Corinthian portico, a late addition to the west facade. 10: The southern entrance. 11: A view from the south-east.

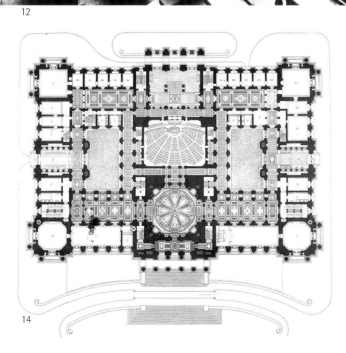

13

12

14

15

16

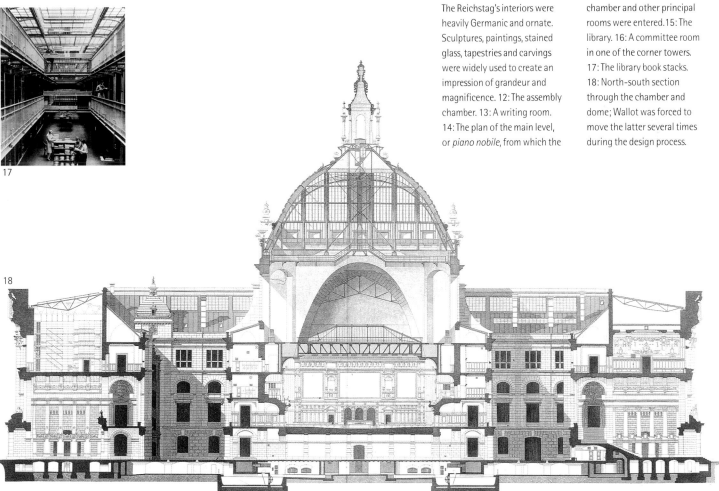

17

18

The Reichstag's interiors were heavily Germanic and ornate. Sculptures, paintings, stained glass, tapestries and carvings were widely used to create an impression of grandeur and magnificence. 12: The assembly chamber. 13: A writing room. 14: The plan of the main level, or *piano nobile*, from which the chamber and other principal rooms were entered. 15: The library. 16: A committee room in one of the corner towers. 17: The library book stacks. 18: North-south section through the chamber and dome; Wallot was forced to move the latter several times during the design process.

Inside the building, the deputies could not agree a course of action. It was only when news came that Karl Liebknecht, leader of the revolutionary Spartacus League, was marching on the Imperial Palace at the head of a group of revolutionaries, ready to declare a Bolshevik republic, that they rounded on Philipp Scheidemann, the leader of the Social Democrats, and begged him to address the crowd. Scheidemann climbed onto the parapet of a first-floor balcony and shouted an extemporised speech. He deplored the war and the rule of the Kaiser and announced the formation of a new democratic regime. His rallying cry – 'Long live the German Republic!' – was taken up by the crowd. Scheidemann was only just in time. Two hours later, from a balcony of the Imperial Palace, Liebknecht announced the birth of a Socialist republic.

The contest in Berlin between the Reichstag Republicans and the Palace Revolutionaries lasted for months, with continual street fighting between rival gangs of Social Democrats and Spartacists. It culminated in the defeat of Liebknecht's Spartacus Uprising of January 1919, a Communist attack which so nearly succeeded in taking control of the city that the Social Democrats were forced to call on units of the German Army to prevent Berlin from going the way of St Petersburg.

As it was, the Reichstag functioned only as a fortified outpost of social democracy because continuing civil disorder prevented Parliament from meeting in Berlin. Instead the new Republic's first parliamentary sessions were held in provincial Weimar. It was not, therefore, in the Reichstag

20

21

22

23

that Social Democrat chairman Friedrich Ebert was elected first President of the Republic. Nor was it there that the first coalition government was formed to pass the Weimar Constitution. Enlightened in many ways, this document called for an elected president and a single legislative parliament elected by proportional representation. Unfortunately it also conferred emergency powers on the President, enabling him to appoint a chancellor and rule by decree should Parliament be unable to form a government with a working majority.

Government or no government, post-war Germany faced enormous problems. Within a month of the Weimar Parliament's return to a Berlin pacified by the army, the Social Democrat-led coalition had lost its majority, creating a situation where more deputies opposed the new constitution than supported it. Nor did the extremist political factions of Left and Right disappear. In the wake of the suppressed street fighting there followed a series of political assassinations culminating in the murder of the Social Democrat Foreign Minister and an unsuccessful *coup d'état* in Munich led by a former soldier and right-wing demagogue, Adolf Hitler. His anti-Republican National Socialist German Workers Party – the Nazis – was destined to grow as the problems of the Republic worsened.

At the heart of Weimar Germany's difficulties was the crushing burden of reparations imposed by the Treaty of Versailles which ended World War I. The Allies were determined that Germany should pay, but with a present-day value of £130 billion the payments swiftly bankrupted the

Although it was threatened by political unrest between the wars, the Reichstag remained virtually unchanged for 40 years after its inauguration. When revolution reached Berlin in 1918, the German Republic was declared from a Reichstag balcony. In the civil disorder that followed, the building was occupied and the deputies fled to provincial Weimar, but they returned soon after and the Reichstag served as the Weimar Republic's House of Representatives for fourteen years. 19: Parliament in session in 1922. 20, 21: The members' dining room on the principal level. 22, 23: The periodicals room.

German state and led, in 1923, to a currency collapse. With the aid of debt rescheduling and American loans, a six-year period of stabilisation followed, during which the extremist political parties were held at bay and the Republican regime was able to survive. Then, in 1930, the repercussions of the Wall Street Crash dragged Germany down again as American loans were repatriated, exports collapsed and German banks began to fail.

The economic crisis soon caused unemployment to soar, and in the parliamentary elections of September 1930 all the extremist anti-Republican parties made gains at the expense of the Social Democrats, so that no workable coalition could be formed. This was the signal for the emergency powers of the Weimar Constitution to come into play. The President — by now the wartime leader Field Marshal Paul von Hindenburg had succeeded the late Friedrich Ebert — appointed his own chancellor to govern by presidential decree. A succession of presidential appointees followed over the next two years but all found it impossible to govern without parliamentary support. Meanwhile, in successive elections, the Nazis had pulled ahead of their opponents, until by the summer of 1932 they held 230 Reichstag seats, making them the largest political party, though still without an absolute majority. The Nazis' parliamentary leader, Hermann Göring, was elected President of the Reichstag in the same year.

By the end of 1932, with the Nazis in control of the Reichstag but unwilling to form a coalition government, and the President unwilling to install Hitler as Chancellor, only frantic poli-

24

25

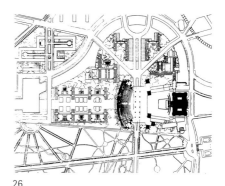

26

ticking could produce a solution. Finally, on 30 January 1933, the President found a compromise. He appointed Hitler Chancellor together with his favourite, Franz von Papen, as Deputy Chancellor, under the misapprehension that the latter would be able to restrain the former. Inevitably the reverse occurred. Notwithstanding the proposals he laid before President Hindenburg, Hitler had no intention of trying to form another parliamentary coalition. Instead he planned to become President himself.

Contrary to popular belief, Hitler never spoke in the Reichstag. He visited the building only once, deriding it as an 'old shack' that had cost less to build than a single battleship. Mysteriously, on the night of 27 February 1933, only one month after Hitler's elevation to the chancellorship, the Reichstag building was severely damaged by fire. Less than 40 years after its completion the building had suffered the second disastrous setback in its history.

Although it was widely believed then and afterwards that the Nazis had connived in the burning of the Reichstag in order to justify the wholesale arrest of Communist deputies that followed, there remains a lack of corroborating evidence. Historians consider it more likely that the Dutch 'vagrant', Martinus van der Lubbe, who was arrested inside the building on the night of the fire, did the deed for reasons of his own. Whatever the truth of the matter the plenary chamber was destroyed and the building rendered unusable. From 1933 until Hitler's death the deputies met — increasingly infrequently — in the

Even when newly completed the Reichstag was too small for its purpose. An extra floor of offices was added in 1912, but by the 1920s more space was required. Competitions for the extension of the Reichstag were held in 1927 and 1929, but the first was inconclusive and the second was derailed by the repercussions of the Wall Street Crash. 24: A drawing by Peter Behrens for the 1929 competition. 25: Hans Poelzig's scheme of 1929. 26: Hugo Haring's proposal for the 1929 competition.

nearby Kroll Opera House. It was there, and not in the Reichstag, that on 23 March 1933 the deputies passed, by a two-thirds majority, the Enabling Act that conferred dictatorial powers upon Chancellor Hitler.

During the Weimar years much thought had been given to the Reichstag's future. In 1927, an architectural competition was held for the extension of the library and members' office areas. No first prize was awarded and the judges concluded that the project should include the redesign of the Reichstag's surroundings. A second competition was held in 1929, this time with the object of creating a larger government quarter around the building. Several of the Republic's leading modern architects, including Peter Behrens and Bruno Taut, rebelled against this glorification of a Wilhelmine relic and proposed to disguise the building by wrapping it in 'modern functional architecture', while Karl Wach went even further, proposing to enclose it inside a large box – ideas that were to emerge in a more serious vein 60 years later.

In 1930, when the competition entries were put on display, two projects excited particular interest. Hans Poelzig proposed a complex of buildings north of the Reichstag in the bulge formed by the bend of the Spree and a new north-south axis connecting the Potsdamerplatz with the Platz der Republik (as the Königsplatz had been renamed) to improve access. In a similar vein Hugo Haring called for the erection of an enormous tribune in front of the Reichstag, creating an arena for public meetings. Behind this tribune Haring proposed an avenue of eight towers to house the various government ministries.

27

28

29

30

But, as in 1912, the course of history ensured that all these suggestions came to naught. With the collapse of the last parliamentary coalition in 1930, Germany entered another period of acute political and economic crisis and public building projects were put aside. Nonetheless the principle of integrating the Reichstag into a larger political complex was not forgotten; it was soon to surface again, even more powerfully, in Albert Speer's plan for the rebuilding of Berlin as 'Germania', upon which work began in 1937 and continued until resources were diverted to the war effort in 1941.

Strongly influenced by Hitler's own architectural ideas, the Speer plan retained a repaired Reichstag, not as a parliament building but as a parliamentary library and monument to the German unification of 1871. He placed at right angles to the Reichstag, held at a distance by two vast projecting colonnades, a tremendous 290-metre-diameter dome set on a massive square base. This monstrous ceremonial structure was intended to accommodate an audience of 180,000 people and, by its sheer size, it clearly solved the problem of the Reichstag's isolation at a stroke, albeit by dwarfing it in the process. Awaiting in vain its incorporation into this grandiloquent scheme, the Reichstag – patched up and made watertight, but without its chamber – was used by the Nazis as a venue for anti-Jewish and anti-Bolshevik exhibitions. Finally, as Germany again descended into total war, it was pressed into service as a temporary maternity hospital and military medical archive.

During the 1920s the National Socialists gradually gained ground in Parliament, exploiting the Social Democrat coalition's inability to resolve Germany's crippling economic problems. By 1932 the Nazis were the largest political party and in January 1933, President Hindenburg reluctantly appointed Hitler Chancellor. 27: Nazi MPs entering the Reichstag after the 1932 elections. 28: Nazi Brownshirts in the Reichstag. 29: Joseph Goebbels in the Reichstag after a Brownshirt walk-out on 9 February 1931. 30: Chancellor Hitler greeting President Hindenburg, 1933.

31

48

32

34

35

33

On the night of 27 February 1933 a fire was started at the Reichstag. A Dutch 'vagrant', Martinus van der Lubbe, was arrested in the building and confessed to the crime, but maintained that he had acted alone. However, Nazi leaders claimed that the fire was the start of a left-wing uprising and arrested prominent Communists. 31, 32: The burnt-out chamber and octagonal hall. 33: Flames still engulf the dome the morning after the fire began. 34, 35: The trial of van der Lubbe. 36: The void beneath the dome; the chamber's glass ceiling has twisted and collapsed.

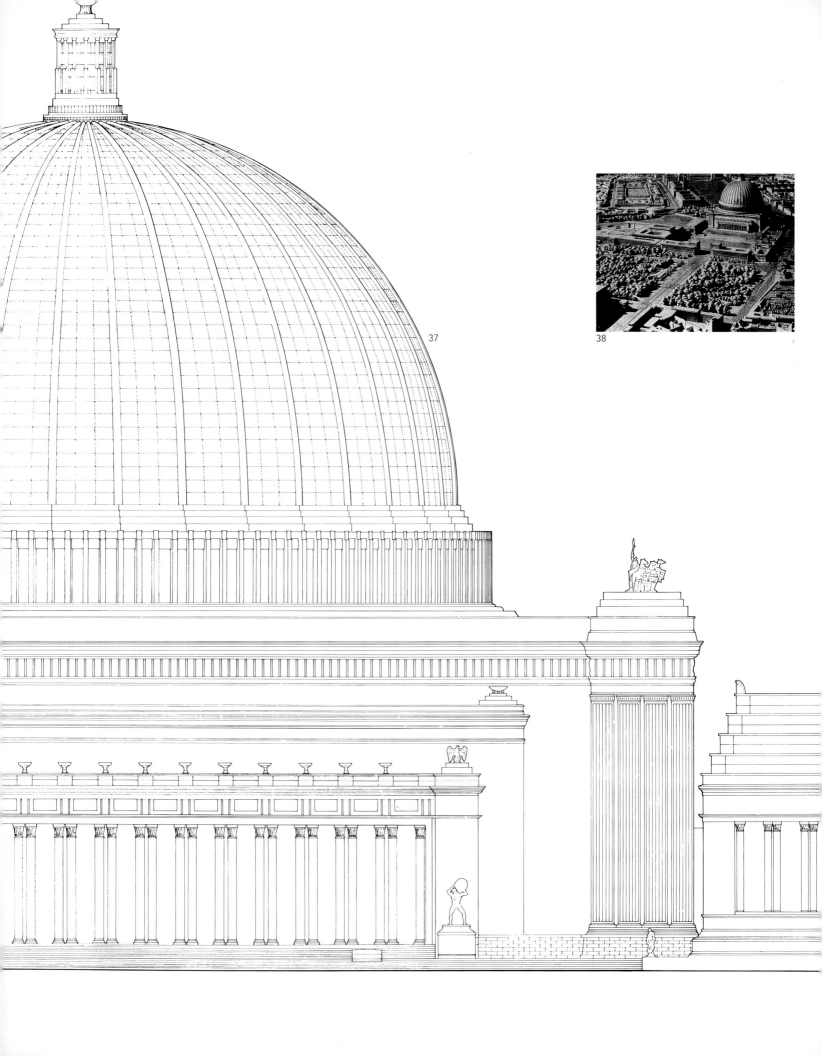

37

38

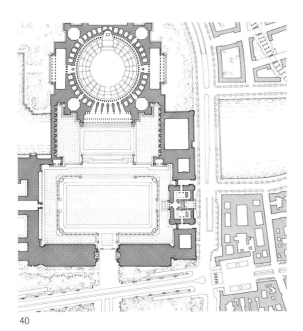

40

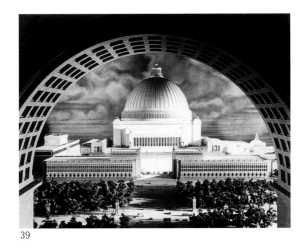

39

After the fire, the Reichstag featured in Hitler's plans as a parliamentary library, subservient to an enormous new *Grosse Halle* — an assembly hall for 180,000 people that formed the centre-piece of Albert Speer's grandiose scheme for the rebuilding of Berlin as 'Germania'. 37: A drawing of Speer's scheme, showing the Reichstag dwarfed by the vast assembly hall. 38, 39: Two views of Speer's model; the Reichstag is set at right angles to the *Grosse Halle*, to the east. 40: The plan of the Speer scheme; the Reichstag would have fitted three times beneath the dome of Speer's great hall.

51

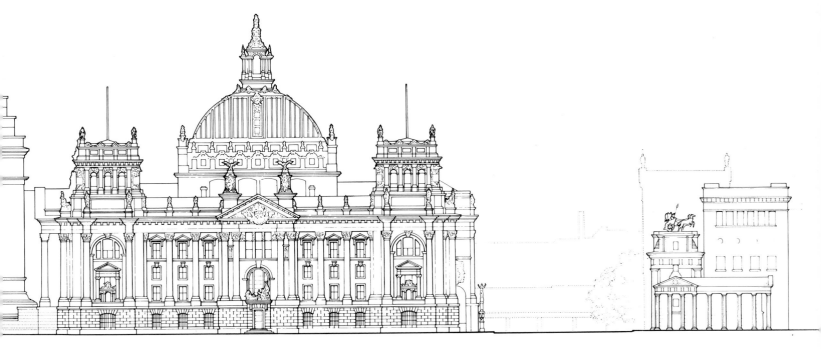

Following heavy air raids in the autumn of 1940, the Reichstag's corner towers were equipped with anti-aircraft guns in early 1941 and its windows were bricked up to save the interior from blast damage, leaving only loopholes to admit light. Then, in March 1945, as part of the defence of the city, the building was designated a strongpoint in fortress zone *Zitadelle* which included all the main government buildings. The troops responsible for the defence of the *Zitadelle* were chosen from crack elements of foreign SS divisions formed to fight with the Germans in Russia, the Reichstag garrison being composed of remnants of the Belgian Walloon Division — desperate men whose homeland had already been liberated by the Allies, and who could be counted on to fight to the death.

By April 1945 the Red Army advancing from the east had crossed the Oder and fought its way into the outskirts of Berlin. At the end of the month Marshal Zhukov was so close to the *Zitadelle* complex that he could target his guns on the Reichstag from the western edge of the Tiergarten only two miles away. The effects of artillery fire combined with bomb damage to remove most of the detail from the building's elevations, leaving it a barely recognisable hulk. There was more to come, however, for a full-scale Soviet infantry assault would be required before the Reichstag's defenders would submit.

The final act was not long delayed. At noon on 30 April, Red victory banners were handed out to assault units of the Russian 3rd Shock Army. Following a prolonged barrage of heavy

52

41

42

43

artillery, tank and rocket fire, small teams closed in on the battered building and wormed their way in through breaches in its walls. By 2.15pm Sergeants Yegorov and Kantariya were able to wave a Red Flag from a window on the second floor but even at 10.50pm, when, according to Stalin's official version of events, a larger victory banner was raised on the roof, there were still defenders holding out in the basement. These were not silenced until the afternoon of 2 May.

Thus came and went the greatest disaster in the history of the Reichstag. Yet the building was still not destroyed. The moment of victory immortalised in Yevgeny Khaldei's celebrated photograph of the Red Flag being raised at the nadir of the building's fortunes also recorded its survival as a symbol that would etch itself into the popular imagination. The Russians were not mistaken in attaching great importance to its capture. Stalin had been a revolutionary in 1917 and his armies of 1945 were the children of that revolution. For them the Reichstag was the obstacle that had prevented Red revolution in Germany. It was a place of martyrdom, forever connected with the arrest, imprisonment and death of the Communist deputies after the fire of 1933; and beyond that it was the nominal home of the German politicians of the Hitler years who willingly supported the savage invasion of the Soviet Union in 1941.

Two months after the German surrender, when US and British troops finally joined the Russians in Berlin, a reporter from *Newsweek* watched with curiosity as lines of Soviet NCOs

With its chamber destroyed, the Reichstag served a series of increasingly ignominious functions. Abandoned by the Nazi regime, which met elsewhere, the building was patchily restored to house propaganda exhibitions before being bombarded during World War II. 41: A Nazi-era postcard showing the Kroll Opera, where Parliament met after the fire. 42: An image from the exhibition 'The Eternal Jew', staged in the Reichstag. 43: The opening of the exhibition 'The Bolshevik Terror' in 1937. 44: British troops take a tea break outside the war-scarred Reichstag in June 1945.

45

47

46

48

50

51

49

The Reichstag provoked much
discussion during the 1940s
and '50s because it was one of
the few Berlin monuments to
have survived the war. In 1954
it was decided to make the
building safe by demolishing
its dome. Dynamite had been
banned in Berlin so a thermal
agent, Thermite, was used in
a process that can be thought
of as 'reverse welding'. 45–48:
Perching 70 metres above the
ground, workers laced two-
metre lengths of Thermite
through the frame. The
Thermite was then electrically
detonated. 49–51: The
Thermite begins to cut
through the frame.

53

52

54

55

56

At a first attempt on 23 October 1954, the steel frame proved unexpectedly resilient; cold weather prevented the Thermite from taking effect as anticipated. A second attempt on 22 November was required to destroy the dome. The heavy steel construction collapsed within 45 seconds. 52: Berliners look on as the dome finally crumples. 53: The remains of the collapsed dome in the Reichstag chamber. 54-57: The dome caves in.

57

removed their boots and formed human pyramids to inscribe graffiti higher and higher on the Reichstag's great columns and across its walls. He remarked on the Russians' lack of interest in less badly damaged buildings such as Hitler's still-intact Chancellery. For the Russians the conquest of the Reichstag had become symbolic of recent victory as well as past defeat.

After 1945 – the year German historians call *Stunde Null* or 'Hour Zero' – the Reichstag lay in ruins. It was derelict when the Iron Curtain came down and Berlin was divided into separate occupation zones – French, British, American and Russian – and remained so when the Berlin Airlift defeated a Soviet effort to starve out West Berlin. It was still an empty shell when the Cold War led to the creation of two rival German states, with the Western capital removed to the distant city of Bonn.

It was not until 1954 that clearing up operations began. In that year the skeleton of the dome was demolished. In 1957 work began on restoring the building envelope. However, another upheaval was about to begin. In the early morning of 13 August 1961, the East German Government, exasperated by its continual loss of population to the West through Berlin – 4.4 million people since 1945 – abruptly closed all crossing points from the Soviet zone and began to construct a 46 kilometre barrier dividing the city. That was followed by a 160 kilometre concrete wall which isolated the whole of West Berlin. The Reichstag was once again on the front line, on the very edge of this jagged border between East and West.

56

58

59

60

61

In the shadow of these events the architect Paul Baumgarten was commissioned to refurbish the shattered Reichstag and – in a brave affirmation of faith in eventual reunification – construct an assembly large enough to house all the deputies from the Federal Republic in addition to the 22 elected in West Berlin. His work began with the removal of massive quantities of masonry to clear spaces that in some cases had been unusable for nearly 30 years. The building also underwent a major external restoration, with the removal of any statuary which had not been obliterated in the war. Baumgarten's remodelling was a wholesale modernisation with little concession to the Reichstag's historical shell.

In 1971, with the acceptance of the Quadripartite Agreement by the Allied Powers in Berlin, the Soviet Union recognised ties between the Federal Republic and West Berlin and agreed to ease access to the city provided that no further plenary sessions of the Bundestag took place there (only one such meeting had been held, and not in the Reichstag building). In that year too came the first proposal by the Bulgarian artist Christo to 'wrap' the Reichstag. For the next eighteen years the building served as an occasional venue for political committees and non-governmental organisations, and became the home of a museum of modern German history that attracted half a million visitors a year.

A new era for the Reichstag lay in wait, however. In 1989 political disturbances reverberated throughout Eastern Europe and the whole mechanism of the post-war Soviet Empire

In 1957 plans were proposed to rebuild the Reichstag to house an all-German Parliament in the event of reunification. Architect Paul Baumgarten won the competition to carry out the work in 1961. His austere building opened in 1971 but the political climate of the Cold War meant that it was not used for its proposed function for 29 years. 58: Baumgarten, centre, and West German politicians with a model for the Reichstag. 59: Workers posing in front of the facade, which was restored before the rest of the building in 1957. 60: A stone-mason works on the restoration. 61: The chamber in 1971.

began to self-destruct. In Berlin the East German regime became less exigent; in the West, open-air concerts were held in the Platz der Republik, their sound systems directed over the Wall at young East Germans. The Soviet leader Mikhail Gorbachev held talks with the West German Chancellor, Helmut Kohl, and toured the capitals of Europe, drawing massive crowds. In November the Berlin Wall was torn down and the road to German reunification, which had seemed closed indefinitely, suddenly opened up. One year later all remaining barriers between East and West were removed. In one euphoric moment Germany was reunited.

In the aftermath of reunification came the inevitable question: should Parliament move to Berlin, or should it remain in Bonn where it had operated effectively since 1949, and where a new parliament building had just been completed? In a close vote in 1991 the Bundestag decided in favour of Berlin; but if Berlin then where should the Parliament be housed? The Reichstag building was an obvious location. Then as throughout its history the building was there: needed but unwanted; available yet unsuitable; historical and yet, as it were, tainted by its own history.

Another close vote in the Bundestag determined that an architectural competition should explore how the Reichstag might be adapted to serve once more as the seat of German Parliament. The competition was open to all German architects together with fourteen invited foreigners. In the event the entry was comparatively small; the brief was requested by 300 German architects but only 80

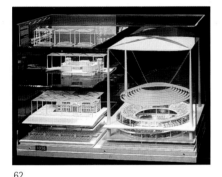

62

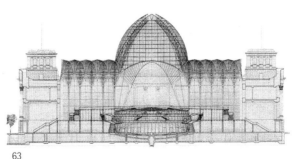

63

64

proposals were submitted. The results reflected a perhaps understandable native reluctance to engage with such a historically problematic building. In the end, three foreign architects — Norman Foster, Pi de Bruijn and Santiago Calatrava — shared the first prize. In the subsequent run-off, the brief was changed and the scale of the project dramatically reduced, and Foster won the second-stage competition.

Foster's appointment in June 1993 almost marks the end of the story of the old Reichstag, but not quite. There remained one outstanding issue from the Cold War years: the wrapping by Christo and Jeanne-Claude. This abstract 'memorial to democracy' for which the artist, with his customary pertinacity, had argued over the preceding quarter of a century, became a reality in the summer of 1995. That event was in its own way as extraordinary as any other episode in the history of this epic building. For just over two weeks in June and July, the still domeless shape of the Reichstag was concealed beneath a vast glistening cloak of silver polypropylene fabric, secured with blue ropes, producing an effect that Christo likened to 'the frosted metal of automobiles'.

Berliners, of course, came to look at this strange phenomenon; but from all over Germany too, visitors descended upon the Platz der Republik to marvel at this strangely demythologised landmark. It was a catharsis. By the time the huge strips of fabric were removed and this strange interlude came to an end, the Reichstag seemed to have recovered its innocence. Its transformation had begun.

In 1992 a competition for rebuilding the Reichstag was announced. Three non-German architects won joint first prize and Norman Foster won the run-off in June the following year. 62: Norman Foster's prizewinning proposals for the first competition. 63: Santiago Calatrava's four-sided homage to the historical Reichstag dome. 64: Pi de Bruijn's submission with its related ancillary structures.

Destruction and Preservation

Rudi Meisel

DEM DEUTSCHEN VOLKE

The first step, before the process of transformation could begin, was to strip the building of its 1960s structural interventions, while preserving what remained of the nineteenth-century fabric. At the heart of the building a Japanese 'masonry muncher', with a 43-metre boom, steadily consumed great swathes of concrete in its steel jaws. Around it, smaller machines nibbled away delicately, bringing the structure of Wallot's building to light. Meanwhile, in the recesses of the building, specialist conservators worked to protect historical wall surfaces and the graffiti that covered them.

Chapter 1

Architecture

The scarred and graffiti-marked fabric of the Reichstag bears the imprint of time and events in a palpable

and

way. It is more evocative than any exhibition. Preserving these scars allows it to stand

History

as a living museum of German history for future generations.

Norman Foster

60   When the second stage of the Reichstag competition came, in March 1993, the political mood was very much 'the morning after the night before'. The cost of moving the seat of government from Bonn to Berlin had begun to spiral and belts were being tightened as the wider economic realities of reunification dawned. To win, I knew that our scheme would have to be affordable and that our ideas would be subject to close financial scrutiny. It was apparent that only a scheme which worked within the walls of the old Reichstag would be viable. The subsequent loss of the 'big roof' was a disappointment, but the ideas behind it — a strong ecological agenda, the use of daylight, a commitment to transparency and public accessibility — remained paramount. Together with a growing understanding of the Reichstag's history, these ideas would go on to inform the design of our new proposals. This chapter charts that evolutionary process.

Seen at night, the Reichstag becomes transparent. Approaching from the west, visitors see through the entrance hall and the chamber to the eastern lobby beyond. The lightness of the new stands in stark contrast to the heaviness of the old.

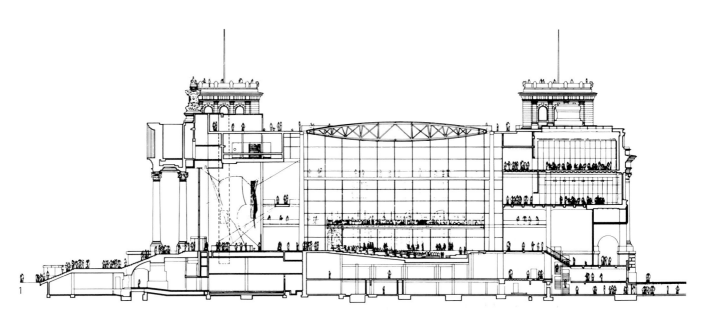

1

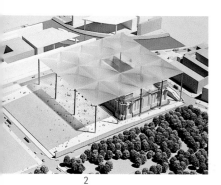

2

3

4

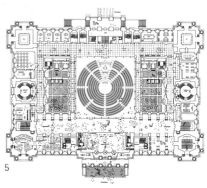

5

On 12 March 1993 a second, two-day, public colloquium began in the Reichstag building. It was a key moment in the course of the competition, an opportunity for its supporters, led by Rita Süssmuth, to reassert publicly their commitment to rebuilding the Reichstag and to bring the decision-making process out into the open. A substantial group of MPs attended and Rita Süssmuth and Professor Karl-Josef Schattner (Chairman of the first stage competition jury) presided. The Schultes-Frank masterplan proposals were on display, together with models of the three prizewinning schemes, and a maquette of Christo and Jeanne-Claude's 'Wrapped Reichstag' proposal, which was about to be realised after more than twenty years of debate.

It had been decided that each architect would make a short presentation. In anticipation of that, and any formal request for changes, we had begun to look at options for reducing the 'big roof', adapting it to fit the Schultes-Frank masterplan. We wanted to demonstrate that we could respond quickly to new requirements or new thinking. The roof in the first stage of the competition comprised four bays of four 'pillows', each measuring 50 x 40 metres. We began by eliminating one bay on the northern edge and studying the effects of that; and then we investigated how it might work as just a single pillow over the chamber itself, without sacrificing the basic principles of the scheme. However, I left the colloquium convinced that a more radical solution was required.

In the wake of the first stage of the competition it became clear that the 'big roof' was no longer viable. 2: The first option was to reduce the roof and podium on their northern edge adjacent to the Schultes-Frank masterplan buildings. 1, 3-5: In the second round of the competition, four 'variations on a theme' were presented. These ranged from modest renovation to full-scale rebuilding. The raised roof element was temporarily absent, reduced to a single glazed 'pillow' above the chamber. It was this scheme that led to Foster's appointment as architect in June 1993.

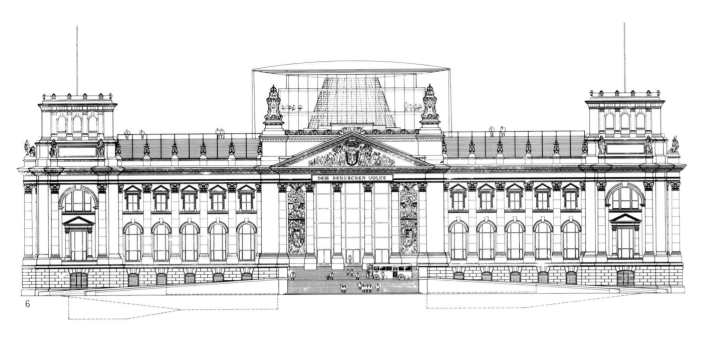

6

7

8

In January 1994, as the scheme developed following the competition, alternative solutions for the roof level were explored which reintroduced a marker on the skyline. 6, 7: The introduction of a conical lantern above the chamber brought with it the idea of a viewing platform with 'pillow' structure roof above, combined with a public restaurant located directly above the chamber. 8: The scheme was revised in April 1994, losing the restaurant but retaining the viewing platform. 9: The first incarnation of the 'lighthouse', which provided a powerful marker on the skyline.

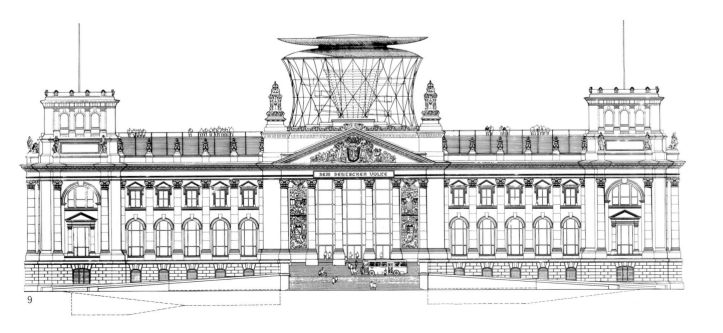

9

It was not until the end of April 1993 – a year after the original competition was announced – that the extent of that rethinking became clear. At a Building Committee meeting in Bonn we were told that the net accommodation required was to be cut by around 60 per cent, from 33,000 square metres to between 9,000 and 12,000 square metres. The existing floor area of the building was approximately 17,000 square metres, so we had gone from 'overfilling the rucksack' to practically emptying it out.

All three winners were asked to submit revised proposals in line with this new brief, but nobody seemed to have a clear idea of a submission date. I was asked how long it would take us to revise our scheme. So I said, 'It takes as long as you want it to take: six days, six weeks, or six months – let's say six weeks', and everyone agreed. I also discovered that although there was a new brief, there was still no agreed budget. However, it was clear to me – if not to our competitors – that each of us would have to cut our cloth dramatically. Our first competition scheme was no longer appropriate. At the time it was hard to lose the 'big roof', but in retrospect it set the agenda for the project that followed. There was a strong element of continuity. Firstly, there was our energy strategy, supported by the enlightened approach embodied in German legislation. Secondly, there was an interest in natural light, a concern which has characterised our work over many years. Thirdly, there was a commitment to public access and the intention to create a transparent, democratic building. These ideas became inspirational as we focused on our new submission.

10

11

12

13

While this process was unfolding, a core group of Building Committee members, led by Rita Süssmuth, visited completed projects by each of the competitors. Peter Conradi had commented sardonically that 'this is going to be more serious than a marriage ... if we want to cooperate with one of these architects, we really have to get to know him.' Having visited de Bruijn, they came to London on 14 June. They would visit Calatrava the following day. They went first to the Royal Academy to look at the Sackler Galleries. Mark Braun and I met them and introduced them to our former client, Sir Roger de Grey, who led them on a tour of the building. The visit over, we invited them back to the studio to get a feel for the way that we worked. It was not clear quite what the correct protocol was, but we assumed that elaborate hospitality would be inappropriate, so we had drinks, and they seemed to enjoy their visit. I remember being struck by their energy and enthusiasm, even at the end of a gruelling day. I heard later that they too had been impressed, not only by 'British understatement', but by the fact that our studio was still buzzing with activity very late into the evening. Conradi recalls sitting with Rita Süssmuth at the end of their tour on the flight back to Bonn and her saying: 'I think we should take the Englishman.'

The key presentation took place three days later on 17 June, in the Bundestag in Bonn, to a committee of 70 people. We reached the Parliament building at the same time as Calatrava and his team. To my amazement, as Calatrava stepped out of his car, so too did Michael Cullen. As

The competition won, Foster and Partners established a studio in Berlin located in the former ballroom of a building on Ebertstrasse. 10,11: The Reichstag team, then fifteen strong, in the Ebertstrasse office. 12: Norman Foster breaks a meeting to take a telephone call. 13-15: Design crits take place in the Berlin studio in October 1995. 16: Lighting consultant Claude Engle discusses the detailed design of the lantern. 17: Design issues raised in the studio are resolved on site in the stripped-out building.

a competition juror, Cullen was an influential lobbyist behind the scenes. He had approached us during the first stage of the competition and had visited the studio in London in July 1992. He had been full of enthusiasm and had offered his services, but I declined. So I was a little taken aback to see that he had switched sides. As it transpired, I need not have worried.

By chance we were the last to present, after de Bruijn and Calatrava, both of whom had produced elaborate models and drawings which were still on view. De Bruijn had modified his scheme, bringing the chamber back inside the building, but Calatrava's scheme was effectively unchanged. Neither architect seemed to have caught the mood of the meeting. Calatrava, it seemed, had focused on symbolism and grandeur which did not go down well.

Instinctively at that point I felt it was important to remove the symbolic 'charge' from our proposals and to focus instead on democracy and the fine print of function, structure, and economics. We opted for a very simple approach, using diagrams and drawings mounted on A0-size boards. Some diagrams were done on the spot. I remember at the last minute writing out the key issues as I saw them: 'Parliament', 'History', 'Economics', 'Energy and Ecology'.

Our research had been very thorough: we had made comparative studies, showing our Reichstag chamber in relation to major parliament buildings from around the world, and had

14

15

16

17

made a detailed study of German parliamentary procedure — so much so that we knew what went on behind the scenes in the Bundestag better than many of its members. We presented the committee with a 'year in the life of the Reichstag' — the cycle of meetings and exchanges, what was happening behind the scenes, the hidden part of the iceberg of which the public, and even the politicians, routinely saw only the tip.

By the time we presented, we had defined a different brief to the one we had been given. It was clear to us that there was space to spare, since the new brief demanded only a fraction of what potentially would go into the container of the old building. We were convinced that certain functions, including the division rooms used by the various political parties — or 'factions' — should be housed in the Reichstag itself and not located in neighbouring buildings as they are in Bonn. There is a ritual on Tuesday afternoons when each of the parliamentary parties convenes, and press and television reporters attend. And so it was natural that we should also include a press lobby and bar in the building where reporters and politicians could meet. With Parliament sitting for only 23 weeks in the year, we wanted to give the building a social life of its own outside parliamentary sessions, but the case had to be argued.

We offered a series of options — four variations on a theme — for rebuilding within the existing walls of the Reichstag and we had costed each of them. At the second colloquium some politicians had advocated patching up the building and using it as it stood. Wolfgang Schäuble, former

18

66 The Reichstag as it stood in 1992, when the Foster team first visited it. There was no sense of the building's history or any connection between inside and outside. Paul Baumgarten's reconstruction in the 1960s had scooped out the remains of Wallot's nineteenth-century interiors and concealed the Reichstag's scars beneath a uniform lining of plasterboard. 18: The first formal session of the Bundestag to be held in Baumgarten's chamber was convened on 4 October 1990 to celebrate German reunification.
19: The second-floor corridor in the east wing. 20: A north-south section through Baumgarten's chamber.

19

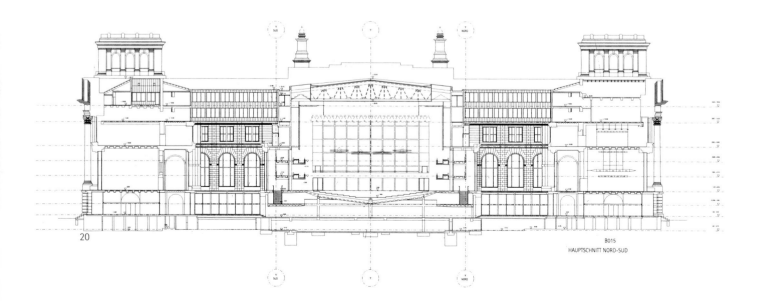

20

B015
HAUPTSCHNITT NORD-SUD

21, 22: Visitors and Members of Parliament throng in the eastern lobby, a space which had been inaccessible at ground level due to the close proximity of the Wall beyond. 23: The President's meeting room in the north-west corner tower on the second floor. 24: A second-floor corridor. 25: A view of the west lobby, then no longer in use as an entrance hall; the main entry to the building was from the south.

22

21

23

24

25

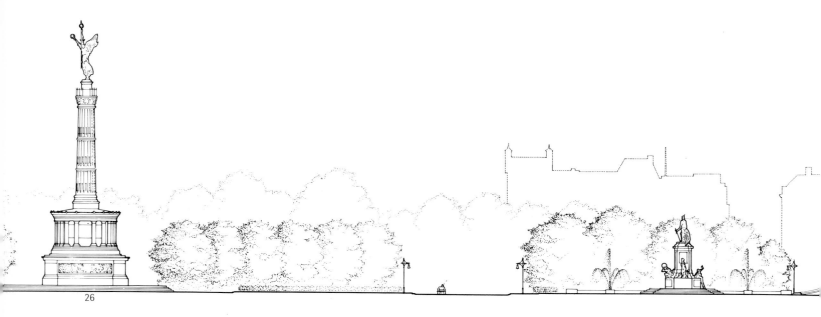

26

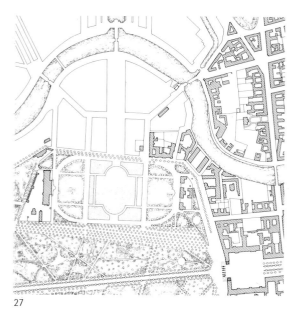

27

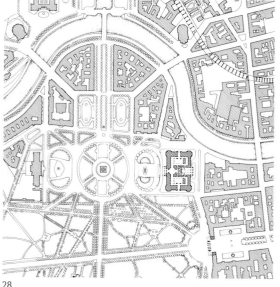

28

Two faces of the Reichstag.
26: East-west sectional elevation through the Königsplatz
and the Brandenburg Gate as
it was in 1901. 27: Plan of the
Königsplatz in 1871 at the
time of the first Reichstag
competition; the Raczinski
Palace provided the site for
the Reichstag. 28: Plan of the
Königsplatz in 1901.

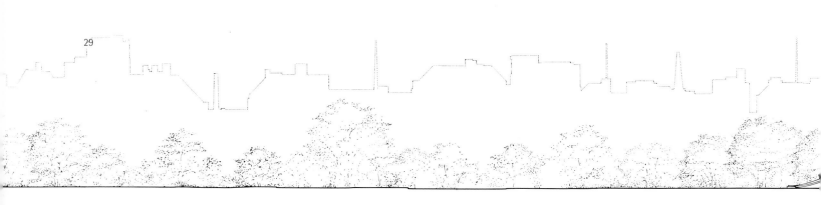

29

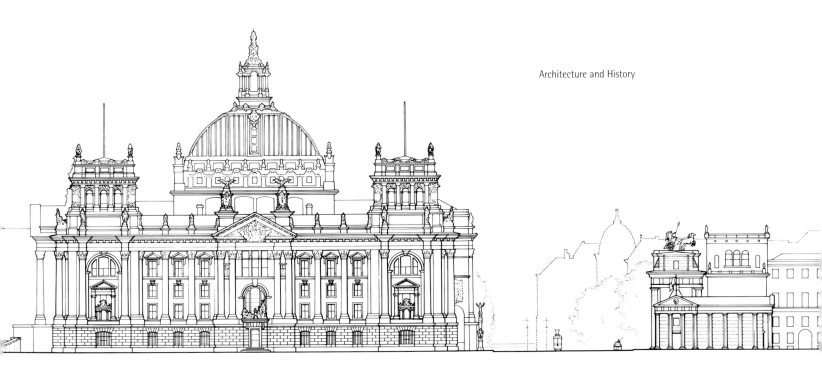

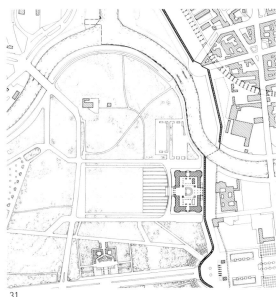

29: A comparative view of 26, above, in 1971, following Baumgarten's rebuilding in the 1960s. 30: The Reichstag and the (renamed) Platz der Republik in 1945; the entire central area of Berlin was left in ruins. 31: The Reichstag and the Platz der Republik in 1962 after the erection of the Wall which cut Berlin in two.

30

31

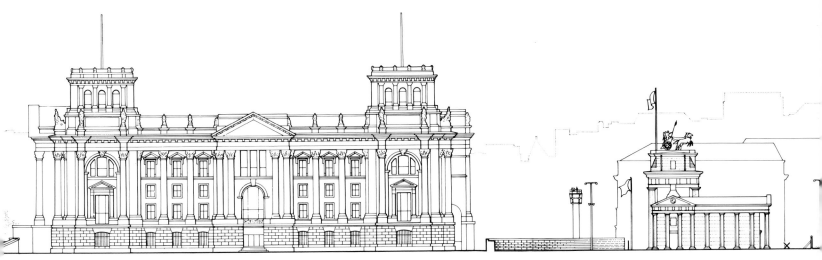

32

70

33   34

35

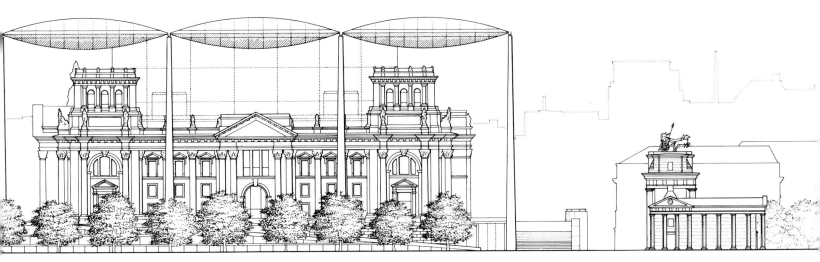

Two approaches to rebuilding the Reichstag. 32: An east-west sectional elevation through the Platz der Republik and the Brandenburg Gate showing the 1992 Foster competition proposals; the Reichstag sits beneath the canopy of an extended roof 'umbrella'. 33: The competition plan in context. 34: The same area in 1999. The Schultes-Frank Spreebogen masterplan, adopted in February 1993, conflicted with the 'big roof' and was a crucial factor in the decision to revise the scheme. 35: A comparative view of 32, above, in 1999 showing the Reichstag and its newly completed cupola. Compare also with 26 on the previous page.

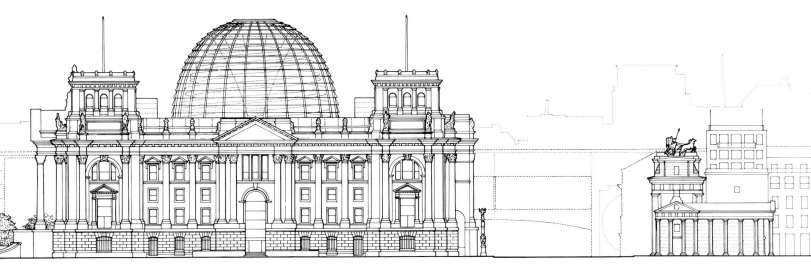

36

37

Paul Baumgarten's extensive use of toxic asbestos in the 1960s meant that the entire lining of his interiors had to be carefully stripped away before reconstruction could begin. This process brought to light unexpected remnants of Wallot's ravaged interiors and other historical traces such as the graffiti left by victorious Soviet soldiers. 36: Norman Foster, David Nelson and Mark Braun inspect the long-forgotten remains of Wallot's decorative scheme in the south-west stairwell. 37: Plaster is stripped from the vaulted soffit of the north corridor.

Chief Whip of the Conservative CDU, said: 'Just paint the walls and we'll move in, we don't want to spend any money on it.' But we were able to demonstrate that even 'doing nothing' would cost millions of Deutschmarks for no real gain. Firstly, huge amounts of toxic asbestos had to be removed before the building could be occupied, necessitating major demolition work and reinstatement; and there would be no possibility of an energy-efficient, environment-friendly services solution if we were to retain the building's existing heavily polluting services installation.

There was the potential for a compromise whereby, for example, the old chamber would stay, but the roof would be reconstructed in a glazed form. Our preferred option was far more radical, however, retaining an echo of our first competition scheme. In this option, it was possible to make the roof level a public place – an objective still very close to our hearts. We presented it in environmental, functional and visual terms, along with detailed reference to cost. And we found that the budget was now uppermost in people's minds.

The next day Mark Braun talked to Peter Conradi. He said it looked as if the competition was between Pi de Bruijn and ourselves; on Monday 21 June at 6.30 there was to be a vote; on 29 June the factions would debate, and on 1 July the Council of Elders would decide. We learned finally that we had won via a statement from the Building Committee. The voting had been sixteen for us, two for Pi de

38

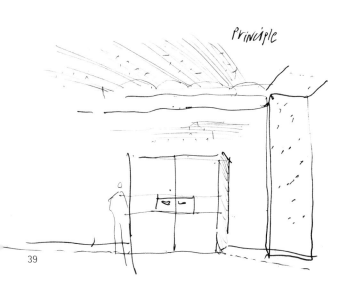
39

Principle

40

41

42

38: A graffiti-covered niche in the north corridor. 39, 44: Norman Foster's sketches of two Baumgarten rooms on the first floor; there was pressure initially to retain elements of the 1960s interiors. 40: Peeling away the layers of history. 41: A section of stonework is revealed. 42, 43: Seeing the building with new eyes.

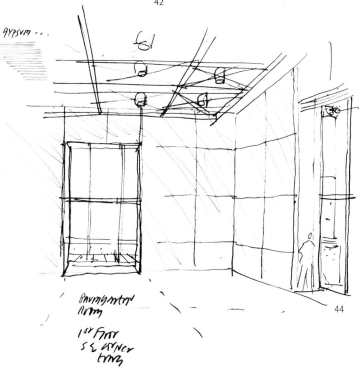
44

43

Bruijn and none for Calatrava. Dietmar Kansy is quoted as saying, 'We had three beautiful girlfriends, but in the end we could marry only one.'

We won, I think, because we listened carefully and did the right research. We identified and understood the core issues. We had a clear philosophy of integrating new and old, based on our experience at the Royal Academy. We were attuned to political sensitivities. And we demonstrated the relationship between capital cost and running costs — principally energy — in a compelling way. In fact the question of energy had come to the fore. The Committee was strongly in favour of our recommended option and rejected out of hand the idea of a 'make do and mend' solution. But many issues remained unresolved.

Two days later we were back in Bonn meeting the Federal Building Ministry (BmBau) to discuss detailed costs. There had been no opportunity so far to carry out a proper study of the existing building and to evaluate its structural condition. Now, with what was seen as a rehabilitation scheme in prospect, the state of everything from the walls and roof to the window frames was clearly a matter of interest. All these factors had to be taken into consideration before the budget could be finalised. Eventually, early in 1994, it was fixed at DM600 million.

Having won the competition, I knew that to control the project, we would have to work from Berlin. We had considerable experience of working in Germany, and many German

74

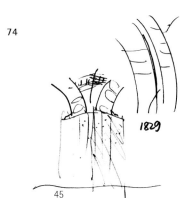
45

46

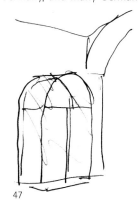
47

48

architects in our studio; and we were used to creating satellite operations around the world — we had done so in Hong Kong, for example, twice in twenty years, the first time to build the Hongkong and Shanghai Bank, the second to construct Hong Kong's new International Airport at Chek Lap Kok.

On 1 August 1994 the fifteen-strong project team moved into a studio in the ballroom of a pre-war building in Ebertstrasse, opposite the Reichstag, in the former East. The following spring Christo and Jeanne-Claude's team for the 'wrapping' joined us in the building and we got to know them very well. I remember it as an eerie and slightly sinister place. I was convinced that it had been used by the Stasi, or some other secret organisation because it had the most elaborately sound-proofed doors. Thickly padded and covered in leather, fixed with fat brass pins, they were quite bizarre but also rather beautiful. We stayed there for two years until the building fell due for renovation as part of the Dorotheenblock development and we moved to a larger office in Giesebrechtstrasse off the Kurfürstendamm.

In Germany it is now customary for the architect to act as 'general planner' for a project, not only coordinating but employing all the other consultants. This was not a role we wanted or could have handled easily. It would have meant assembling a multi-disciplinary team in Berlin and diverting our attention from the key task of designing the building. To complicate matters the old BBD, with which we had dealt in the early days of the project, was in the process of being replaced on the Reichstag by the BBB — the *Bundesbaugesellschaft Berlin* — an independent body intended to apply a market-oriented man-

While elements of the design were being finalised, the demolition of Baumgarten's chamber proceeded with destructive precision.
45, 47, 50: Norman Foster's sketches exploring how new doorways and partitions were to be integrated within the vaulted ground-floor level.
46, 48, 49: The 'masonry muncher' weaves its way through the building like a dinosaur on the prowl, consuming vast chunks of concrete in its steel jaws. 51: Norman Foster sketches as the building comes down. 52: A sketch of the newly revealed Wallot vaults in the eastern lobby.

agement approach to public building projects. The issue was finally settled when the Munich-based Michael Kuehn, who at that time was the services consultant for the Reichstag project, assumed, in effect, the general planner's role. This meant that the government had two main contracts, with Kuehn and with us. My colleagues Graham Phillips and Mark Sutcliffe have vivid memories of the negotiations with the BBB on this issue, which were tougher and longer than any they can remember.

When the commissioning process began, it was arranged in phases for the various stages of the work, the first formal commission coming in September 1993. At that point we had to establish a work routine with the client, and a regular monthly meeting — a *Jour Fixe* as it is called — was agreed with the Building Committee under Dr Kansy. It was at those meetings, over the next five years, that every detail of the project was discussed and approved.

The Building Committee comprised senior parliamentarians from all parties — many of them also members of the Council of Elders — each of whom reported back to his or her party hierarchy. As architects coming face to face with this powerful political machinery for the first time, we began to appreciate the extent to which people discuss things and come to their own agreements behind the scenes. There was a huge amount of lobbying and rehearsing of arguments outside of the formal Committee meetings. At first we found this disconcerting — an individual might like what we had done, but have

49

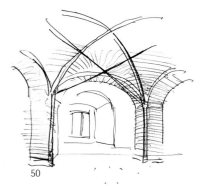

50

51

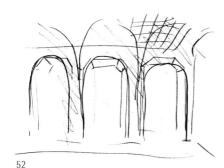

52

to vote against it to maintain the party line — and so we had to learn not to take it personally. There was bureaucracy, of course, and many upheavals, but we also encountered a genuine open-mindedness and a desire to achieve the best solution. I was struck by the dedication of all those involved in what was often an exhausting process; meetings with the Building Committee and its advisors would typically begin in the afternoon and extend into the late evening. But it was also a very rewarding process.

Politically, on the other hand, it was a very sensitive climate. I think that in some instances decisions made by the Building Committee really reflected the political flavour of the moment. For example, when measures were introduced by the Conservative (CDU) Government to restrict social services, it sparked a sequence of protests in Berlin. The miners went on strike; so too did the steelworkers. I remember one Committee meeting in Bonn where protesters were marching up and down outside.

Unemployment in the German construction industry was also rising. In one celebrated moment the Reichstag itself became a symbolic focus for protest against the use of illegal foreign labour; the site was invaded and temporarily occupied by rioting building workers.

It was around that time that we were trying to get approval for our choice of stone in the building. We specified a French stone which is more durable than its German equivalent. But, quite naturally, the Building Committee was heavily pressurised by the German stone lobby to use a local material. I felt that as foreigners in that equation we were in a very difficult position. In the end we settled for a Bavarian stone, although some Spanish stone was used and installed by German labour. By a nice irony, however, the German-supplied stone we battled over was installed by armies of Polish craftsmen. So in the end it was very much an international effort.

As the project progressed our detailed understanding of the Reichstag began with research into Wallot's building, which had been exhaustively photographed prior to the 1933 fire. Originally, the principal rooms, including the chamber, had been located at first-floor level, accessed on all four sides by grand staircases. Subsidiary areas were located on the ground floor. The other major rooms, including the extraordinarily elaborate library, were ranged around the chamber, or placed at second-floor level. Wallot had been preoccupied with display, but beneath his highly elaborated decorative scheme there was a well-planned and logical building.

The Reichstag as we found it was scheduled as 'a building worthy of protection' and the Heritage Department in Berlin had to be consulted on any proposals affecting its character. Such safeguards had not existed in the 1960s when the masonry guts had been torn out of the building in an act of civic vandalism more devastating than anything wrought by the Red Army. A huge amount of historical detail that had survived the war was destroyed in this process; for example, corridors were arbitrarily

76

54

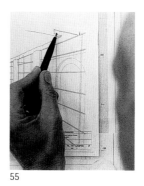

55

56

53

constructed across the internal courtyards and great staircases that had survived the bombardment were needlessly demolished and replaced by new structures.

Paul Baumgarten's reconstruction was at odds with the original form of the building. His planning was horizontally constrained, with little vertical connection or emphasis. New third and fourth floors were introduced and the upper levels were clogged with plant. The building's internal logic was consciously disregarded so that its coherent circulation pattern was lost. You entered the building from the south, at undercroft level, without any sense of occasion – you might have been entering a subway station. The interior of the Reichstag, as I first saw it, reminded me of a convention hotel or a municipal baths. I could not imagine anything interesting ever having happened there.

However, to everyone's astonishment, as we peeled away the plasterboard and asbestos lining of Baumgarten's interiors, the bones of Wallot's Reichstag gradually came to light. This process was carried out with almost surgical precision. Each new incision revealed striking, even bizarre imprints of the building's past, including fragments of nineteenth-century mouldings, masons' marks and the graffiti chalked on the walls by victorious Soviet soldiers in 1945. I was struck by how affecting these graffiti were – each message a coarse reminder of a painful human story, otherwise long forgotten. You could tell whether a message had been written by a soldier or an officer: the soldiers had to make do with charcoal, while the officers used the coloured crayons they carried for marking map positions as they advanced on Berlin.

Following the move to Berlin the Ebertstrasse studio became the principal forum for detailed design work, which was examined and progressed through a series of crits. 53-56: Modifications are agreed at a design meeting in September 1994.

I came to realise that the Reichstag's fabric bears the imprint of time and events more powerfully than any exhibition could convey. I was convinced that it should not be sanitised. Preserving these scars allows the building to become a living museum of German history.

The fact that this approach was accepted proved to me what an extraordinarily open and democratic society Germany has become. Not everyone shares that view, of course. The *New York Times* of 6 March 1999 complained:

Certainly there is something 'open', if not plain masochistic, about Chancellor Gerhard Schröder going past Russian obscenities to reach his blue-doored parliamentary office. Schröder's father died in 1944 on his way back from the Russian front.

It is worth noting, however, that Chancellor Schröder is an ardent supporter of our approach. For him, as for many of his generation, it was important that memories of those dark days were kept alive.

As demolition work began, the decision to retain these historical traces led to quite extraordinary scenes. Standing at second-floor level I remember looking down into a gloomy void 20 metres below which had once been the chamber. A great Japanese 'masonry muncher' with a 43-metre boom

57

58

59

60

— one of only four in Europe — crept along on its caterpillar tracks, greedily consuming vast chunks of concrete in its hydraulic jaws. All around it other dinosaur-like machines nibbled away delicately at what remained. And only feet away from this mayhem, specialist conservators in goggles slowly scraped away layers of grime from the original stonework, operating with almost watchmakerly precision to protect the fragile graffiti.

Throughout the rebuilding we followed a clear ethos of reconciling our new interiors with the historical fabric. Junctions between old and new work are expressed and where the existing fabric has been repaired the junction is clearly articulated with a finely incised shadow gap, so that each layer of intervention in this architectural palimpsest can be understood. The only exception to this rule is in the two recreated courtyards where the upper levels had been unsympathetically rebuilt. Here we followed the example of others in repairing the facades and opted for restoration following the pattern of the original.

We have worked within the discipline of the old shell, respecting the historical floor levels and their expression in the facades. Where Wallot's ruined corridors have been retained, you can feel the history of the place particularly strongly. The corridors leading to the east lobby feel almost sepulchral, like an ancient Egyptian catacomb. Great cyclopean boulders of stone around the newly reopened doorways are all that remain of once ornate architraves. As you rise through the building, however, its history is less evident, and there is instead an unfolding sense of lightness, growth and change.

As design intention progressed closer to reality, regular presentations were made to members of the Building Committee. 57: Norman Foster and Mark Braun present a mock-up of the chamber seating and desks to the Building Committee in December 1997. 58: Norman Foster and Mark Braun present proposals for the chamber eagle to the Building Committee in Bonn, September 1997. 59, 60: with the cupola framework approaching completion in January 1998, Committee members, MPs and journalists make a tour of inspection.

The reconstructed building takes organisational cues from Wallot's original intentions, reinstating the subtleties of axial door and window alignments and the resonances of his planning grid. In other significant ways, however, our approach represents a radical departure. Spatially, Wallot's Reichstag was highly compartmentalised; the chamber itself was a flat-ceilinged room despite the looming presence of the dome above. We have gouged through the building from top to bottom, opening it up — especially the chamber — to natural light and views. Members of Parliament on the floor of the chamber can now look up directly to see people on the ramps in the cupola, the highest point of which is more than 40 metres — the equivalent of thirteen domestic storeys — above their heads. The strength of this connection between the chamber, the cupola and its surrounding public roof terrace is crucial.

Our first competition scheme had proposed a viewing deck at roof level where visitors could look out over Berlin's skyline, symbolically placing the public above the heads of their political representatives. This principle was extended in our second scheme and we explored the idea of allowing the public beyond the tribunes in the chamber, making the Reichstag itself, in part, a public place.

Organisationally the building is now layered in a way that reflects the alternately public and private, separate and interlocking activities that take place within it. The principal parliamentary and public entry level forms a *piano nobile* above a ground floor of services and subsidiary functions

78

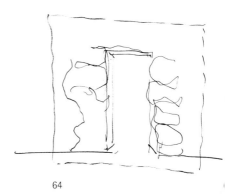

61 62 63 64

as it did in Wallot's day. From this main level, MPs enter the floor of the chamber, or branch off to reception rooms and members' dining rooms, while the public are directed via glass-fronted lifts in the lobby to roof level or to the mezzanine from where they enter the tribunes in the chamber. The second floor is the presidential level, with offices and formal rooms for the President of the Bundestag and the Council of Elders. On the third floor — a new level located behind the parapet of Wallot's facades — are the faction rooms and press lobby. Parliamentarians, public and press each have their specific spaces; sometimes they are kept distinctly apart, sometimes their realms overlap, and there are emphatic moments of 'punctuation', focused on the cupola and the chamber, where parliamentarians and public, parliamentarians and press, respectively come together.

The original Reichstag chamber was famously destroyed in the 1933 fire. The dome was demolished a little more than twenty years later and the huge masonry piers which supported it were removed as part of the 1960s reconstruction. So we had a clear zone at the heart of the building in which to create an entirely new space. It occupies the full width of the plan between the two surviving courtyards, and is physically and visually integrated with the nineteenth-century fabric.

In moving from Bonn to Berlin MPs wanted to maintain a degree of familiarity in the layout of the chamber. In most European Parliaments, cabinet members sit on the floor of the chamber with their colleagues. But in Germany, where it was historically appointed by the Kaiser, the cabinet

The scarred remains of Wallot's nineteenth-century interiors have a tremendous poignancy; in the east corridor the cyclopean stone surrounding once elaborate doorways has an archaeological quality reminiscent of some ancient historical site. 61: A mezzanine-level walkway in the east corridor accesses a new door opening aligning with a reopened historical doorway below. 62: Retained graffiti in the east corridor. 63, 64: Detail and sketch of a newly reopened doorway in the east corridor. 65: Where the new meets the old the junction is clearly articulated.

Смирнов

43 РВО

Слава героям
...рушили знамя
...ди над Бер...

Шляндрев
Александров
...Калмыкко

ФОМ

67

68

69

70

The east corridor rises through three levels, a legacy of the Baumgarten reconstruction in the 1960s which entirely disregarded Wallot's vaulted nineteenth-century spaces. 66: A view from the east corridor into the east lobby. 67: The same view in the early 1970s. 68: A view of the east corridor at second-floor, presidential level. 69: In Baumgarten's refurbishment, a glass-block floor slab cut this space in two horizontally. 70: The east corridor at first-floor level as it survived the war; battle-scarred but essentially intact, it was needlessly swept away.

71

72

73

The north corridor is among the best preserved of Wallot's nineteenth-century spaces.
71: The niches and walls in this space carry the marks of Soviet soldiers; the scars left in the masonry date not only from the war, however, but also from the 1960s when all the ornamental carving was chiselled away.
72, 73: Comparative views in 1972 and 1959 respectively.
74: The north courtyard which abuts the north corridor.
75, 76: Steel bridges allow public access to the tribunes in the chamber; these lightweight structures contrast deliberately with the heaviness of the retained stonework.

74

75

76

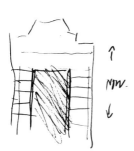

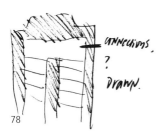

79

New staircases occupy Wallot's nineteenth-century stairwells. Wallot's great granite stairs survived the war but were swept away in the 1960s remodelling, justified by an arbitrary change in floor levels. 77, 79, 81: The line of Wallot's original stairs can be traced in the repaired wall surface. The positions of ornate pilasters and cornices are revealed by the scars left when they were chiselled away. 78, 80: Norman Foster's design sketches exploring how the staircases are isolated from the surviving fabric. Here, as elsewhere, new interventions are clearly articulated, allowing the building's many historical layers to be read simultaneously.

78

81

80

has traditionally sat in front of Parliament, not as part of it. That was the model followed in the old Waterworks in Bonn, where the Bundestag was based until it moved into Behnisch's new building. Behnisch's innovation was to challenge that convention, and to seat everybody democratically in a true circle. However, that arrangement proved both unpopular and impractical, especially at Question Time, and so we developed our proposals along more traditional lines, testing our ideas against the experience of both locations.

Unlike the House of Commons, where there is a scramble for seats — even on the front benches — in the Bundestag every MP is provided with his or her own seat, and the respective party groupings have to be observed. The German system of parliamentary committees, which meet on the floor of the chamber, means that often there will only be a small group of MPs present and they will move forward to occupy vacant seats close to the podium. At other times the chamber will be packed. Even when largely empty, we wanted the chamber to feel intimate and to avoid the sense of an 'inner core' superior to the rest. When there is a vote, MPs will come to the chamber, temporarily leaving their offices or faction rooms, and they typically have only eight minutes to get to their seats, so circulation routes had to be legible and direct.

For Members of Parliament the chamber is the natural focus of the building. It was important for us and for them that members of the public coming to the chamber to listen to debates should be involved in proceedings and not feel like detached onlookers. The elliptical configuration of the

86

82

83

84

chamber seating and the arrangement of the public tribunes is therefore designed to engender a close relationship between public and parliamentarians. Weaving the network of connections which allows such public access has led to the creation of some dramatic spatial effects. For example, from the new mezzanine-level connecting bridges which lead to the tribunes, there are striking views down into the east entrance foyer, a space intended for formal 'red carpet' occasions as well as for everyday use by MPs and staff.

In our rebuilding we wanted to banish any feeling that there were secret domains, or hives of bureaucracy. For security reasons, not every part of the Reichstag can be open to the public, but we have ensured that where possible it is transparent and its activities are on view. It is a building without secrets. The broad ambulatory of the press lobby, for example, focuses on the glazed soffit of the chamber and from here journalists can watch proceedings below.

The idea of public and politicians entering the building together, through the 'front door', was equally important. To my amazement, when I first walked in eager anticipation up the grand western staircase I found the main entrance locked and barred. It had not been used since the late 1950s when reconstruction work on the building began. We decided that it should be opened up for everybody. It is fundamental to the architectural 'promenade' of the building and epitomises the new attitudes of openness and democracy in Germany. Helmut Kohl himself said that the Reichstag must be for a new

The shape of the chamber and the layout of the members' seating — circular versus elliptical — was a matter of protracted debate. 82, 83: Such was the profile of this debate that cartoons appeared in the press satirising the issue. 84: Former Bundestag President Rita Süssmuth discusses proposals for the elliptical seating arrangement in Foster's Berlin studio.

generation of Germans and this has very much been a guiding principle. The entry sequence up these steps now culminates in a 30-metre high, light-filled lobby which is dignified yet, I hope, free from the pompous connotations of power that previously attached to the Reichstag. In Baumgarten's reconstruction the podium of the Bundestag chamber had been relocated on the western side of the building. We have restored it to its original position to the east which means that those entering the building are confronted, through glazed partitions, with a direct view through to the seats of the President of the Bundestag, the Chancellor, and other national leaders.

Beyond the chamber are other spaces which form part of the parliamentary machinery: the President of the Bundestag needs dignified spaces in which to entertain; the press has to be accommodated; there are also committee rooms and places where MPs can eat, drink and refresh themselves in breaks during long sessions. We conceived the Reichstag not as a sequestered chamber building, but rather as a gathering place where encounters are encouraged between MPs, the public and the press; so on top of all these working levels, the public realm reasserts itself in the great roof terrace and a restaurant which MPs, the press and members of the public can share.

The roof level — what Le Corbusier identified as the 'fifth elevation' — is a crucial but frequently under-designed element of a building. All too often it is filled with services and barred

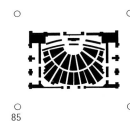
85

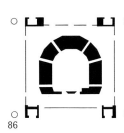
86

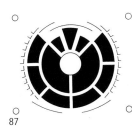
87

88

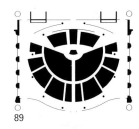
89

to the public. Getting people onto the roof of the Reichstag — with its marvellous views of the city — and into what became the cupola was always a part of our vision. The exploration of various options for the roof was to pave the way for what, for me, is the central achievement of the entire project — the way in which it embodies the principles of public access and democracy.

As we worked on the revised scheme, in the early summer of 1993, we began to explore ways in which a new raised element — not yet a cupola — could be developed at rooftop level. As we progressed our daylighting studies and investigated ways in which top-light could be brought into the chamber, we saw that views down into the chamber from above could also be opened up. The possibility of integrating these ideas within a new cupola emerged gradually in response to a dialogue with the politicians. The evolution of the cupola's design and the political climate in which it was conceived are related in Chapter 2.

When we embarked on the second round of the competition, I had not foreseen that we would go in that direction. But I felt strongly that our transformation of the Reichstag into the new Bundestag should have a marker on the Berlin skyline, communicating the themes of lightness, transparency, permeability and public access that underscore the project. I saw it as an opportunity, conceiving of the new structure as a 'lantern' with all the architectural and metaphorical associations which that term implies. Our next task was to give that concept appropriate form.

Comparative plans of the chambers in the Reichstag in Berlin and the Bundestag in Bonn, charting the evolution of the seating arrangement. 85: The original Reichstag chamber as completed by Paul Wallot, 1894. 86: The Reichstag chamber as reoriented by Paul Baumgarten, 1971. 87: The circular form of Günter Behnisch's Bundestag seating in Bonn, 1992. 88: The first Foster Reichstag competition scheme, 1992. 89: The oval seating form in the Reichstag as built, 1999.

90: The chamber under construction in August 1997. The shell is complete and the steel framing of the floor and tribunes is in place.

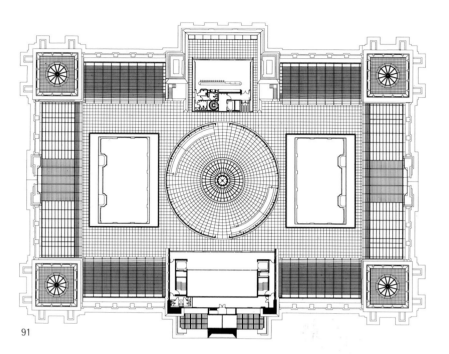

91

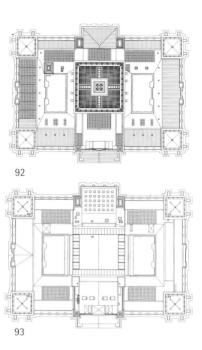

92

93

90

91: Plan at roof level. 92, 93: Comparative plans by Wallot and Baumgarten in 1894 and 1971 respectively. This is the building's principal public level. In Wallot's scheme the roof was inaccessible; in Baumgarten's reconstruction new lightwells served a floor of offices. 94: Plan at third-floor level; this is a new floor housing faction rooms and the press lobby. 95: Comparative plan by Baumgarten; there was no Wallot equivalent.

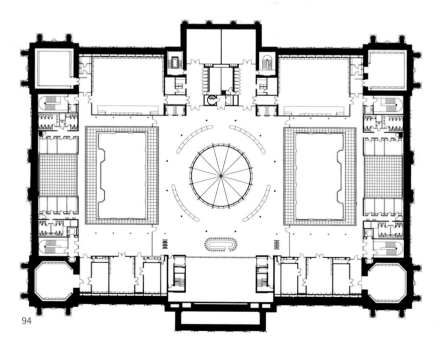

94

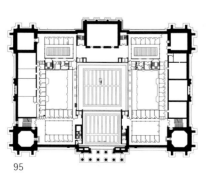

95

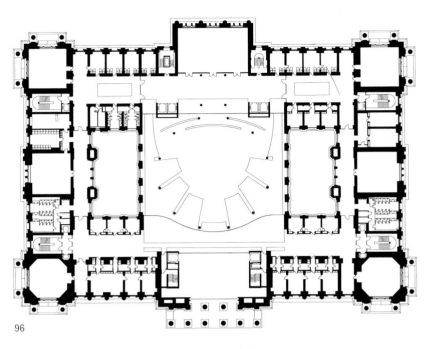

96

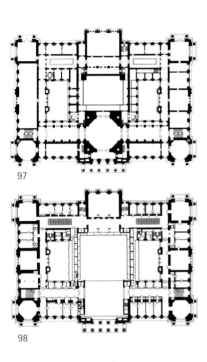

97

98

91

96: Plan at second-floor level.
97, 98: Comparative plans by
Wallot and Baumgarten in 1894
and 1971 respectively. This is the
presidential level. Wallot's
octagonal entrance hall, which
dominates his plan, was
demolished as a preliminary
to Baumgarten's rebuilding.
99: Plan at mezzanine level;
from this level the public have
access to the tribunes in the
chamber. 100, 101: Comparative
plans by Wallot and Baumgarten.

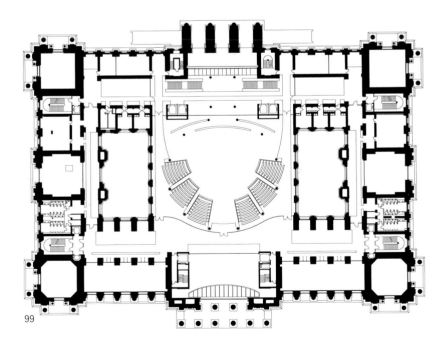

99

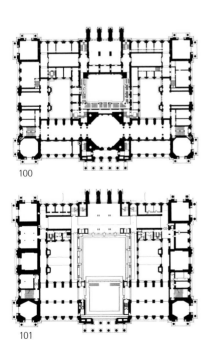

100

101

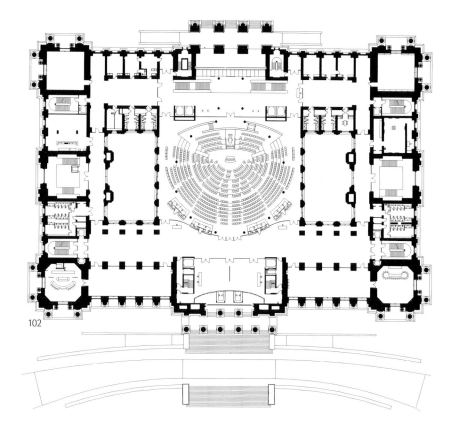

102

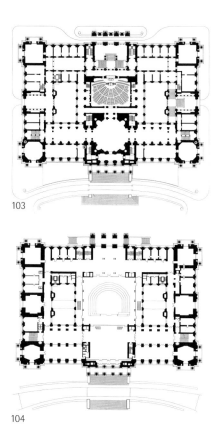

103

104

92

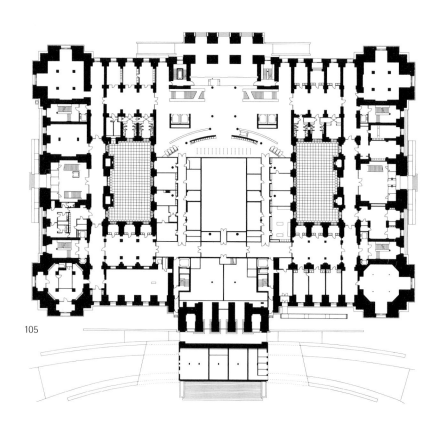

105

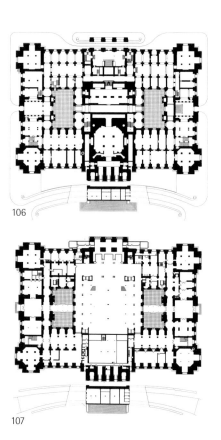

106

107

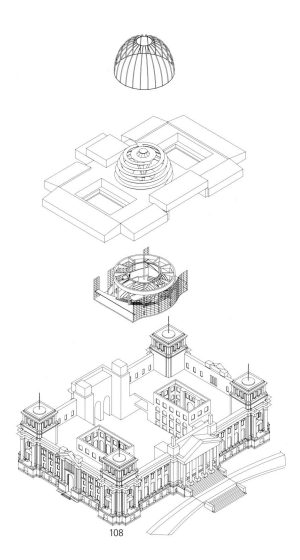

108

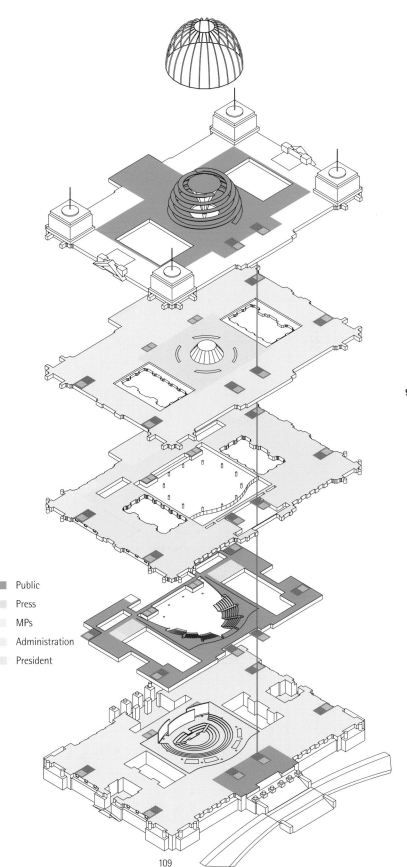

93

102: First-floor plan; this is the principal parliamentary level. 103, 104: Comparative plans by Wallot and Baumgarten, in 1894 and 1971 respectively. Baumgarten's chamber was oriented so that the Speaker faced east. 105: Plan at ground level. 106, 107: Comparative plans by Wallot and Baumgarten.

Two exploded views of the Reichstag. 108: New into old; the chamber occupies the heart of the existing building created by Baumgarten's reconstruction in the 1960s. 109: The distribution of functions and public accessibility. From the western entrance visitors ascend by lift to the mezzanine-level tribunes or to the roof.

■ Public
▨ Press
▨ MPs
▨ Administration
▨ President

109

Visitors to the Reichstag.
110: Members of the public
enter the building as equals
alongside MPs up the grand
flight of steps from the west.
They are taken by lifts either to
the tribunes in the chamber,
or to roof level and the cupola,
111, with its panoramic
viewing deck.

110

111

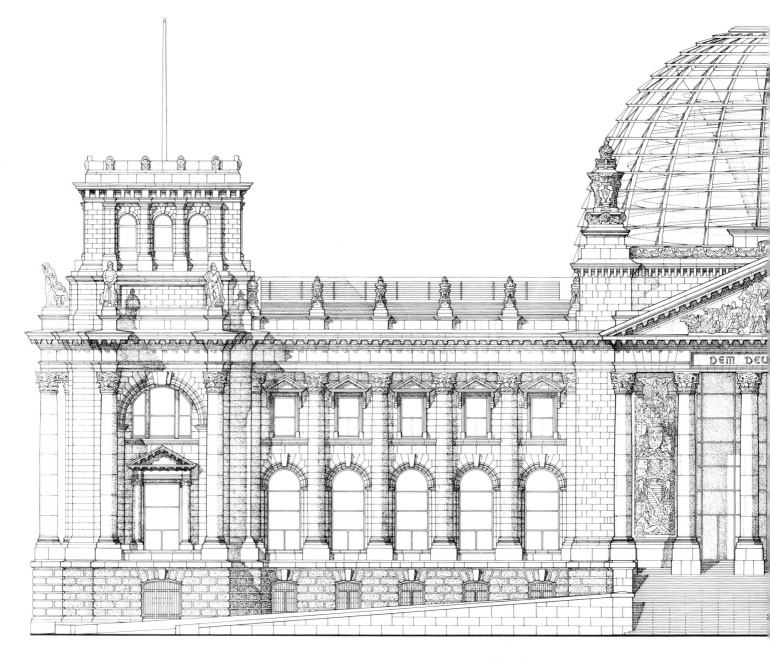

DEM DEU

112: The west elevation.
Surviving in a much reduced
form, Wallot's nineteenth-
century facades appear
forbidding and severe.
The lightness of the new
interventions within is signalled
externally by the glassy
structure of the cupola and the
opening up of the west facade
behind the portico.

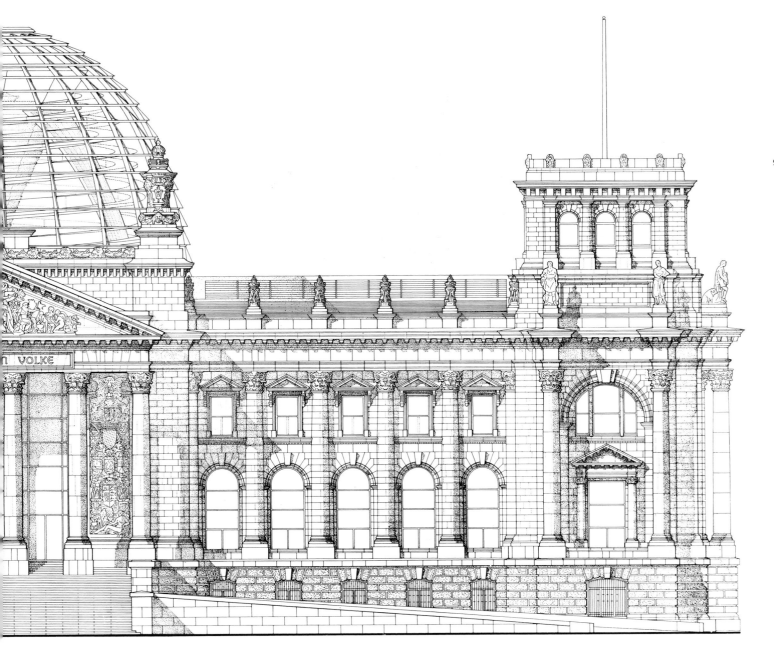

113

114

115

116

The west entrance hall and lobby. 113: Looking north along the west lobby at first-floor level. 114: Arriving visitors have a clear view of the seats of the Chancellor, the President of the Bundestag and other national leaders. 115, 116: Comparative views of the west entrance hall and lobby as completed by Baumgarten in 1971. 117: A view out through the west portico from the mezzanine-level bridge that gives public access to the tribunes in the chamber.

117

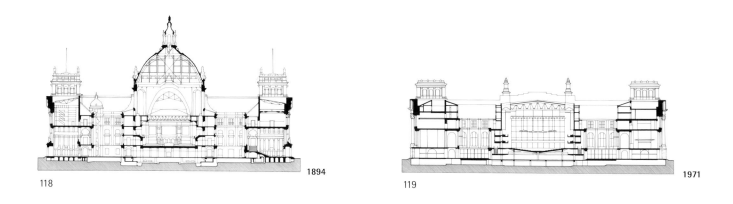

118   1894   119   1971

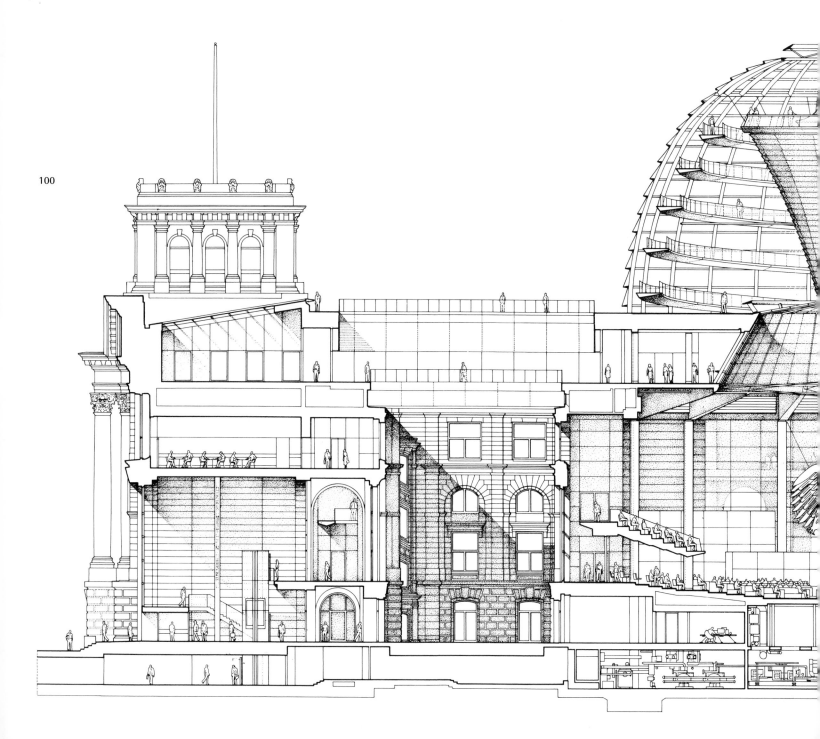

100

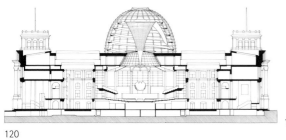

120

1999

North-south section through the chamber, facing the Speaker's chair, 121, and comparative sections through the Wallot, Baumgarten and Foster schemes respectively, 118, 119, 120. The symbolic heart of Wallot's Reichstag was torn out prior to Baumgarten's rebuilding; the historical dome was demolished in 1954. The new cupola signals the Reichstag's transformation but avoids the empty rhetoric of Wallot's dome.

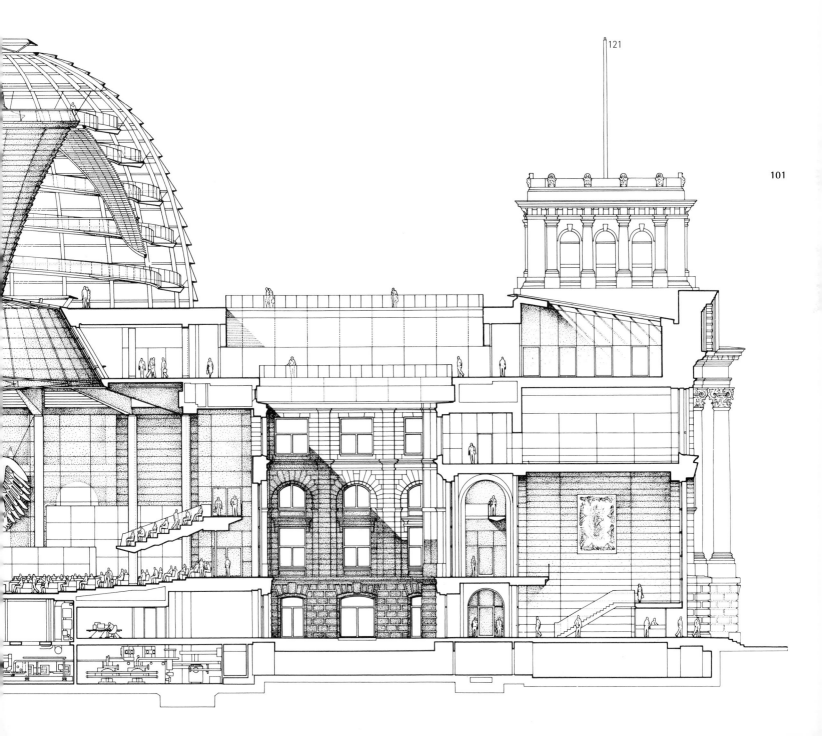

121

101

122: A view into the chamber from the west lobby. Where possible the building is transparent and its activities are on view.

125

124

126

The east lobby, behind the
Bundestag President's chair, is a
private entrance, for use by MPs
and their staff. Entry is at street
level; two broad flights of stairs
lead up to the first-floor
chamber level. 123: A view
along the east lobby at first-
floor level, looking north.

124: A comparative view of the
east lobby as reconstructed by
Paul Baumgarten in the 1960s.
125: A view into the chamber
from behind the eagle. 126: The
opposite view out through the
three arched openings of the
east entrance portico.

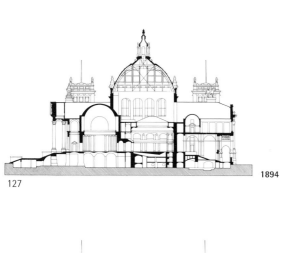

127   1894

128   1971

106

129   1999

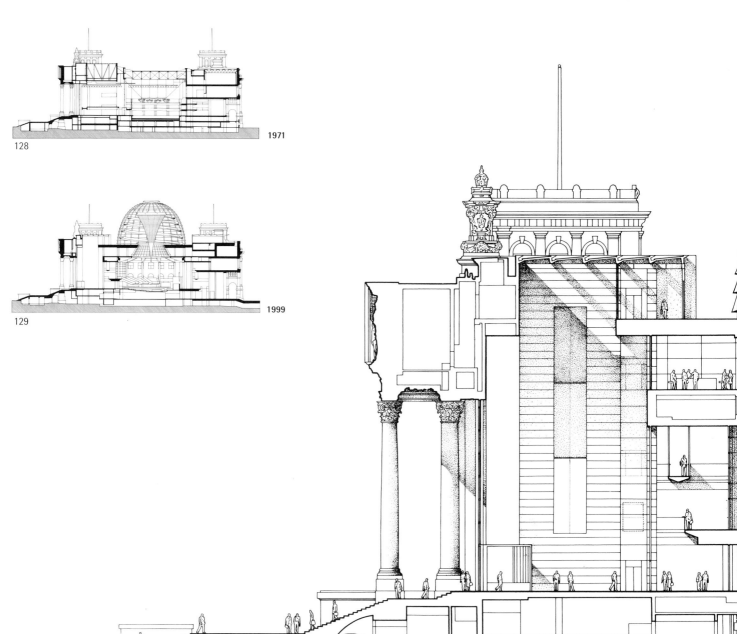

130

Cross-section through the east and west lobbies and the chamber looking north, 130, and comparative sections through the Wallot, Baumgarten and Foster schemes respectively, 127, 128, 129. Wallot's main entry sequence up the grand flight of steps from the west is reinstated; so too is his principal parliamentary level which forms a *piano nobile* above a floor of services and subsidiary accommodation. The spatial grandeur of Wallot's building was crushed by the uniform horizontality of Baumgarten's new floor levels; the new chamber and cupola cuts through these levels to provide a powerful vertical emphasis.

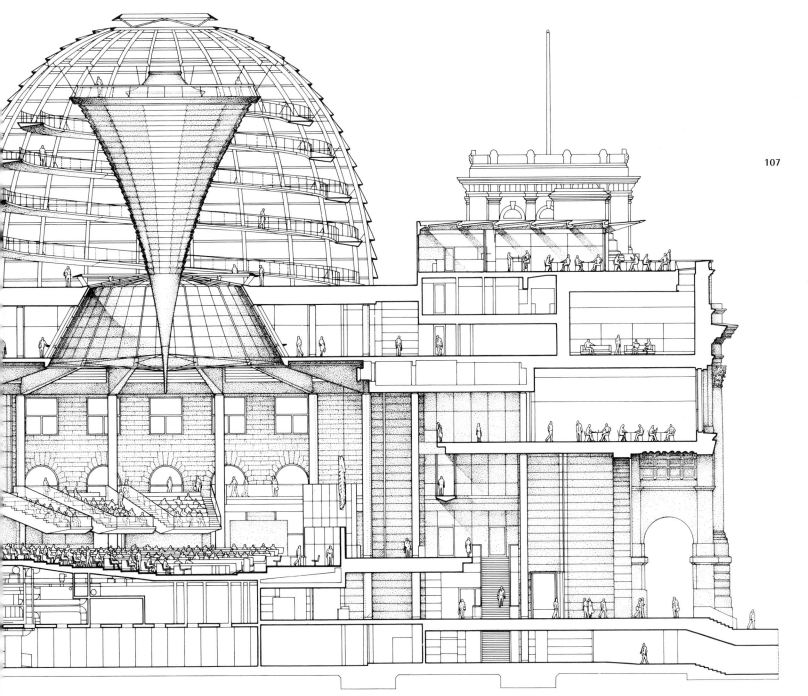

131

The parliamentary chamber
occupies the full width of the
plan between the two surviving
nineteenth-century courtyards.
131: A view of the public and
press tribunes at mezzanine
level. 132: Looking north
into the chamber. 133: A
comparative view of
Baumgarten's chamber in 1971,
looking in the same direction;
he reoriented the chamber so
that it was focused to the west
with the Speaker symbolically
facing towards the Wall.
134: Looking towards the seats
of the President of the
Bundestag, the Chancellor,
and other national leaders.

133

132

136

137

The press lobby, at third-floor level, sits directly above the chamber and has unobstructed views down into it. The political factions also have their meeting rooms and boardrooms at this level, and there is a bar where the press and MPs can meet informally. 135: A 'bird's-eye view' down into the chamber through the inclined glazed screen of the press lobby and the 'bicycle wheel' bracing of the cone. 136, 137: At this level the lightness and transparency of the new interventions are most apparent: all the building's processes are on view — it has no secrets.

138

Individual parties — or factions — have their meeting rooms and boardrooms on the third floor. The tower rooms at this level have been brought into use for the first time in their history. 138: View of the Green Party faction room. 139: Detail of the juxtaposition between new panelling and existing brickwork; there were no finishes in these rooms historically — the brickwork has simply been painted. 140: A view up through the skylight of one of the tower rooms. The flag-poles continue in miniature the theme established by the cone in the chamber and penetrate the glass soffit.

139

140

Conserving Graffiti

Rudi Meisel

Throughout May 1945, Soviet soldiers thronged to the Reichstag to leave their mark on a monument seen as the bastion of German national authority. Almost every inch of the interior was marked with inscriptions. Conserving these graffiti, as one of the vital layers in the Reichstag's history, was a specialist task that demanded the development of new techniques. After fixing the chalk or charcoal surface of the graffiti, the surrounding stone surface was cleaned with an abrasive powder in a micro-jet instrument that could be directed close to the contours of the lettering.

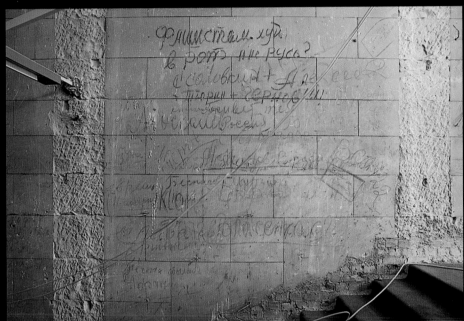

The

When work began on the Reichstag's interiors, traces of the past emerged: shell marks from World War II,

Marks of

graffiti scrawled by Russian soldiers, and remains of the original architecture. These scars have been

History

conserved, allowing the Reichstag to function as a living museum of German history.

Helmut Engel

116   On 2 May 1945 *Pravda* ran a leader, backed by an aerial photograph, announcing that the Red Flag was flying from the historical Reichstag building, and that 'the lair of the Fascist monster' had been taken. It was obvious that, for the Soviets, it had become more important to capture the Reichstag than to take Hitler's Chancellery, the *Reichskanzlei*. It was the Reichstag which, once taken, became the symbol of the victory over Fascism. As soon as the Reichstag was occupied a veritable stream of Red Army pilgrims made its way to this symbolic building. Every element of the Red Army was represented, and each man wanted to leave his mark for posterity. This helped to ensure that the 'Battle for the Reichstag', as dramatised in Soviet collective memory, was written into history, becoming the subject of museum installations and artists' panoramas.

Soviet soldier Igor Usachev proudly writes his name and the date, May 1945, on a wall in the newly captured Reichstag. The writing medium varied according to rank: soldiers used charcoal or chalk, while officers wrote with the coloured crayons they carried for marking map positions.

Today it is almost impossible to comprehend just how much of the building was marked with inscriptions, but it can be said with some certainty that the whole interior was covered, to above the height of a man (in some places even to ceiling height) with Cyrillic writing. The inscriptions appear to have followed definite patterns. Rare examples are dated, the earliest giving the date 2 May [1945]. Often, visitors recorded nothing more for posterity than their names — usually in charcoal or wax crayon, though occasionally in white chalk or lead pencil. (The medium of each inscription tells us something about its author – soldiers only had access to charcoal, while officers wrote with the wax crayons that they used to mark map positions.)

Many named the points in this patriotic struggle at which the fortunes of war had begun to turn in favour of the Soviets, and the German aggressors had begun the withdrawal through Eastern Europe which would culminate in their defeat. It was as if they wanted to suggest the size of the victory through the distances covered in the struggle: 'Caucasus – Berlin'; 'Odessa – Berlin'; 'Moscow – Berlin and back'; 'Krivoy Rog – Ordzhonikidze – Berlin'; 'Stalingrad – Berlin 22.6.41 – 8.5.45'; 'Sverdlovsk'; 'Moscow – Smolensk – Berlin'; 'Brest – Luza – Lvov – Berlin'.

Many of the places given, such as Charkow or Odessa, could simply be the home towns of soldiers. The fact that Berlin features repeatedly at the end of the lists of names reveals not

118

1

2

3

4

only the paramount political goal of Soviet strategy — to take the capital — but also the general degree of Soviet awareness of the significance of Berlin.

The alcoves in the Reichstag evidently tempted some members of the Red Army to inscribe their names in a positively proprietorial fashion, if not quite with a sacred flourish, right across them, as in the western alcove in the northern corridor on the first floor. First the words '2 May Leningrad' and the names 'Kossourow, Juditschew, Beskrony', were inscribed. Then two entries were made under '9 May'. The first, obviously the earlier of the two, reads 'The veterans of Stalingrad in Berlin', and has eleven names inscribed below it, in two columns: two captains, three lieutenants, four sergeants and two privates. Then later, between the two blocks of names, someone added 'The defenders of Moscow were here', and a total of ten names.

These inscriptions, with their clear references to Leningrad, Stalingrad and Moscow, then of course attracted various, what might be called explanatory, comments: 'They certainly paid for Leningrad! Stenischen'; 'Hello Moscow! Berlin's had it'; or 'This is where I fetched up and threw up — Gornin'. The writing in the eastern alcove on the same corridor probably also dates from 1 or 2 May, and reads: 'On the day of the victory over Fascism we send battle greetings to all members of the glorious Red Army! The lieutenant-colonels of the Guards Signals'.

Paul Wallot's interiors were scarred first by the fire of 1933, then by bombardment in 1945 and finally by the inscriptions of Soviet soldiers. 1: The eastern entrance hall shows the grandeur of Wallot's scheme. 2, 3: A comparison of this space before and after World War II shows the damage wrought by fire and shells. 4, 5: Two views of the southern entrance hall show the extent of the Cyrillic graffiti. Graffiti were also left by British and American servicemen; the soldier posed here is British. Interestingly, this photograph indicates the wealth of nineteenth-century fabric that survived the war.

The messages for posterity therefore ranged from the cursory to the cere-monious. Only rarely do the inscriptions appear to have betrayed any malice on the part of the victors towards the defeated: 'On 3 May 1945, Peskin from Odessa and Shitmarow from Leningrad inspected the ruins of Berlin. This made them glad and gave them satisfaction.' Only one of the preserved inscriptions resorts to the repertoire of Russian obscenities invoking the mother figure.

Examples such as 'Our path led us from the Caucasus to the Reichstag in Berlin', and 'We made it to the Reichstag — Hitler's lair', allude to the Reichstag's role as the Soviet's prime target. For the Soviets, the Reichstag symbolised Germany itself, as indeed it had been designed to do. The supreme goal of the mighty building, and especially of its pictures, statuary, artworks and stained glass, was to be a symbolic statement, rising above party strife, of the imperial unity achieved by Germany after the Franco-Prussian War of 1870-71. This is how we should read and understand all those imperial crowns and eagles, both on and in the building, the allusions to the federal nature of the empire in all those coats of arms and emblems — of the federal states themselves and also of the cities — and the allegories of the rivers.

The four corner towers, for example, should be interpreted as signifying the four kingdoms of Prussia, Bavaria, Saxony and Württemberg which were the backbone of Imper-

120

6

7

8

9

ial Germany. Symbols to ward off the evil of internal strife included St George — here given the features of Bismarck — slaying the dragon, and mighty eagles pinning down the snakes of discord with their talons. The relief on the pediment over the west entrance was central to this 'programme' in its representa-tion of the symbol of thriving art and industry under the auspices of the German Empire. The figure of a victorious Germania on horseback towered above the gable and the inscribed dedication, *Dem Deutschen Volke*, which was added belatedly in 1916.

Another recurrent theme in the imagery was the allusion to war and peace, and to power and strength. As part of the pictorial statement, statues symbolising the bedrock of the state — agriculture, industry, trade, art, literature, justice, statesmanship and the defence of the empire — surrounded and symbolically linked the four corner towers, representing the four German kingdoms. The allusions to the roots of Imperial German history inherent in the figures of the German emperors from Charlemagne to Maximilian I, the symbolic images of the various epochs of the old imperial state, and the statues of the spiritual heroes of German history, lent legitimacy, through the past, to present and future commitments.

It was, of course, traditional to depict virtues such as justice and wisdom, harmony and intelligence, bravery and love of peace, as fundamental attitudes for mankind. The allusions to

Wallot's original building was elaborately decorated. Its extensive iconography included coats of arms symbolising the various mini-states that made up the German Empire. 6: A stained glass window with an allegorical figure, one of many such windows that added splendour to the interiors. 7: Most of the Reichstag's stone carving and statuary was executed by the workshops of Reinhold Begas and Rudolf Maison. 8, 9: One of two panels on the west facade, combining coats of arms with allegorical figures, shown as it left the workshop and as it survived World War II (8).

10

11

12

13

14

15

16

17

The iconographic programme was intended to symbolise Germany's new unity and might. The vast array of sculpture included statues of Teutonic heroes, linking the new Parliament to the great deeds of the past. 10-12: Each of the corner towers signified one of the four major kingdoms of Germany. 13, 14: The chamber was also highly decorated, including a personification of modern communications holding a telephone receiver. 15-17: Imperial eagles and crowns featured often, as on the south pediment. The eagle with a snake in its talons was a symbol to ward off discord.

19

20

21

22

23

24

25

26

The octagonal entrance hall bears witness to the Reichstag's mutilation. Having survived fire, war and defacement, the hall was finally destroyed as part of Baumgarten's rebuilding in the 1960s. 19, 20: The statue of Kaiser Wilhelm I, centre-piece of the hall, was beheaded and knocked off its pedestal in 1945. 22, 23: The entrance hall and surrounding ambulatories in their original state. 18, 21, 24, 26: Views of the same spaces after the war, and during rubble clearances in the 1950s. 25: The south ambulatory during the 1960s rebuilding, its high vault cut through by a flat ceiling.

the elements were also traditional. The front wall of the parliamentary chamber — the 'shrine' — was decorated with images of significant events from the history of the young German Empire.

For nearly 40 years, from its inauguration in 1894 until 1933, the Reichstag served first as Parliament to the empire and then, after the 1918 revolution, as the House of Representatives of the Weimar Republic. Throughout this period it underwent little alteration. The destruction and damage to the Reichstag by the fire of 1933, the war in the air — increasing in intensity from 1943 — and the final battle of May 1945, not only marked a watershed in the development of the building's historical significance: the fabric of the building had now been breached as well. And so the imagery with which the historical Reichstag had been endowed was almost completely lost.

For Germans, the Reichstag building has held a varying significance in different periods of its existence. In the nineteenth century it was a symbol of hard-won German unity. For the Nazis, the building was regarded contemptuously as a talking shop for democrats, something to be replaced by dictatorial will in a totalitarian state. After the division of Berlin and the construction of the Wall, the Reichstag also became — like the Brandenburg Gate — symbolic of the division of Germany, because of its location hard against the border with the East. Only for the Soviet Union did the Reichstag remain as testimony to the defeat of Fascism.

124

27

28

29

30

When it came to rebuilding the Reichstag in the 1960s, the urge to obliterate its troubled past and to introduce a 'democratic', transparent glass architecture, meant that a large proportion of its inner fabric was destroyed. 27-29: Views of rubble clearance show that much of the building was damaged but still restorable. 30, 31: The 1960s rebuilding began with extensive demolition: the interior was completely gutted and vast quantities of masonry removed.

The Cold War prolonged the Reichstag's role as a parliament building in waiting. Once again it acquired a high symbolic value which, in anticipation of reunification — perceived as inevitable in the national consciousness — was bound to lead to the building's refurbishment.

The Reichstag's rebuilding in the 1960s involved a level of structural intervention that showed little respect for its historical form as designed by Wallot. Attitudes which had persisted since the 1920s towards the historicism of the nineteenth century ensured that the remains of its external ornament would be erased and, on the inside, the fabric destroyed — purportedly for the sake of functional improvements — and a new access system introduced.

All these measures were supposed, as 1960s thinking would have it, to lend the Reichstag the character of a building fit for a modern democracy in which glass had now acquired the meaning of transparency and openness. Never again — as had been the case during the years of the Third Reich — was the fate of the people to be decided behind closed doors. And of course the meaning of the word parliament was to be expressed in the architecture of the building itself, and not in the surface embellishments of pictorial decoration or sculpture.

In this climate, the historical architecture of the Reichstag had no role to play. Perfectly restorable nineteenth-century architecture was, therefore, treated with a ruthlessness

incomprehensible today. Much of the war damage, itself an equally meaningful record, was also lost in the process. It is said that the Soviet Union secretly pleaded with the West German Government against the scope of this work because it effectively destroyed the memorial to their victory in 1945. It was only with the reunification of Germany in 1990 and the final conversion of the building into the seat of the Bundestag that these traces were once more revealed.

Paul Baumgarten's design has now been lost and with it a whole historical perspective. Although the Berlin conservation body had initially been in favour of preserving elements of the 1960s refurbishment, particularly on the floor where the parliamentary chamber is situated, there were overwhelming functional reasons why elements of Baumgarten's work could not be retained. These included the spatial requirements of the parliamentary chamber itself, and the necessity of removing the large amounts of toxic asbestos introduced as a lining material in the 1960s. The decision was more than justified by the fact that large parts of Paul Wallot's original architecture, widely assumed to have been destroyed, were dramatically brought to light.

The approach to conservation in refurbishing the Reichstag was necessarily based on two criteria. Firstly, the original fabric was to be retained as far as possible, and secondly, the building was to some extent to assume the role of 'history book'. Beneath Baumgarten's panels, elements of the

126

32

33

34

35

nineteenth-century fabric had been preserved to a surprising extent. Wallot's access system had been completely lost with the introduction of the enclosed central lobby on the ground floor. But when the intermediate ceilings in the old entrance areas on the north and south sides of the building were removed and the eastern entrance opened up, the original spatial qualities could once more be appreciated, allowing access within the building to be restored to its original layout.

The Cyrillic inscriptions of Soviet soldiers also deserved a place in the history books, as did the marks left by shrapnel and the intense heat of burning fires on the natural stone surfaces of the two eastern halls. Additionally, the traces of destruction to the original fabric of the building, which were the legacy of the 1960s, were retained as historical proof of the lack of understanding for Wallot's nineteenth-century architecture.

Added to the principle of retaining the original fabric, which proved impossible to apply to anything rebuilt after 1945, was the clear architectural concept of not reinstating fabric of which nothing — or only fragments — remained. This meant not replacing items such as broken cornices, mouldings or architraves in their presumed — but in fact unknowable — original form. It also meant not reconstructing whole sections of the building as, regardless of prevailing conservation doctrine, this would have largely meant the destruction of the Reichstag as a historic monument to the struggle of 1945.

For the 1990s rebuilding, the plaster and asbestos lining of the 1960s interiors had to be stripped away before reconstruction work could begin. When the plaster was peeled away, imprints of the past were brought to light that had been hidden for over 30 years. 32-35: Cyrillic graffiti and traces of Wallot's original ornate interiors emerged from behind the plaster lining.

Throughout the building a clearly delineated incised detail between the existing fabric and new repairs ensures that a clear reading of the historical layering at work here is possible.

Once it was accepted that the Russian graffiti would be retained, the specific problem of cleaning the surrounding natural stone surfaces and preserving the inscriptions had to be addressed, together with their protection as demolition work progressed. When the painstaking process of conservation began, it was found that the wall surfaces and therefore the inscriptions had been damaged by exposure to lime, cement, plaster, dust and water, as well as by the marks of plaster wire from the 1960s rebuilding.

Through experimentation, conservators discovered that any surface roughness could be removed using scalpels and fine glass paper, and an air gun with fine tuning used at low pressure was sufficient for removing dust. The wax crayon and pencil could be cleaned using soft paintbrushes, and the dust was in any case barely visible on the white chalk inscriptions.

After much preliminary testing it was found that the inscriptions in charcoal, which had very little surface cohesion, could be fixed with a paraloid solution without producing surface shine or causing the colour to run. The white chalk inscriptions were fixed with an aqueous solution. After fixing, it was possible to clean right up to the contours of the lettering, using a micro-jet instrument

36

37

38

39

with a calcium-based powder as an abrasive. This conservation work has created a unique and highly symbolic document of Germany's recent past.

Today, in the light of the rebuilding of the Reichstag, one question still needs to be asked: what message does the new home of the Bundestag convey? It can of course be seen as an empirical statement — the logical result of the building's history. What is far more important, however, is what message from this 'living museum' of German history will find its way into the collective consciousness not only of the German public but of people all around the world. And how, in particular, will it be received, heeded and respected by the representatives of those people — the politicians who have to work in the building? Will misguided national perceptions mean that some people will be interested only in a literal understanding of the inscriptions themselves, and regard the chisel marks on the broken cornices and door surrounds as unsightly scars which ought to be removed, having no merit other than their ugliness?

In the end, perhaps the most important message to be transmitted by the building in its new form should be an optimistic one: that, despite allusions to it in the Reichstag's nineteenth-century imagery, the historical existence of a once expansionist and aggressive German Empire has no contemporary relevance to a reunited, democratic and European Germany.

36-39: Conservators worked with watchmakerly precision as the building was demolished around them and new techniques were developed to preserve the Reichstag's past.

Modelling the Lantern

Rudi Meisel

In the middle of a freezing continental winter, on 5 February 1996, twelve large crates containing a 1:20 scale model of the Reichstag chamber and cupola were hoisted onto the roof of the north-east corner tower. The model was precisely detailed and designed to test the mirrored cone in real conditions under the Berlin sky.

Claude Engle, the lighting
consultant, measured the light
being reflected into the
chamber model and
pronounced the experiment
a success. A system that had
begun life as a hunch — against
all conventional wisdom — had
been proved effective.

Architecture

As night falls and the glass bubble of the lantern glows, Berliners know that the Bundestag is sitting.

and

For them — and for a far wider public — the building has become a beacon signalling

Democracy

renewal and the vigour of the German democratic process.

Norman Foster

130   Long before the first Reichstag competition, controversy had begun to grow about the building's lost dome and proposals for its reconstruction. There was a vociferous lobby in favour of reinstating the dome exactly as it had been a century earlier. Advocates of the historical dome argued not only that it was symbolically desirable, but that it was also technically feasible. Among them, Oscar Schneider — a CSU representative on the Building Committee — gave an impassioned speech to his party on the subject. They and their CDU colleagues voted overwhelmingly to support the dome's reconstruction. I was passionately opposed to that idea. Many German politicians, I know, shared my concerns. It had worrying overtones; it went against the *zeitgeist*; it would have been an empty historicist gesture; and it would have been fundamentally at odds with the whole ethos of our scheme. This chapter describes that unfolding debate and the new cupola that resulted from it.

The new cupola can be read at many functional and symbolic levels. It signals renewal; it is fundamental to the Reichstag's daylighting and natural ventilation strategies; and crucially it is a new public space where the citizens are encouraged to climb onto the roof of their Parliament.

Looking through my sketchbooks, in preparation for this book, I found a sketch of the Reichstag drawn after my first visit to the building in July 1992. I remember sheltering in a café with Mark Braun and my partner, Spencer de Grey, and exchanging our first impressions of the building while it poured with rain outside. We talked about the missing dome and whether it should be replaced. I wrote against the sketch: 'Put it back in glass — lighter?' That sketch got forgotten but it posed a question that we would answer in due course.

For me the starting point was that any new roof structure should signal change; it should tell the world that the Bundestag had moved into the Reichstag. Structurally it should be transparent, in the spirit of our reconstruction. Functionally it should be clearly related to the chamber below and be a generative element in the internal workings of the building. In fact, as the design of the cupola — or 'lantern' — developed, it became a key component in our light and energy-saving strategies.

For some our new cupola is evocative of the original dome, but it is as light as its predecessor was heavy. Paul Wallot's dome was entirely symbolic, fulfilling no practical function. It enclosed only an enormous void, an arrangement that can be appreciated clearly in post-fire photographs. There was an opaque glass ceiling between the dome and the chamber which admitted no fresh air and little daylight and gave that space a box-like quality. The dome was even problematic in compositional terms. We

132

know that it was repositioned at least once during the design and construction of the building and, in its final alignment, it was not even placed symmetrically above the chamber. In fact the dome seemed to me to be the weakest element in Wallot's scheme. Furthermore, following the dome's demolition in 1954, the four corner towers had been lowered, irrevocably altering the formal dynamic of Wallot's composition. A historically accurate restoration would have required not just the recreation of the dome, but the reinstatement of the towers, together with a great variety of hugely complex and elaborate decorative work and statuary in both stone and metal. It would have been vastly expensive and with no practical gain. Working against the background buzz of this debate, we began to explore different ways in which all the themes that inform the lantern's design — natural lighting, transparency, energy efficiency, public access and the celebration of democracy — might come together in a unified whole. The models we made in the studio during late 1993 and into January 1994 record the unfolding of the design process.

With the move to Berlin in prospect, politicians spoke fondly of the atmosphere in Bonn as relaxed and friendly, almost joyful, and reminisced about what Peter Conradi (after Milan Kundera) has characterised as the '*Rheinische* Lightness of Being'. We wanted to recreate some of this Bonn lightness in the new Reichstag chamber, exploiting the lantern's potential as a major source of daylight. Our earliest attempts at forging a relationship between the chamber and a rooftop structure of some kind were

From its earliest days, Foster and Partners' architecture has been informed by an understanding of how natural light can be used or 'sculpted' to modulate and enrich a building's spatial characteristics; this is allied with an acknowledgement of the benefits daylight brings from an environmental point of view. 1: Natural light and sunlight played a vital role in the design of London's Third Airport, Stansted, completed in 1991. 2, 3: For the Hongkong and Shanghai Bank, 1979-85, a 'sun scoop' was developed to throw sunlight deep into the building's atrium.

hampered by the fact that the form of the chamber was not yet resolved at ceiling level. It was only when we identified the need for a press lobby and located it directly above the chamber, where it could relate to the third-floor faction rooms, that the chamber felt contained as a space. However, while we had successfully capped the chamber's proportions – creating a space slightly higher than the chamber in Bonn – we had reduced its exposure to the sky. Despite the two courtyards on either side, to achieve the degree of lightness that we wanted within that great solid masonry shell, we knew that much of the daylight simply had to come from above. And so we had to think about ways in which we could draw daylight down into the chamber through a relatively small opening.

At the same time we were considering the roof level and how it could be used. We had already identified it as a public level along the lines of the first competition design. In our thinking we equated the roof of the Reichstag with that of the Arc de Triomphe in Paris. It is not like the Eiffel Tower which lifts you away from the city at a huge remove; instead it raises you just above treetop height so that you can see and feel the whole city at much closer proximity. The Reichstag's roof offers a unique vantage point over Berlin. To the west you look out over the whole of the Tiergarten to the Congress Hall, the Bell Tower and across to the new Chancellery buildings. The new commercial towers on the Potsdamer Platz lie to the south, and in the foreground, very close to you, is the Brandenburg Gate. To the

4

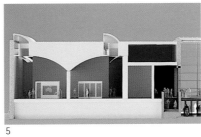

5

6

east you see the whole of the historical quarter of the city. It is a wonderful place to be, and so it seemed natural to add to the excitement and drama of being on the roof by projecting a structure above the parapet that would provide a public viewing platform with uninterrupted 360-degree views.

Responding to a dialogue with the Building Committee, in April 1994 we presented a series of costed alternatives. These included a glazed 'pillow' in the spirit of the earlier 'big roof', and the first incarnation of the 'lantern' idea as a glazed drum-like form, capped by a disc-shaped wind scoop to increase natural ventilation and air extraction from the chamber. The latter became known as the 'lighthouse'. It explored a prototype of the ascending public route and viewing platform that we would finally adopt. Alongside that we investigated more recognisable cupola forms, each time testing their relative performance in daylight and energy terms and exploring their relationship with the organisation of the chamber. The political debate about the dome overlapped with the equally politically charged decision-making process about the seating arrangement in the chamber: circular versus elliptical. This, of course, raised a further question about where the cupola's structure could fall. Structure, services and architectural expression were always integrated in our minds.

We were working towards a crucial presentation to the Building Committee on 28 April 1994. What we did not know was that as Committee members arrived from Bonn for that

4: A very early project, an office building located deep in a Norwegian forest, for Fred Olsen, 1973, used rooftop mirrors to throw scarce sunlight into the building's interiors. 5: At the Joslyn Art Museum, Omaha, Nebraska, 1992-94, rooftop reflectors keep direct sunlight out but allow daylight in and 'bounce' it around the galleries to give even distribution. 6: First impressions: a sketch made by Norman Foster at the time of the first site visit to the Reichstag in July 1992 which was to prove prophetic; the note asks of the dome: 'Put it back in glass – lighter?'

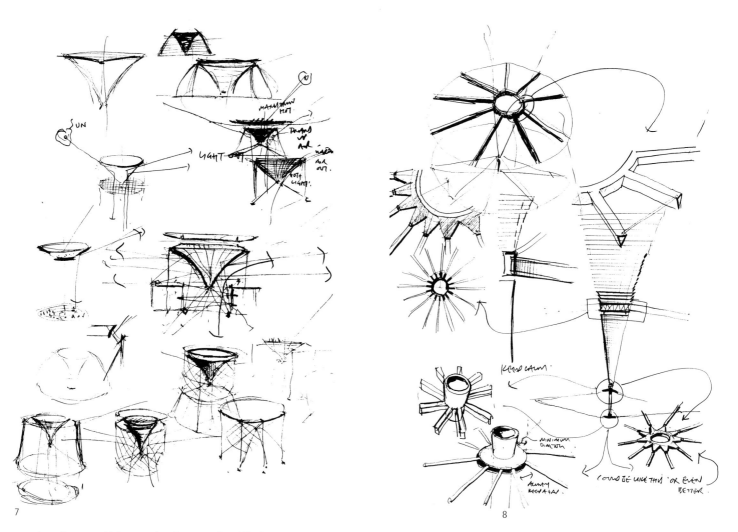

7

8

meeting they would be met by Conservative MP Oscar Schneider, handing out updated copies of a 1986 architectural and engineering report from Georg Kohlmeier, which suggested ways in which the historical dome could be rebuilt. This was despite the fact that its supporting structure had been removed in the 1960s, and its whole *raison d'être* had disappeared. Schneider waved his report in the air and announced to the press that the dome was still feasible, a claim that sharply contradicted our own research.

Not surprisingly, that meeting was stormy. There was a coalition at the time between the Conservatives (CSU/CDU) and the Liberals (FDP). The Conservatives came to the meeting prepared to vote for the dome. But there was nothing in the Liberals' agreement which bound them to support that view and they took an independent line. Chaos reigned; so much so that at one point, the Chairman, Dietmar Kansy, called for an adjournment to allow 'five minutes of debate'. Ultimately it was the Liberal Speaker, Jürgen Starnick, who brokered a compromise with the Social Democrat (SPD) members of the Committee in support of a 'modern dome', although none of the politicians at the time seemed to have a clear idea of what that might be.

A few weeks later, in early June, I was invited to lunch in Bonn with a small group of Building Committee members. I was asked directly by Oscar Schneider if I would be prepared to develop a dome. I refused outright to contemplate rebuilding the historical structure, but agreed to

An idea develops. 7, 8: Sketches by David Nelson, partner in charge of the project, in which he explored the detailed development of the light reflector. Its design sprang from the notion of rotating the curved light reflector used at the Joslyn Art Museum to form a cone — an idea for which there was no tried and tested precedent (7). It developed through experimentation to a point where its efficiency was proven and the details of its construction could be explored and refined (8).

134

investigate our cupola options further. Throughout the project we had not shown the Committee a single idea that did not carry our absolute conviction. I knew that if we were to develop a cupola design for presentation we would have to be prepared to build it.

Towards the end of June we narrowed our options down to two: the 'lighthouse', and a parabolic cupola with a truncated top which contained the essence of the scheme that was eventually built. Both options featured spiralling ramps culminating in a public viewing gallery and incorporated a prototype of the mirrored, light-reflecting 'cone' which is so critical to the success of the entire project. I still preferred the 'lighthouse', since it seemed to offer greater potential for lightness and transparency of construction. The political consensus, however, was for something more 'dome-like' and so we pursued the latter option. On 29 June, following a vote in Parliament by all 672 MPs, the Council of Elders formally ratified a decision in favour of a more dome-shaped scheme.

The decision was made, but as we refined our proposals we still faced rearguard action from the Conservatives and a surprise attack from Santiago Calatrava. One acerbic opponent referred to our truncated cupola as 'an English boiled egg', while Calatrava rather alarmingly accused us of having 'stolen his dome'. He also made an abortive attempt to sue the German Government for damages for allegedly appropriating the main elements of his design.

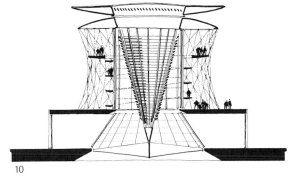
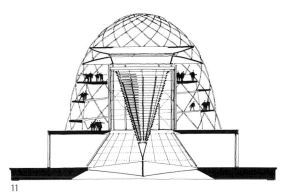

9

10

11

It was a sad case of sour grapes, but it led to a prolonged period of excited and unhelpful press activity culminating in an interview in the *Tagesspiegel*, on 9 July 1996, in which Calatrava baldly accused us of plagiarism. In response to one journalist, who pursued the story, I pointed out that there are 22 domes on the Berlin skyline — on churches, synagogues, public buildings and museums — and suggested that Calatrava might like to claim copyright for those too. It is significant that he had pursued a dome which was square on plan and absolutely without function; it was an empty rhetorical gesture in the spirit of Wallot's original. (Interestingly, Michael Cullen, who had been Calatrava's advisor at the second stage of the competition, had always favoured reviving the historical dome.) However, it soon became clear to impartial observers that Calatrava was misguided, and even the *Tagesspiegel* was sceptical. Eventually the press lost interest in what was really a non-story and the controversy died away.

Altogether it took ten months of consultation with the Building Committee over the detail and nuances of the lantern's design before it was finally approved. We had modified its profile — giving it a rounded top — by extending the secondary structure beyond the level of the viewing platform, and glazed the whole thing. On 9 March 1995, our proposals were formally accepted by the Council of Elders. The question of a replica historical dome had at last been laid to rest. On the same day the question of the chamber layout was resolved when MPs voted for an elliptical arrangement.

9: The first practical experiments to develop the light-reflecting cone were made by lighting consultant Claude Engle using a small model, which he set up on the tip of Gibson Island in Chesapeake Bay where the 360-degree horizon of Berlin could be reproduced. The mirrored cone became a constant element in the different options considered as the design of the lantern developed during the spring of 1994. 10: The cone sits at the heart of the 'lighthouse' which for a while was the design team's preferred solution. 11: An early incarnation of the cupola.

12

13

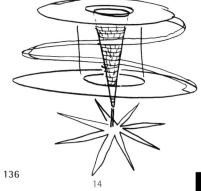

136

14

15

16

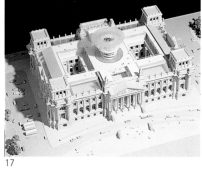

17

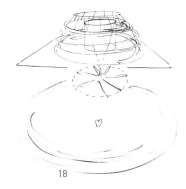

18

19

20

21

The design of a new rooftop feature — not yet a 'dome' — grew out of a sense that the Reichstag should declare its transformation on the skyline. During spring 1994 two options were explored in detail: a cylindrical structure known as the 'lighthouse' and a cupola, initially with a truncated top. 12, 13, 15, 16, 19, 21: Many variations on the 'lighthouse' theme were explored using detailed models. 17: A 1:200 scale model showing the 'lighthouse' in context. 20: The same model featuring an earlier cylindrical solution. 14, 18: Norman Foster's design sketches.

6. The inner one is tighter and therefore steeper

7. The outer one is more shallow

8. In between the two is the supporting structure.

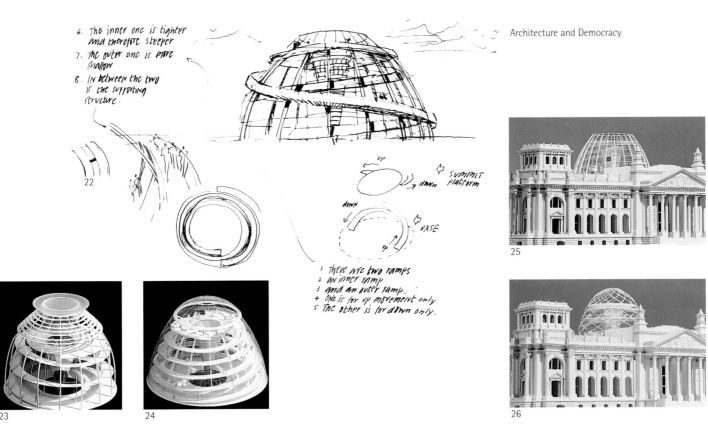

22

up

down ⟸ SUMMIT PLATFORM

down

⟸ BASE

up

1 There are two ramps
2 An inner ramp
3 and an outer ramp.
4 One is for up movement only
5 The other is for down only.

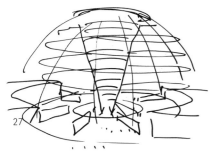

23   24

25

26

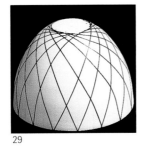

27

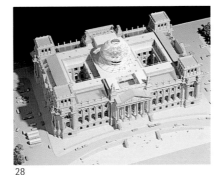

28

In response to the Building Committee's request for a more 'dome-like' solution, the cupola option was progressed. The spiral ramps, mirrored cone and public viewing platform were constant features. 22: Norman Foster's design sketch from January 1995 explores the idea of inner and outer ramps. 23, 24, 29, 31, 32: The design progressed through a series of 1:200 scale models. 27, 30: The cupola approaches its final form. 25: The truncated dome is tested on the 1:200 model. 26: An earlier option with a lattice structure. 28: A model of the approved solution in which the cupola was 'rounded up'.

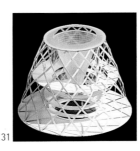

29

of note in this approach it also easy to interpret ... up platform arrive. is now 1st level.

30

31   32

The 'lighthouse' was undoubtedly rooted in the ideas of Buckminster Fuller. But Bucky, I believe, would also approve of the lantern that we went on to build. There is, for example, more than a hint of the geodesic Solar House — designed with moveable, sun-screening inner skin — that we developed together in 1983, shortly before his death. For me, with its environmental and democratic agenda, the lantern is certainly more closely related to Bucky's humanist vision than to the symbolism of the nineteenth century. It represents the ultimate synthesis of old and new in the building and brings together all the elements which make up our programme of transformation. Its circular plan unifies the interlocking geometries of the spiral ramps, the mirrored cone and its supporting structure.

The idea of the reflective cone provided the solution to lighting and ventilating the chamber and forged the vital architectural connection between the chamber and the lantern. The light reflector — a light 'sculptor' and a sculpture in its own right — is a concave, faceted cone covered with a battery of 360 angled mirrors which together form a giant Fresnel lens, just as you would find in a searchlight or a lighthouse. In fact it works like a lighthouse in reverse, directing horizon light down into the chamber. Berlin is a low-rise city; there are very few tall buildings on the horizon, and none close to the Reichstag, and so we had a full 360 degrees of sky to play with. The system brings in light so effectively that it allows us to rely on controlled daylight in the chamber on all but the gloomiest days of the year. In ventilation terms, it

33

34

35

also enables us to rely to a high degree on natural sources. The disc, or 'halo', which hovers over the top of the cupola works aerodynamically and was developed through extensive modelling in wind tunnels. It is designed to draw out stale air from the chamber below, the chamber and cone together performing like a solar chimney. This aspect of the cupola's design is discussed more extensively in the following chapter.

The sun-shade, which runs on a track inside the dome, is a vital ingredient of our strategy. Powered by photovoltaic cells on the roof, it is really a mobile curtain, made up of tubular aluminium blades and controlled by electronic sensors which allow it to track the path of the sun to prevent the penetration of solar heat and glare. In winter, and at the beginning and end of summer days when the sun is lower, the shield can be moved aside to allow softer rays to dapple the chamber floor; it is another aspect of the animation of the lantern. It sounds elegantly simple now, but conceiving the daylighting system and proving its effectiveness was truly a process of discovery. Looking at our work, people tend to focus on technology, but that is only part of the story. The daylighting concept for the Reichstag is unique to Berlin, suggested by its uninterrupted skyline. The same approach would not have worked in, say, Frankfurt. In that sense the lantern is very much of its place. The same is true of other projects. Our daylighting strategy at Stansted Airport, for example, was a specific response to a northern climate; we could not have applied the same thinking in a Mediterranean context such as our Carré d'Art in Nîmes.

Each of the three principal rooftop options was explored in comparative photomontages. 33: The lattice structure of the 'lighthouse' was topped by an aerofoil 'flying saucer' which reads very clearly on the skyline. 34: The truncated form of the intermediate dome, which was described by one critical MP as an 'English boiled egg'. 35: The cupola as approved by the Building Committee in March 1995; only the details of its structure and glazing remained to be finalised.

In the Reichstag, and each of these buildings, you have a strong sense of place, of the outside, of the changes in nature and the quality of light; aspects that lift the spirit, but which you cannot quantify. It is very difficult to convey in words the act of design; it involves a lot of value judgements, some of which can be measured, others of which are quite visceral. In truth a powerful part of ourselves finds its way into design, whether we articulate it or not. It is not just about technology and efficiency. For example, if at the Reichstag, sunlight sparkles and dapples the floor of the chamber at a certain time of the day, it is because a conscious decision was made that sunlight should be an essential ingredient of the interiors. It is not accidental. The sun-shade is specifically designed to allow some sunlight through. It has all been thoroughly modelled and explored. It comes out of a passion for the quality and animation of that space.

We began at the Reichstag by looking at analogous situations: the ways, for example, in which natural light is reflected into art galleries. I cast my mind back to Alvar Aalto's galleries in the Art Museum in Aalborg, which I first visited in the 1970s. Aalto's galleries are cleverly top-lit, with a rich variety of reflectors that direct and control the light without blanking off the sky or excluding a glimpse of the sun. Seeing the building on a late October afternoon — and this is a northern latitude where winter daylight is scarce — the quality of light was such that only afterwards did I realise that it was windowless in the accepted sense of the word. Similarly, in his Stockmann Bookshop in Helsinki, Aalto provides great prismatic

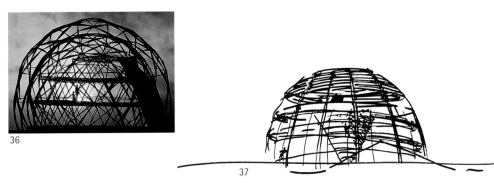

36

37

139

38

rooflights which combine banks of lights with an occasional welcome burst of sunlight. These rooflights must surely be the twentieth-century equivalents of chandeliers: sculptural, functional and decorative.

Collectively, we also drew on our own experience from earlier projects. For example, in the Hongkong and Shanghai Bank, completed in 1985, we developed a 'sun scoop' which tracked the sun to bring light down into the heart of the atrium. Similarly, in a project for Fred Olsen designed in the 1970s for a deep forest setting in Vestby, Norway, we proposed using mirrors to throw skylight into the building's interiors. And in terms of gallery design, at the Carré d'Art and in our Joslyn Art Museum Addition in Omaha, Nebraska, in the United States, we had developed rooftop reflectors to keep the sun out but allow daylight in and 'bounce' it around to give even distribution in the galleries. (The Joslyn Art Museum was under construction while the Reichstag was being designed.)

Sitting in a plane one evening with my partner, David Nelson, we discussed the Reichstag. David sketched out the curve of the Joslyn light reflector and rotated it to form a cone. It was an intriguing idea, but neither of us knew whether it would work. Back in London we explored the concept with Claude Engle, our lighting consultant on the Joslyn Art Museum and the Hongkong Bank and many other projects besides. He saw immediately that we were onto something. He knew that the Reichstag's reflector would have to be a sky-oriented system — like the Joslyn's — rather than reliant on the sun; the sun to some extent

The cupola as it developed was based very much in the thinking of the late Richard Buckminster Fuller — Bucky — with whom the practice collaborated on a number of early projects. 36: Notable amongst these was the geodesic Solar House, featuring a moveable sun-screening inner skin, which was designed with Bucky in 1983 shortly before his death. 37: Norman Foster's design sketch of the Reichstag cupola; the formal similarities with the Solar House are striking. 38: Norman Foster studies the 1:100 model of the Reichstag in the London studio.

39

would be the enemy. And he was convinced that horizon light — which is soft and even — could be reflected into the chamber. Conventional wisdom, however, was to the contrary: that only directional light — a beam, or ray of sun — could be concentrated and redirected in a controlled way. So we had to prove our case.

In densely planned medieval cities, angled mirrors were traditionally hung below the windows of buildings on constricted streets to reflect light into their interiors. I can still remember narrow thoroughfares in the City of London with white panels fixed at an angle below the windows to reflect in a little more light. Following that principle, David Nelson did his own ad-hoc experiments, using a flat mirror to throw skylight into a dark basement room and proved to himself that, while daylight cannot be focused, it can certainly be redirected. It was then really a matter of degree; the question was whether we could redirect *enough* horizon light to create a 'sky-catcher' in the Reichstag.

The detailed development of the cone into a Fresnel lens was really Claude Engle's brainchild. Claude is a passionate sailor, whose motto is: 'If you've got a sail, why use the motor?' Wherever possible he likes to work using the real sky rather than a computer simulation. He conducted the first practical experiments using a small model of the reflector constructed from metal foil, which he set up on the tip of Gibson Island in Chesapeake Bay. This was the closest place to his studio in Washington DC that he could simulate the 360-degree horizon of Berlin. He came back confident that it would work. From that

'Hey presto'. The design of the dome is decided. 39: Norman Foster explains the principles behind the cupola to a visiting journalist, who remains off camera.

point on the cone became the common denominator in our various cupola options. Finally, having refined our proposals and focused on the cupola, we decided to build a large-scale mock-up of the chamber and the reflector and to test it on site.

So it was, on a freezing winter morning in February 1996, that we hoisted twelve large crates on to the north-east tower of the Reichstag. They contained the components of a huge 1:20 scale model of the dome and chamber, minutely detailed and big enough for us to stand inside, which would provide us with conclusive evidence. All of us involved in the experiment, including Claude, David, Mark Braun and myself, were wearing our ski outfits against the ferocious cold. In fact one of my colleagues stood too close to the gas heater that was saving us from extinction, and his jacket caught alight. That provoked the first flurry of excitement. The next thrill came when, using a light-meter, Claude measured the light being reflected into the chamber. The cone worked beautifully — our instincts had proved to be correct.

That winter's day was a landmark — every element of the design was in place. A month later, with demolition work complete, the shell and core contractor started work on building the new structure. The first task was to lay the foundations for the twelve fair-faced spun concrete columns in the chamber — each weighing 23 tonnes — which support the reinforced concrete ring beam on which the dome rests. In April a huge tower crane was positioned in the centre of what would become the chamber

floor. It had a 60-metre boom and could lift up to 30 tonnes. Smaller cranes occupied the south-east, south-west and north-west corners of the building. As the superstructure progressed the contractor would sometimes stay on site welding steel beams late into the evening. You would see a lone man sitting in a cage hanging from a crane, the sparks raining down against the night sky.

While that was going on, the lantern's structure was being finalised in collaboration with our remarkable German structural engineers, Leonhardt Andrä and Partner. Construction began in June 1997. Completed, its steel structure looks almost fragile, though it weighs over 800 tonnes. The ramps were erected first, supported on temporary steel formwork. These were followed by the lantern ring at the top of the cone, and the 24 catenary shaped meridian ribs — triangular in cross-section — from which the ramps are ultimately suspended. Then came the horizontal ring beams, which are trapezoidal in cross-section and spaced 1.7 metres apart; rigid interconnections are made between the ribs and the ring beams by means of cast steel connectors with welded joints. Next came the framing for the cone which is 15 metres in diameter at the level of the public platform, tapering to 2.5 metres at the point where it punctures the chamber ceiling and is braced by a 'spider' of stainless-steel cables. With all these elements in place, the formwork was dismantled and brought down through the open soffit of the chamber. Finally, the dome was glazed using laminated safety glass — some 3000 square metres in all.

The progress of the dome's design, and the political debate surrounding it, was followed avidly by German cartoonists; some were acerbic, some scatological. 40: Bundestag President Rita Süssmuth wears a Christo 'Wrapped Reichstag' gown and a Foster cupola as a hat. 41: The Reichstag dome as adapted to suit different German tenants; clockwise from top left: for the Finance Ministry, the Interior Ministry, to celebrate the World Cup, and for the Chancellor's office (Chancellor Kohl was regularly depicted by cartoonists as a pear). 42: A reference to the cupola's ability to expel hot air.

Crucially, all the elements that comprise the cupola are interdependent. The ramps, cone and framing interlock in a delicate structural balance: you cannot modify the whole without destabilising it. The suspended ramps, for example, apply vertical loading on the cupola on the one hand, but they also provide lateral stiffening within the overall composition; take them away and the entirety fails. The lantern grows out of the building; physically and symbolically it integrates old and new.

With the first ribs in place, on 18 September 1997 the client held a traditional 'topping-out' ceremony. An immense wreath – formed into a mini-dome – was hoisted up to the top of the cupola, and we had our first cue for a party. For the next two days the building was thrown open to the public and 60,000 people climbed up to the roof to get a first glimpse of the new cupola. That figure, although astonishing, was easily exceeded in the four public open days following the building's inauguration when 150,000 people – many of whom queued for several hours – climbed up the ramps to enjoy the first privileged views across Berlin. Today the figure has settled down to a more manageable but still remarkable 8000 per day and the Reichstag has quickly established itself as one of Berlin's most visited landmarks.

The idea of encouraging a steady stream of visitors to climb on top of the parliamentary chamber – 'Allowing the citizens to climb on our roof', as Rita Süssmuth described it – was always seen as radical. It is a great credit to the politicians that they supported this idea rather than under-

142

43

44

45

46

mining it, which they could have done at any point. Sceptics, of course, pointed to a number of potential problems, one of which was noise: would the tramp of feet be heard in the chamber? You cannot create a major public attraction, then place overbearing constraints on the way it is used, and so we had to be absolutely certain that noise transmission would not be a problem. The solution was to 'soundproof' the ramps by isolating them on neoprene pads and to create a noise-absorbing sandwich within the structure of the ramps themselves. Now, should MPs care to look up, they can clearly see the constant stream of visitors above their heads but they cannot hear them.

In certain light conditions – at dusk and especially when television lights are in use – visitors on the roof can see down into the chamber. Television lighting, in fact, was an important consideration. A constant criticism of the chamber in Bonn from television crews was that the tops of the politicians heads were too brightly lit. To achieve the optimum effect on screen you need to create a balance between natural front-lighting and artificial top-lighting. The cone is designed to spread light in the chamber, illuminating the edges of the room more than the middle, and this provides the best effect for television.

The concept that informed the design of the cone as a daylighting device also suggested other, external lighting ideas. If light can be reflected in, then – pursuing the association with searchlights or a lighthouse – it can also be directed out. Taking this as a cue, we experimented with a

All the structural elements that make up the cupola were fabricated in the workshops of Waagner-Biro in Vienna throughout the spring and early summer of 1997. 43-46: The spiral ramps were prefabricated in short sections to allow them to be transported by truck to the site where they were welded into continuous lengths.

number of ways in which the lantern might be lit at night. The normal arrangement, when Parliament is in session, is for the cupola to be evenly illuminated. This is achieved using a ring of spotlights to illuminate the cone, which appears as a brightly lit filament in the huge 'chandelier' of the lantern. On special occasions – as a backdrop to general elections, or the election of the President, and on Reunification Day – a symbolic wreath of light is created around the cupola. At such times twelve high-intensity xenon lamps – christened affectionately by one MP as the 'Twelve Apostles' – which are positioned at the foot of the cone, are directed vertically onto its uppermost mirrors. They project dazzling beams of light four kilometers out into the night sky, creating a new symbol of Parliament and an ethereal landmark that can be seen all over Berlin.

I have seen this idea grow from a vague technical possibility into something that has a powerful symbolic force, and that is a very special experience. But I also remember that it took a lot of lobbying before the politicians could be persuaded to buy into the idea. I felt so strongly about the issue that we decided we would fund the first lighting experiments ourselves to try to prove our case – successfully as it transpired. I remember particularly standing on the bridge over the Spree on the night of the first lighting test in June 1998, with members of the Building Committee. Rita Süssmuth, looking up at the glowing halo around the lantern, said: 'I know it was not your first choice, but it looks fantastic, you know'. I am reminded also of her words a few days earlier at the ceremony to celebrate the lantern's completion,

48

49

50

held shortly before the general election that was to see her party removed from power. Questioned by one journalist about her prospects she said: 'Let's not talk about the elections today, and let's not talk about money. Let's talk about the fact that here ... in Berlin we have created a building which will be a symbol of the openness and transparency of our parliamentary democracy in the coming millennium'.

Certainly the lantern itself has been adopted as a popular symbol of the new Berlin. A colleague reported a conversation with the archetypal Berlin taxi driver, who proudly pointed to the lantern as the city's latest landmark. And I was fascinated to see that when *Die Zeit* ran a series of articles about the new Berlin Republic they used a drawing of the lantern as a 'signature' for the articles. The building was not finished at the time, but the lantern had already become an accepted icon. It is, incidentally, a very economical new landmark, accounting for just five per cent of the building's budget. I think that Peter Conradi summed it up very nicely when he said: 'I feel that it is witty in a way, and so different from Wallot. Every visitor will know on first sight that this is not the historical building. It is absolutely clear that this is an altered building: a building with a history'. The cupola is a symbol of renewal and democratic openness, but it is also a testament to a tremendous *open-mindedness* in government, without which the project would not have been possible. As Dietmar Kansy very kindly put it: 'The cupola is a perfect example of how something magnificent can come out of political wrangling'.

With all the structural elements of the cupola in place the process of installing its faceted glazing panels and the mirrors that comprise the Fresnel lens of the cone began. 47: Glazing the cupola. 48: The glass panels forming the chamber soffit are sealed in place. 49, 50: The mirrors which line the cone are secured in place and adjusted individually to ensure their optimum efficiency.

51

52

54

53

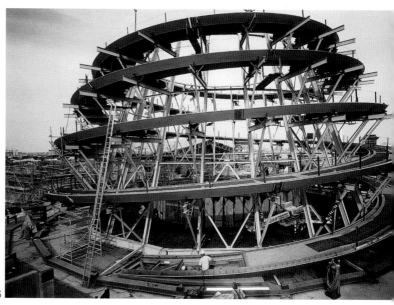

55

Construction of the cupola began in June 1997 and was completed in September 1998. As seen now its steel structure looks almost fragile, although it weighs in excess of 800 tonnes. 51, 52: The first step involved the construction of the temporary steel formwork on which the ramps were supported during the course of their assembly. 53-56: With the formwork in place the ramps gradually climb up to the level of the public viewing platform.

56

57

58

59

With the ramps complete, the lantern ring at the top of the cone was installed, followed by the meridian ribs from which the ramps are ultimately suspended. 57: The first ribs are secured in position. 58, 59: The horizontal ring beams are installed; spaced 1.7 metres apart, they are secured to the ribs by means of cast steel brackets. Inside the cupola the cone framing can be seen taking shape. 60: The structure is complete and the glazed skin is in place. 61: A view up inside the cupola as construction nears completion.

60

61

62: A view up through the open top of the cupola, seen through the lattice structure of the temporary formwork, in October 1997.

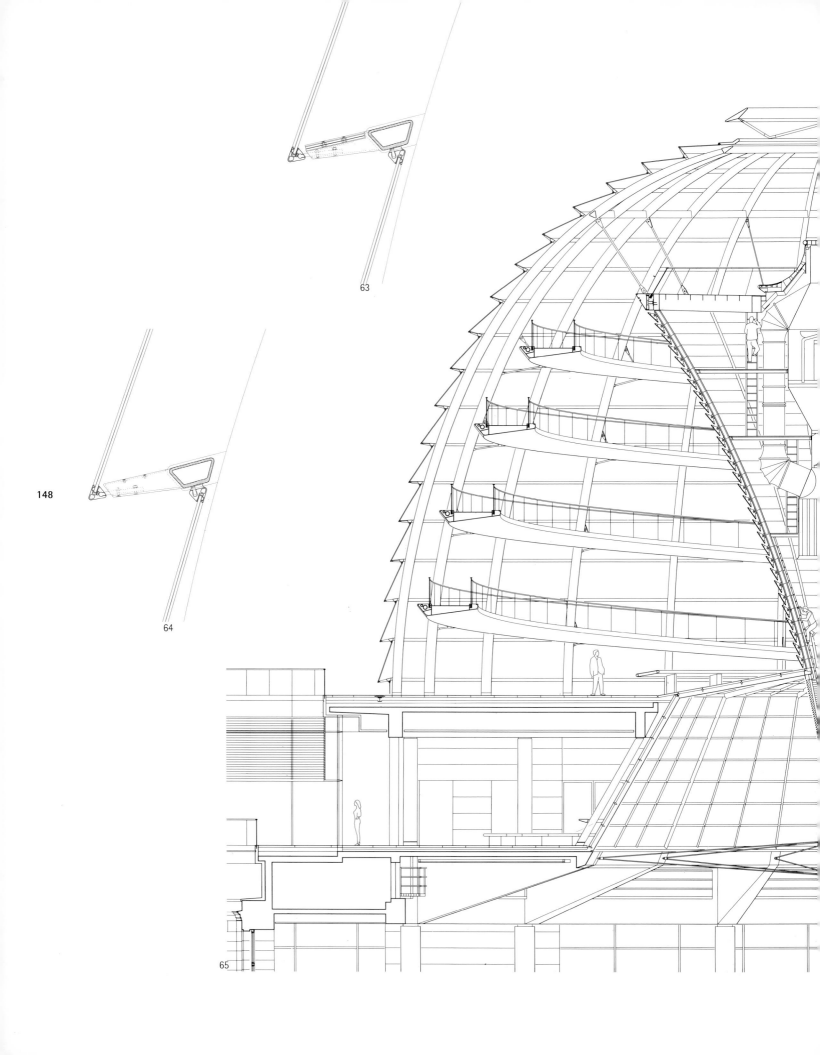

148

63

64

65

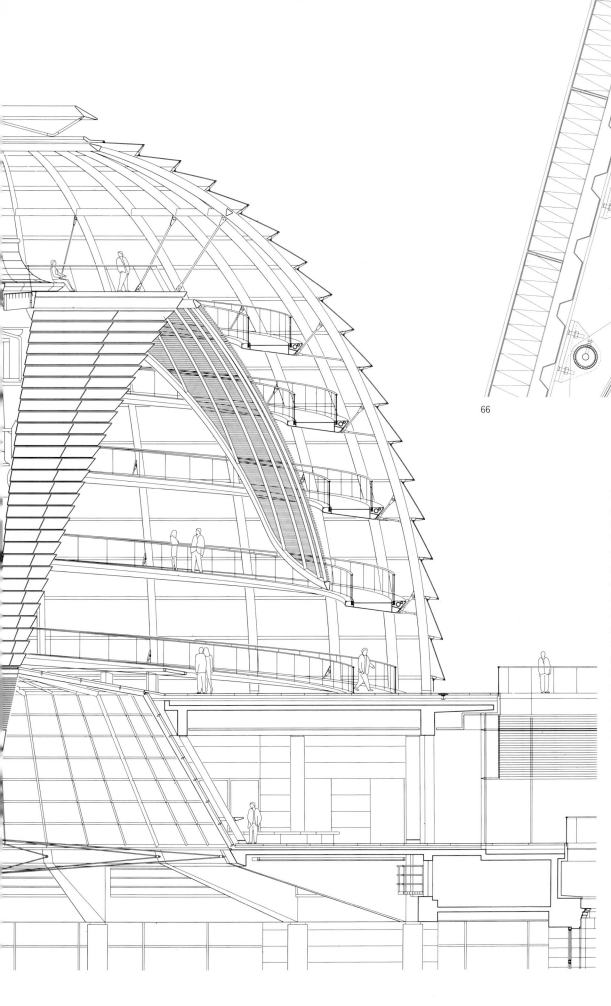

66

Details of the cupola with **149**
glazing and mirror assemblies.
63: The cupola's faceted glazing
is formed from two laminated
sheets of 12mm-thick safety
glass, secured with extruded
aluminium glazing bars. 64: At
intervals the horizontal glazing
between facets is omitted to
assist ventilation through the
dome. 65: A detailed cross-
section through the cupola; the
mirrored cone is cut away
to reveal the air-extraction
plant. 66: Detail of the mirror
assembly. Each mirror is
pivoted individually.

67: The cupola is brought alive by a constant stream of visitors coursing up and down its ramps, their forms reflected to kaleidoscopic effect.

68

69

Within the cupola a sun-shade, controlled by electronic sensors, rotates to track the path of the sun. 68, 69: The sun-shade runs on rails at the top of the cone and is powered by photovoltaic cells on the south-facing section of the roof. Its tubular aluminium blades are designed to screen out solar heat and glare while still admitting sunlight to add sparkle in the chamber below. 70: Norman Foster's sketch which anticipated the mirrored cone. 71, 72: Views down into the chamber and from the chamber floor up into the cupola.

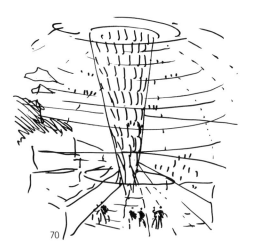

70

71

72

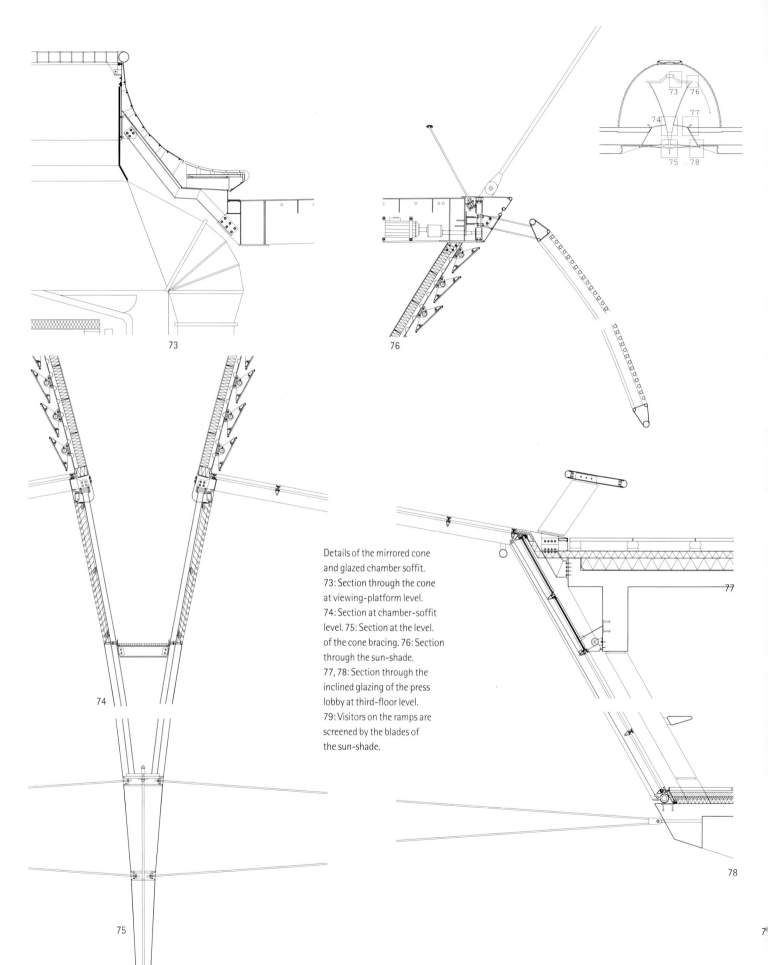

73

76

Details of the mirrored cone
and glazed chamber soffit.
73: Section through the cone
at viewing-platform level.
74: Section at chamber-soffit
level. 75: Section at the level.
of the cone bracing. 76: Section
through the sun-shade.
77, 78: Section through the
inclined glazing of the press
lobby at third-floor level.
79: Visitors on the ramps are
screened by the blades of
the sun-shade.

74

77

75

78

80

The cupola is open to the elements at its top. The spoiler or 'halo' which caps the dome works aerodynamically to encourage air-flow up through the cupola and helps to draw exhaust air from the chamber out through the vent at the top of the cone. 80: A detail of the structure at the top of the cupola. 81: The ramps are suspended by tie-rods from the cupola's ribs. 82: A typical section through the ramp assembly. 83: The cone assembly is also hung from the cupola structure. 84: A section through the head of the cupola showing the aerofoil spoiler. 85: Visitors on the public viewing platform.

81

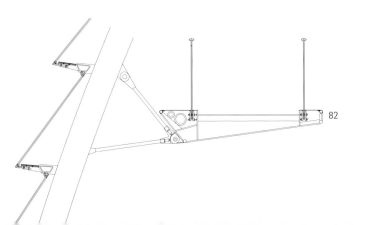

82

83

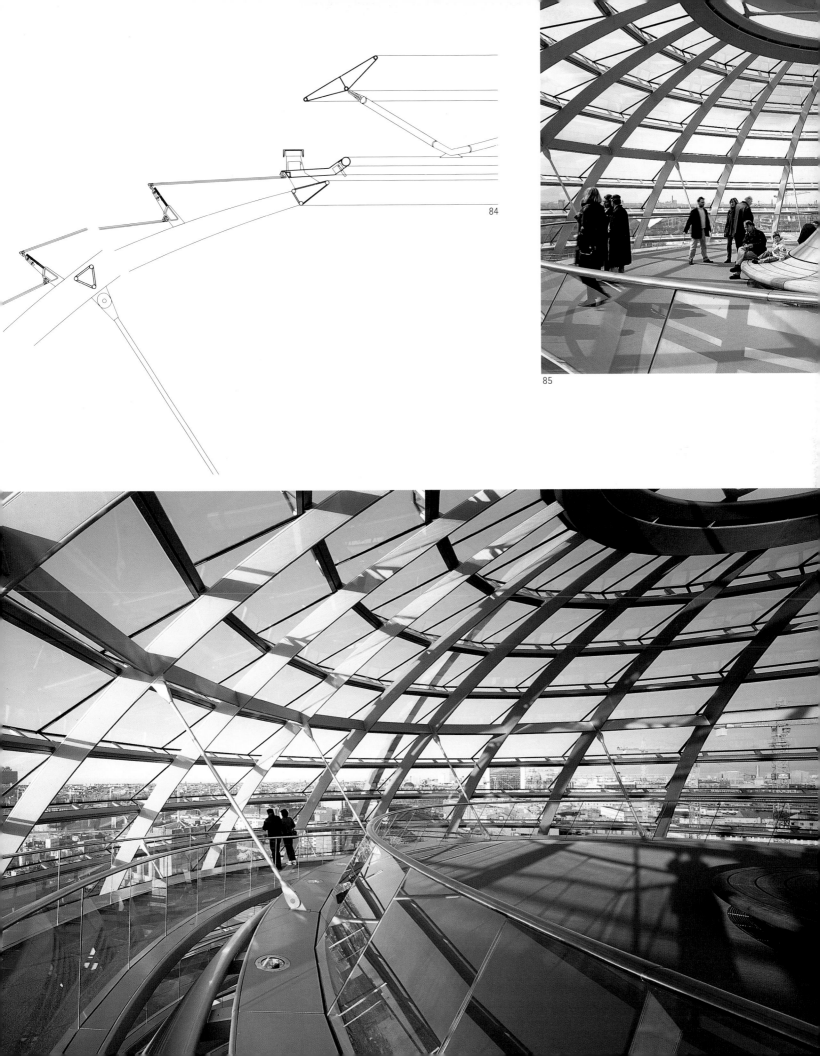

84

85

86

The roof of the Reichstag represents a major new public and civic space in Berlin. 86: The roof-level café is a popular attraction, offering spectacular views of the eastern part of the city. 87: A detail of the third-floor terrace and shaded glazing; this is the level where the political parties have their meeting rooms. The full-height glazing at this level maintains a strong visual connection between public above and politicians below. 88: An early sketch by Norman Foster of the cupola and roof terrace. 89: Citizens on the roof.

88

87

8

Topping-out Ceremony

Rudi Meisel

On 18 September 1997, with the ramps and the first of the cupola's ribs in place, a topping-out ceremony was held in which a traditional wreath — in the form of a dome — was raised to the top of the cupola. Speaking at the ceremony, Bundestag President Rita Süssmuth said: 'This dome ... is a symbol of our freedom, this city and this country ... Here the citizens literally have the opportunity to climb onto our roof to see politics from above and not just from below.' For the next two days the Reichstag was thrown open to the public and 60,000 people slowly wound their way to the top of the building.

When
Democracy
Builds

Some of the twentieth century's most prominent architects have created landmark parliament buildings,

which embody democracy in architecture itself. The new Reichstag forms part of this tradition,

drawing lessons from the transparency and public accessibility of its predecessors.

Peter Buchanan

164 The seat of a national government is one of the most symbolic of buildings, if for no other reason than that it inevitably comes to represent its country. It is also a repository of the nation's traditions and ideals, and the place where its destiny is determined. Such a symbolically loaded building might, therefore, seem unlikely to be commissioned from a foreign architect. This might be expected to be particularly true of a country such as Germany where the sense of nationhood has historically been rooted so much in 'blood and soil', in contrast to countries such as Britain, France or the US where it has rested much more in democratic institutions. Yet it is precisely this elevated status of the democratic institution, the Bundestag, and its democratic processes that the transformed Reichstag now so aptly houses and symbolises, by introducing a dialectical play between old and new, solid and transparent, vertical and horizontal, and by evoking the German ideal of the *Stadtkrone*.

Recent parliament buildings have sought to embody democracy in architecture itself, rather than in surface embellishments. The democratic dedication on the Reichstag, 'To the German People', was belied by the Kaiser's initial refusal to allow the inscription, its egalitarian spirit having provoked his disdain. It was belatedly inscribed as a patriotic gesture in 1916, in the middle of World War I.

Yet there are many twentieth-century precedents of national parliament buildings designed by foreign architects, although they are mostly for ex-colonies, built by architects from the colonising country. The three most famous were all designed for outposts of the former British Empire, but by non-British architects. The Punjabi and Bangladeshi Governments turned respectively to the Swiss-French, Le Corbusier, and the Estonian-American, Louis Kahn, for assembly buildings in Chandigarh and Dacca. Two of the most revered of modern architects, Le Corbusier and Kahn were to help advance these countries into the modern age. Yet ironically, both designed buildings that even at the time seemed more archaic than modern, and to many today seem excessively primitive. They are, however, also highly charged and timeless masterworks, not least because they deliberately evoke local tradition.

Both Le Corbusier and Kahn drew on historical themes from East and West to symbolise the dignity, solemnity and seriousness of government. At Chandigarh the plan evokes the Classical elements of K F Schinkel's Altes Museum while the portico is capped by an Indian parasol roof which, seen end-on, suggests the horns of the local cattle Le Corbusier liked to sketch. Dacca's plan recalls compositional themes found in Mughal and Roman architecture. Both buildings play circular forms against rectilinear; each of their assembly chambers is circular in plan (that at Dacca is chamfered into a polygon), organised around a vertical axis that rises to a distinctive lantern filtering natural light down into the hall.

166

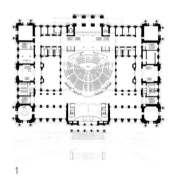

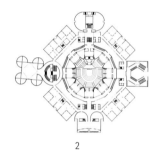

1

2

3

4

The invitation to those entering to lift the eyes, and the emphasis on the vertical axis, inspire awe and spiritual aspiration, raising these halls into hallowed precincts where debate should be measured and inspired. The lantern, in each case, also announces externally the presence of a chamber that is otherwise buried among surrounding spaces. At Dacca the circular hall rises above the surrounding spaces. At Chandigarh, this theme is extended; besides the dominant form of the projecting assembly chamber, there is a smaller pyramidal roof above the council chamber.

The third former British colony in this selection, Australia, chose through competition the Italian-American architect and acolyte of Kahn, Romaldo Giurgola, to build its new Parliament House in Canberra. His design fuses architecture and topography, burying the building beneath the existing Capital Hill. This richly allusive building evokes key elements of Western architectural history, from Queen Hatshepsut's Temple onwards, as well as depicting Australian and Aboriginal motifs. The public can walk up the hill to a four-legged flag-pole which marks both the summit and the Members' hall between the House of Representatives and the Senate chamber below. As now at the Reichstag building, people can ascend above the politicians visible in the hall beneath them. They can also circulate around the complex at first floor level and look down on the politicians from galleries around the central Members' hall and the two chambers. Like the chambers at Chandigarh and Dacca, these are capped by, and top-lit

There are two notable precedents for the interplay between circular chamber and rectilinear enclosure at the Reichstag. 1: The plan of the new Reichstag. 2: The plan of Louis Kahn's Dacca Assembly in Bangladesh. 3: The plan of Le Corbusier's Chandigarh Assembly in the Punjab.

through, conspicuous and distinctive lanterns that are substitutes for a form which has generally been taboo for modern architects: the dome.

Throughout the twentieth century, architects sought less symbolically fraught alternatives. Consider how Erik Gunnar Asplund's Stockholm Library focuses on a drum with a white interior which is an apt metaphor for Scandinavia's pale and misty skies; or the billowing cloud-like ceiling of Jørn Utzon's otherwise Islamic-inspired Bagsvaerd Church in Copenhagen; and the poignantly 'missing' dome of James Stirling's Staatsgalerie in Stuttgart. There are, of course, some exceptions – such as the buildings of Frank Lloyd Wright in his dotage – and there are domes by engineers such as Buckminster Fuller and Pier Luigi Nervi. But for our purposes the most significant exception is Oscar Niemeyer's National Congress Building in Brasilia, another twentieth-century parliament building of international repute. Here too the public has access to the roof via an external ramp to an elevated plaza from which springs a pair of domes. The larger dome, above the chamber of deputies, is inverted (so evoking, according to Niemeyer, the cumulonimbus cloud forms of Brazil's high plateau) and the smaller dome of the Senate chamber is merely a fomal counterpart to it. Little wonder that Foster was for so long reluctant to reinstate a dome on the Reichstag. But these are now Pluralist times, and Modernist taboos are giving way to more conventional responses to decorum and context.

5 6 7 8

Chandigarh and the renovated Reichstag might be thought of as polar opposites. The Reichstag is as technologically sophisticated as the Chandigarh Assembly is primitive (although, more accurately perhaps, both buildings reflect the level of technology then readily available in their respective countries). And while the Reichstag draws in as much natural light as possible, Chandigarh, like Dacca, shuts out the bright glare and heat outside to become a cool, shadowy refuge. Yet there are also some curious parallels between the two buildings. Both chambers are circular – or implicitly so – in plan, are naturally top-lit, and have an emphatic vertical axis crowned by a lantern that announces the presence of the chamber on the roofline. And, just as the Reichstag chamber draws warm air up and out through its lantern, so the Chandigarh chamber was consciously inspired by power station cooling towers, which are profiled to channel warm vapours upwards. Furthermore, many of Le Corbusier's design sketches show a ramp spiralling around the exterior of the lantern, rising from a roof terrace to which the public would have had access to enjoy solar and lunar festivities.

One of the last generation of architects to be fully educated in the Western Classical tradition, Le Corbusier still valued the distinction between exoteric symbols, whose meaning could be readily grasped by all, and the esoteric, to be understood only by deserving initiates. Intentionally hermetic, Le Corbusier's symbolism was conscious and complex (far too much so to be discussed here), and its

Modern architects have explored lanterns, drums and other structures as alternatives to domes. 4: The funnel of the Chandigarh lantern signifies the presence of the chamber externally and is complemented by a small pyramid. 5: The chamber at Canberra is marked by a four-legged flag-pole. 6: At Dacca the circular form of the chamber is extended above the surrounding spaces. 7: The drum of the great library reading room in Stockholm by Gunnar Asplund. 8: Oscar Niemeyer's National Congress in Brasilia, where the shallow dome is overshadowed by its larger, inverted counterpart.

cosmic connections were carefully calculated; for example, a direct shaft of sunlight focuses on a statue beside the Speaker's chair in the Chandigarh chamber on the exact day and hour of the opening of Parliament each year. Such focused shafts of light are a theme in Hindu temples; and the sculptural element of the chamber's roof, which controls the incoming sun, suggests such historical Indian observatories as the Jantar Mantar. Le Corbusier had visited this site and noted in his sketchbook: 'The astronomical instruments of Delhi ... point the way: re-link men to the cosmos'. These elements give the assembly building further resonances with local culture and mythology.

Foster's appointment as architect for the Reichstag renovation was not without direct precedent. The Reichstag was originally built as a triumphalist monument to Germany's belated unification and burgeoning imperial power. Yet the country still felt culturally insecure and uncertain of how best to symbolise these twin achievements. Hence, when the Reichstag project was first proposed, the design was put out to an international competition in which the British architect Sir George Gilbert Scott won second prize.

The eventual building was in a bombastic Italianate style, ornamented with German iconography and statues of Teutonic heroes, and capped by a dome. Built of steel, clad in copper and glass, and square in plan, this dome was hailed at the time as modern. It also rivalled in height and

168

9

10

11

12

prominence the domes of Berlin's Royal Palace and Cathedral, so announcing the importance of the newly emergent Parliament alongside the established institutions of the monarchy and the Church.

Following the reunification of Germany in 1990, and the decision to return the seat of government to Berlin and the Bundestag to the Reichstag, Germany again opted for an international competition to select an architect to rebuild the Reichstag. This was to emphasise the country's transcendence of nationalism in favour of international cooperation, as well as its continuing commitment to being enmeshed in Europe. But it probably also revealed again an uncertainty as to how Germany should represent itself and tame or exploit the association-laden hulk of the Reichstag building.

Compounding such conundrums, renovating the Reichstag would mean coming to terms with more than one building. Once Norman Foster had won the competition and the design was progressing through numerous revisions and refinements, it must have become increasingly apparent that he was dealing with the memories of, and associations with, four quite different buildings: the original Reichstag, its fire and war ravaged hulk, Paul Baumgarten's 1960s conversion and Günter Behnisch's new Bundestag building in Bonn, completed in 1992.

Of these four, much the least important was the building immediately to hand, Baumgarten's renovation. Ranking equally with both the original and the ravaged Reichstag was the

The lanterns above these parliamentary chambers establish a strong vertical axis, suggesting lofty ideals and spiritual aspiration. At the Reichstag this is combined with a horizontal emphasis: the glass walls allow light and views to flood the chamber, creating a sense of transparency and openness. 9-12: The chambers at Chandigarh, Dacca, Canberra and the Reichstag, respectively.

Bundestag in Bonn, then occupied by the politicians. Contrived as the ultimate expression of democracy, this building forsakes any vertical architectural emphasis in favour of a uniform horizontality and transparency, symbolising openness to scrutiny, accountability and accessibility.

The equation of transparent or glass walls with open political process goes back to Hannes Meyer and Hans Wittwer's entry in the 1927 League of Nations competition. This key precedent to the sort of High-tech architecture of which Foster is the leading exponent, was to have been built of standardised repetitive components that minimised expressions of hierarchy as well as suggesting the factories of the proletariat. Meyer's report stated that: 'If the intentions of the League of Nations are sincere, then it cannot possibly cram such a novel organisation into the straitjacket of traditional architecture ... No back corridors for backstairs diplomacy, but open glazed rooms for public negotiation by honest men'.

The transparent enclosure of the Bonn chamber also reveals a bucolic backdrop of landscaped grounds and the Rhine. The ultimate model behind Behnisch's design is, then, not Meyer and Wittwer, but the original seat of democracy, the ancient Athenian Pnyx where political meetings were held in the open air against a panoramic backdrop.

Foster's original design solution, offered in the first stage of the Reichstag competition, might seem to have drawn less on Behnisch's design and more on the temporary arrangement

13

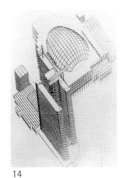
14

15

16

for the 1949 inaugural session of the Bundestag in a converted teachers' college in Bonn. For this occasion bleachers had been erected outside the chamber to allow the public to view proceedings inside. Foster's first scheme proposed a podium wrapped around the Reichstag, reaching to the top of its original plinth, equivalent to first floor level. This provided a public esplanade around the building aligned with the bottom of the huge windows around its *piano nobile*. Rising from the podium were immense columns supporting a canopy that sailed high above the building. Thus was the mighty Reichstag tamed. What appeared to be the lower part of the building was now invitingly open and porous and the whole of the historical structure was reduced to the status of a relic on protective display. The building's bombastic rhetoric would lose all its force. Moreover, people promenading on the podium and on the Reichstag's roof would — though outside the building — still come within its embrace, and to a larger degree take command of 'their' Parliament.

The built solution is very different, not least in being contained within the shell of the old building. A key design strategy has been to fuse, by bringing into dialogue, contrasting formal themes and their various implicit meanings. The most immediately obvious of these is to be found in the interplay between the thick, heavy and solid enclosure of the existing building and the transparency and lightness of the new insertions. This represents a dialogue of the legacy of the past, couched in Classical rhetoric, with the present's very different aspirations for the future voiced in a more 'space age' language.

The use of glass to engender openness and accessibility has many twentieth-century German precedents. 13: The upper level public lobby outside the Reichstag chamber. 14: Hannes Meyer and Hans Wittwer's entry in the 1927 League of Nations competition. 15: The chamber of Günter Behnisch's Bundestag building in Bonn. 16: The 1949 inaugural session of the Bundestag; bleachers were erected outside the temporary chamber to allow the public to view proceedings.

The dominant sense is of a forward-looking lightness and buoyant optimism overcoming the heavy and claustrophobic constraints of the past. The renovated building also cleverly combines the vertical emphasis (with its connotations of higher purpose and cosmic connections) found in the chambers of Chandigarh and Dacca with the horizontal emphasis (with its secular and democratic connotations) found in Behnisch's chamber at Bonn. This is clearly apparent in the chamber, but it is a theme that recurs in the general organisation of the building, and again on the roof.

The result is an aesthetic and technical *tour de force*. Moreover, many aspects of the scheme are symbolically apt and resonant. The light reflector that intrudes into the chamber not only brings energy savings but also makes manifestly clear how it does so, thus becoming a potent symbol of very topical concerns. However, many other aspects of the scheme could be construed as being symbolically ambiguous. It is difficult to predict the meanings that might finally be ascribed to these elements, or whether they will remain teasingly uncertain. It is also unclear whether the agreed meanings will be those the public decides ring true, or those it is persuaded to ascribe as intended and therefore correct.

For example, upon entering the Reichstag, members of the public are offered a clear view into, and through, the chamber via the glazed screen that closes the tall lobby, and another that forms the back of the chamber. This view introduces the theme of transparency and so of the

170

17

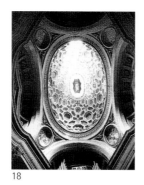

18

19

20

accountability of politicians. Yet this same device could just as easily be read as a tantalising glimpse that emphasises physical inaccessibility. Such are the quandaries faced both during and after design. The architects did in good faith what was possible, within the constraints set by the demands of security and the limitations of the existing building, to achieve transparency: perhaps it is now up to critics and the public to interpret the results in similar good faith.

For those who can penetrate further on the ground floor, the sense of transparency and openness as well as of light and lightness that has been achieved within the massive walls of the old building is amazing. The chamber is flooded with natural light; the space itself seems drawn into the corridors in front of it and behind it and into the courtyards on either side. Here is the horizontal sweep, the views in and out, that in Bonn have been equated with democracy. Yet the space also soars upwards, and the eye is drawn with it, to the lantern and the inverted cone of the reflector that protrudes downwards from it. This, with the light it reflects down and its energy-saving functions, gives an exalted sense of connection to sky and sun, and even to the cosmos. Yet the 'cosmic carrot' of the reflector, with its tapering point stabilised by only the most slender of ties, also lends a sense of the precarious. In this hall, you feel, thought should take wings, and debate be imaginative and responsible, the latter not least because inappropriate comment might be punished by the skewering descent of the rapier-pointed reflector.

The Reichstag's cupola draws the eye upwards to the light and evokes historical associations with Le Corbusier's lantern at Chandigarh, sculpted to correspond with solar and cosmic cycles, and Baroque domes where *trompe l'œil* figures circulate above the heads of those below. 17: The Reichstag's lantern seen from directly below. 18: The dome of Francesco Borromini's S. Carlo alle Quattro Fontane in Rome. 19: The lantern at Chandigarh seen from below.

Yet, for all the space age imagery and concern with the environment, both within the chamber and around, the lantern evokes surprising historical associations, with the Baroque no less. The view up through the dome to the people on the ramps is reminiscent of frescoed ceilings, such as those of Veronese, with skies full of leaning and flying people. And the trick of reflecting down so much light would have been the envy of architects such as Neumann and Bernini, who might conceivably have added a few putti flying around the reflector. Now, perhaps, it is the public — in some celestial realm above the ceiling — who themselves stand in as putti constantly circling in a *tableau vivant*.

The compressed circular layout of the seats is not as extreme as the complete circle found in Bonn (and in the self-consciously non-hierarchical chambers of the United Nations Assembly and the European Parliament) which for Behnisch epitomises democracy in both function and symbolism. He imagined politicians forsaking their tradition of speaking from the privileged position of the rostrum and addressing each other from their seats. But when they continued to speak from the rostrum, those behind the speaker had a disadvantaged view. This is why in the Athenian Pnyx, which served also as a theatre, the seating was arranged in a semicircle: in this first democratic forum it was deemed important not just to hear the words of the speaker but to judge the totality of the performance and of the character who advanced an argument. Now, of course, for such an intimate judgement of politicians, most of us rely upon

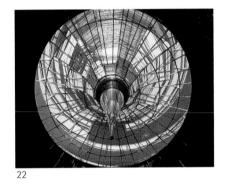

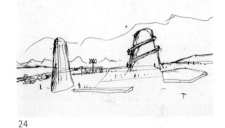

21

22

23

24

television, that ultimate extension of the horizontal, 'democratic' domain. In the Reichstag, it is through closed-circuit television that the press, sequestered on the top floor, will follow debates, as will many of the politicians in their committee and faction rooms.

The raised tribunes in the chamber, which seat invited members of the public, follow the curved geometry of the seating on the floor below. This was the solution Behnisch had first intended in Bonn, but he discarded it in favour of tribunes aligned rectilinearly with the walls of the chamber. He reasoned that the public and press on these galleries are not directly part of the proceedings below and this divorce should be made symbolically clear. But it could just as convincingly be argued that the invited members of the public are very much part of the proceedings: the politicians merely represent their democratic will. Given such a reading, the solution at the Reichstag would seem more truthfully to represent the spirit of democracy than does that in Bonn.

The invited public circulates on bridges that run within the same high-vaulted corridors used by the politicians. The symbolism of this device and the experience it offers — which inevitably informs and adds resonance to any potent symbol — seems again ambiguous: is it a privilege (or a democratic right) to promenade in the same spaces as the politicians, or is the public again simply placed at a tantalising remove?

Public accessibility and transparency are extended as far as security will allow. 20: The public circulates in the same high-vaulted corridors as the politicians, but on separate bridges. 21: The raised public tribunes project into the chamber, set above the MPs' seating. 22, 23: The public circulating on the ramps of the cupola are visible to the MPs in the chamber and can in turn look down through a glass soffit to their representatives below. 24: Le Corbusier's sketches for Chandigarh show a spiral ramp around the exterior of the lantern rising from a public roof terrace.

Clearly visible from this vantage point are the carefully preserved vestiges of war damage: defaced ornament, the scorch marks of flame-throwers, and Russian soldiers' graffiti. Today, the conservation of all traces of the past has become an almost reflex reaction, although in this context, the decision to preserve the past is probably more easily made by a foreign architect. But again this conservation is a gesture that could be seen as fraught with ambiguities. At one level it can be seen as a mark of maturity, and an unflinching commitment never to forget even the worst of the past. At another level, however, it might be interpreted as verging on collective self-abasement; this applies particularly to the preservation of graffiti, which is the equivalent of tribal or animal territorial markings. To erase the past with a seamless restitution of historical fabric and detail is one thing; not to clean up what are merely territorial markings might be seen as another.

The one part of the building to which the public has free access is the roof, including the interior of the dome, the pronounced central axis of which stands against the horizontal sweep of the panoramic view. Traditionally in architecture the roof — as with the original Reichstag — was the realm of gods and heroes, whose images would have adorned the parapets and pinnacles. This was an association that Le Corbusier exploited most explicitly at the Villa Savoye, where the rich disported themselves in Olympian detachment from the world around. On the roof of the Reichstag, against the sky and

172

25

26

27

28

with Berlin spread out all around, members of the public may feel exalted too as they ascend the ramps within the dome to arrive at a spectacular viewing platform. And yet, again, they may also feel excluded, particularly from the politicians whose activities are visible through the glass ceiling of the chamber below.

The dome fulfils multiple functional purposes. Yet its forms are so striking that they invite speculation as to what they might symbolise, and clear meanings are elusive. Commanding particular attention is the faceted, mirrored reflector. This is reminiscent of that of a lighthouse, although it reflects light down and in rather than out, except when it functions as a beacon after dark, announcing that the Bundestag is in session. Both this — and even more so the computer-controlled mobile sun-shade — would have appealed immensely to Le Corbusier, both symbolically and technologically. Not only was he obsessed with cosmic and solar cycles and their symbolic potential, but he was constantly frustrated in his early years because the technology was not yet available to realise many of his pioneering ideas for environmental control systems.

Inside the dome, at the head of the reflector, a wooden bench surrounds the vent through which stale air from the chamber is exhausted. People sitting on this bench look away from each other, making dialogue — the stuff of political process — difficult, while the implied consequence of debate below is that it produces so much hot air, fit only to be whisked into oblivion by upward currents

Traditionally filled with services or inhabited only by statuary, the roof in architecture has been sorely neglected. At the Reichstag the roof is a completely public domain, which includes a restaurant and offers panoramic views of Berlin. 25: Wallot's original roof, populated with statues of Teutonic heroes and gods. 26: The roof of Le Corbusier's Villa Savoye — a playground for the privileged. 27: The ramps inside the Reichstag cupola which ascend to a public viewing platform.

accelerated by the Venturi effect. Such interpretations might be preposterous. But they bring home the impossibility of avoiding the symbolic, particularly with a building like the Reichstag. No matter what functional intention determined its forms, people will inevitably seek and attach meanings to them, and so the architect must anticipate and shape these too.

Yet it is probably the distant view of the new dome atop the Reichstag, an image that will soon symbolise Germany as much as the Capitol dome symbolises the United States or Big Ben symbolises Britain, that will provoke most speculative interpretation. Though it sits comfortably on the old building, it clearly belongs to a very different architectural language and epoch. In contrast to the original dome which, though also glass and steel, seemed to weigh heavily on the Reichstag, the new dome not only looks light but almost seems to be rising as if emerging from the building. Could its egg-like form be seen to symbolise the rebirth of a unified Germany — the eagle has laid?

The dome may also be seen, in a way that reinforces rather than contradicts this interpretation, as a belated but very apt realisation of the proto-modern vision of a *Glasarchitektur* put forward by the poet Paul Scheerbart and the architect Bruno Taut. Scheerbart's utopian novel of that title, published in 1914, claimed that: 'In order to raise our culture to a higher level, we are forced, whether we like it or not, to change our architecture. And this will only be possible if we free the rooms in which we live of

29

30

31

32

their enclosed character. This, however, we can only do by introducing a glass architecture which admits the light of the sun, of the moon and of the stars.' Such a vision was originally hatched in Berlin. But it was realised only in Taut's Glass Pavilion, built for the Deutsche Werkbund Exhibition in Cologne in 1914. This too was crowned by a faceted glass dome around the base of which were emblazoned such aphorisms by Scheerbart as: 'Glass brings us the new era, brick culture only does us harm'.

Such associations might suggest that Foster's light and transparent crystal lantern is more essentially German than the heavy Beaux Arts bombast of the original dome, which some parliamentarians argued should be reinstated. This lineage further suggests a reading — even more resonant — of the lantern as a crystaline *Stadtkrone*, or city crown, without which, Taut argued, no city could fully achieve its identity. This modern secular and spiritual equivalent of the Gothic cathedral — which Scheerbart and Taut, like Gropius at the time he founded the Bauhaus, saw as symbolising the deepest collective aspirations of the German *Volk* — was dreamt of by its proponents as a new civic and communitarian element that would raise German culture to a new and more emancipatory level. Even if not consciously intended, are not such resonances with local culture and myth rather similar to those that raise the assembly buildings by Le Corbusier and Kahn into masterworks? And could any symbolic interpretation be a more appropriate encapsulation of the intentions and hopes behind the rebuilt Reichstag?

The Reichstag's new glass dome echoes early German Modernists' visions of a crystalline architecture representing collective cooperation and spiritual aspiration. 28: The dome of Bruno Taut's Glass Pavilion for the Deutsche Werkbund Exhibition in Cologne in 1914. 29: The interior of Taut's Pavilion with its spiral staircase. 30: Bruno Taut, illustration from *Alpine Architektur*, 1919. 31: Lyonel Feininger's woodcut for the Bauhaus manifesto, 1919. 32: The Reichstag lantern at night with xenon lamps projecting a dazzling crown of light across the skyline of Berlin.

First Light

Rudi Meisel

On 15 June 1998 a mock-up of the cupola's night-time illumination was staged for presentation to the Building Committee. Ordinarily, the cupola is evenly lit using a ring of spotlights to illuminate the core, which glows like the filament in a chandelier. But on special occasions, to mark

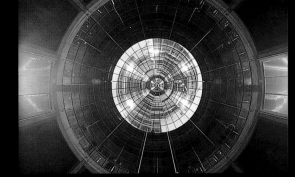

elections or red letter days in the German calendar, twelve high-intensity xenon lamps — the 'Twelve Apostles' — are directed upwards onto the cone's topmost mirrors. They project dazzling beams of light horizontally into the night sky. It is a new symbol of Parliament and an ethereal landmark in Berlin.

Chapter 3

Architecture

The Reichstag eschews wasteful technologies and relies on alternative techniques for energy production.

and

In its vision of a public architecture which redresses the ecological balance, providing energy

Ecology

rather than consuming it, lies one of its most intrinsic expressions of optimism.

Norman Foster

176 Germany has led Europe in the responsible attitude of its environmental legislation and the encouragement of renewable energy sources. From the outset we aimed to demonstrate in the Reichstag the potential for a wholly sustainable, virtually non-polluting public building. We wanted to push the boundaries, to set the trend for public buildings well into the twenty-first century. Buildings currently account for half the energy used in the Western world; and three-quarters of the world's annual energy total is presently consumed by just one-quarter of the Earth's population. Consider those facts and note that, as yet, one-third of humanity has no access to energy beyond burning natural materials, and the implications for energy management are obvious. If this situation is to be addressed, architecture itself must change. This chapter describes our environmental strategy for the Reichstag and the trends it sets for the future.

The Reichstag's cupola provides a symbolic marker on the skyline, signalling renewal, but it also plays a key role in the building's daylighting and environmental strategies.

In energy terms the Reichstag is firmly focused on the future. Its extensive use of alternative resources, together with combined systems of heat and power generation and heat recovery, ensures that the minimum amount of energy achieves the maximum effect at the lowest cost-in-use. It uses daylight, solar power and natural ventilation to provide lighting, hot water, warmth in winter and summer cooling. In fact, because its own energy requirements are sufficiently modest, the Reichstag is able to perform as a local power station, supplying neighbouring buildings in the new government quarter.

The term 'environment-friendly' is now used so widely, and sometimes so casually, that it is perhaps worth restating precisely what it means. The oil crisis of the mid-1970s made many people in developed countries question for the first time the source of their power, light and heat. Then, as now, the bulk of our energy was derived from fossil fuels — chiefly oil — which are a finite resource. As a result of this dawning awareness, efforts began to be made to reduce our reliance on those fuels, both by economising on their use, and investigating alternative energy sources.

From my first days in practice, environmental issues and a concern for economy of means have been a fundamental part of my thinking. It was the late Buckminster Fuller who asked — far from rhetorically — 'How much does your building weigh?' What he wanted to know, of course, was how efficient it was. The story of progress is one of 'doing the most with the least', with more efficiency,

178

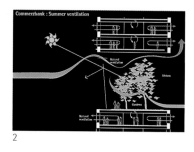

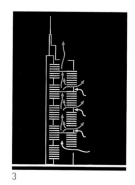

1

2

3

4

from buildings to mobile phones, and that has long been a guiding principle. One of our early buildings, the Willis Faber & Dumas headquarters in Ipswich, designed in 1970, anticipated the oil crisis by pioneering the use of natural gas; that, together with the building's compact form and the insulating quilt of its landscaped roof, meant that it was highly energy efficient. The Willis Faber building attracted as many awards for energy conservation as it did for architecture.

Another early project, a planning study for one of the Canary Islands, Gomera, was undertaken in 1975 in response to a commission from our client, Fred Olsen, who ran commercial cruises to the Canaries and sought to explore the island's tourist potential. Olsen shared our concern for environmental issues long before they were on the agenda of most large corporations. We investigated the use of alternative energy sources — wind and solar power, and methane production from domestic waste — to reduce the island's reliance on imported oil and encourage self-sustaining development.

In many of our projects we ask questions at the most fundamental level; we go back to first principles. For example, the Third London Airport at Stansted, which we designed and built between 1981 and 1991, was the first British airport terminal to take the environment into consideration. We stood the accepted conventions on their head, placing all the building's plant and services in an undercroft, which freed up the roof level, allowing the concourse to be naturally top-lit. In fact, the

The practice's drive towards ecologically sensitive buildings gained ground in Germany, where alternative energy sources are encouraged. 1-3: The Commerzbank tower in Frankfurt, 1991-97, is pioneering in its reliance on natural ventilation; the 'sky-gardens' that spiral up the building act as its 'lungs', while the atrium performs as a distributor. 4, 5: The Business Promotion Centre in Duisburg harnessed solar power, developed the technology to reclaim the heat from extract air, and used an absorption cooling plant to convert excess hot water into cold to cool the building in summer.

concourse is so well daylit that supplementary lighting is required on only the most overcast of days. This has significant energy and cost advantages, because fluorescent lighting, in addition to consuming large amounts of energy, also generates heat, resulting in the need for mechanical cooling. All this adds up to remarkable savings: the running costs are half those of any other British airport terminal. Stansted has since become a design model for other terminals worldwide.

Working in Germany has been important in allowing us to develop our expertise, providing the stimulus to develop still further our philosophy and practical application. The Commerzbank in Frankfurt, for example, completed in 1997, is the antithesis of the gas-guzzling office towers of North America. The client was committed to an environmental programme which went beyond the existing German legislation. We introduced natural ventilation on all 50 floors using the open atrium at the core of the building as a distributor, and introduced internal 'gardens in the sky' opening onto the office floors.

Three buildings in Duisburg, constructed between 1990 and 1993 — the Business Promotion Centre, the Micro-Electronic Centre and the Telematic Forum — produced new thinking about energy and user comfort. We were familiar with the technology of harnessing solar power, but in Duisburg, in collaboration with Norbert Kaiser — an inspirational member of the Reichstag design team in its early stages — we went a stage further, developing the technology to reclaim the heat from extracted air

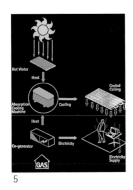

5

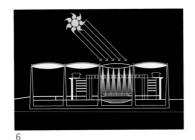

6

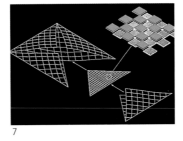

7

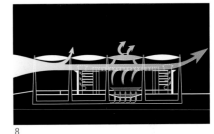

8

and to convert hot water into cold — using an absorption cooling plant — to cool down the building in summer. And we discovered ways of storing hot and cold water for future use.

The 'big roof' — or ecological umbrella — that we proposed in our first Reichstag competition scheme made a symbolic statement about democracy and public accessibility, but it was also a key part of our energy strategy. Many ideas that we explored in the final building first came together under that roof: it encouraged air movement and thus facilitated natural ventilation; it provided shading from the sun and a means of directing natural light; it collected rainwater, which could be drawn into a subterranean storage tank to be used as 'grey' water to flush lavatories, thus reducing the building's water demands; and it harvested energy using photovoltaic cells that convert sunlight into electrical power.

An enormous amount of research went into the development of that roof. Initially, we proposed something that resembled a chessboard: squares carrying photovoltaic panels alternated with others designed to admit carefully controlled daylight. Later on, we developed those pillow-like squares so that each one combined an energy-generating and daylight-control function. Nothing about that first scheme was superfluous. For example, the great stainless steel columns on which the roof was carried functioned as reverse chimneys, drawing down cool air which could then be used to ventilate the chamber. We also explored the concept of storing excess hot and cold water below ground.

The first Reichstag competition scheme — the 'big roof' — established an environmental strategy which is developed further in the final building. 6: The roof filtered sunlight to provide daylighting in the chamber while eliminating solar heat and glare. 7: Photovoltaic cells — which convert sunlight into electricity — would have supplied the building with electrical power. 8: The roof also worked aerodynamically, aiding a system of natural ventilation: the stainless steel columns functioned as reverse chimneys, drawing down cool air to ventilate the chamber.

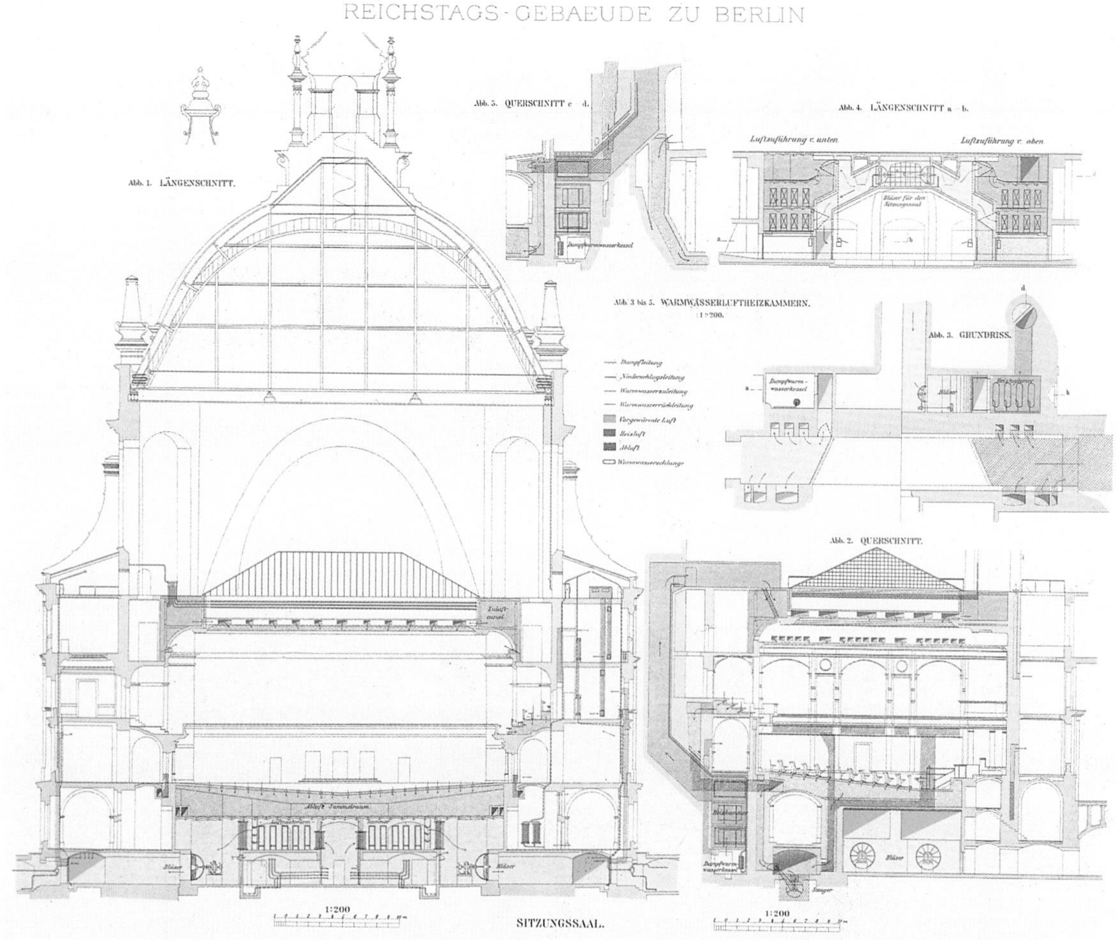

180

REICHSTAGS·GEBAEUDE ZU BERLIN

Abb. 1. LÄNGENSCHNITT.

Abb. 5. QUERSCHNITT c d.

Abb. 4. LÄNGENSCHNITT a. b.

Luftzuführung v. unten   Luftzuführung v. oben

Dampfkesselwasserkanal

Abb. 3 bis 5. WARMWÄSSERLUFTHEIZKAMMERN.
1:200.

Abb. 3. GRUNDRISS.

1:200

SITZUNGSSAAL.

Abb. 2. QUERSCHNITT.

1:200

9

REICHSTAGS GEBAEUDE ZU BERLIN

MITTELTHEIL DES KELLERS IN DER HAUPTQUERACHSE VON W. NACH O.

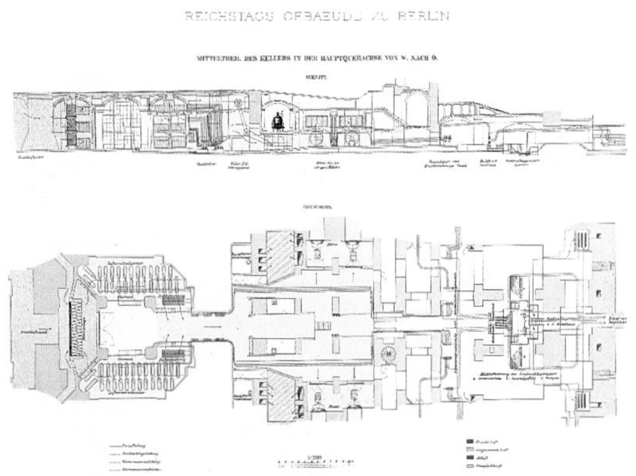

10

11

12

The services installations in the Reichstag, as completed in the 1890s, were designed by the American engineer, David Grove, and were considered 'state of the art' at the time. 9, 10: Extracts from the original services drawings; the chamber was naturally ventilated via a large plenum beneath the chamber floor. Fresh air was drawn down into this plenum through ducts concealed within the west portico and pediment. 11: A view of the Reichstag's original boiler room which was located to the east of the building behind the Reichstag President's Palace.

However, at the second stage of the competition we were confronted with a new brief that required only a fraction of the accommodation originally specified. The chief implication of this was that our revised scheme would have to work entirely within the shell of the Reichstag building. We therefore began to look at ways in which we could work within the nineteenth-century walls whilst applying an energy strategy in tune with contemporary standards. Large historical buildings of this type generally have thick walls, with a relatively low ratio of window openings to facade. The structure keeps out a lot of summer heat, but in winter the building can take a long time to warm up. Berlin can be very hot in summer and extremely cold in winter. Because of its great thermal mass the Reichstag responds only slowly to changes in temperature, which is both a problem and an opportunity, allowing passive systems of temperature control to be exploited. Removing the 1960s lining of plaster and asbestos and exposing the 'heavy' structure behind was a necessary first step towards releasing the building's thermal potential.

In recent years our understanding of environmental issues has become more sophisticated. We have begun to acknowledge the fragility of the natural world and the harmful impact of our industrial installations. We know, for example, that power stations that produce electricity by burning oil or coal are inherently wasteful and environmentally damaging. In Berlin it is estimated that around half the energy consumed to create electricity is expended in the form of waste heat, which is

13

14

15

16

dumped by power stations into lakes and rivers, thus harming their natural ecology. In addition, fossil fuel-burning power stations deposit large amounts of carbon dioxide — a 'greenhouse gas' — into the atmosphere, causing long-term environmental damage. This has been a crucial factor in global climate change.

The new Reichstag works independently of these power stations, eschewing a reliance on traditional fossil fuel-burning installations, and minimising carbon dioxide emissions. The Reichstag as we found it had a very different story to tell. In the 1960s, when it was rebuilt, there was little understanding of, or interest in, environmental issues. The building used oil-fired heating boilers that produced an alarming emission rate of 7000 tonnes of carbon dioxide annually and it was reliant on the national electricity grid to power its air-conditioning and lighting. There was no attempt to make optimum use of natural light. It was a dinosaur in terms of attitudes prevailing in Germany in the 1990s, consuming enough energy annually to heat 5000 modern homes. Like a lumbering supertanker it was also slow to respond to controls; raising the internal temperature by just one degree on a typical mid-winter's day required a burst of energy sufficient to heat ten houses for a year. The status quo was clearly unacceptable.

During our presentation to the second-stage competition jury — which included the politicians on the Building Committee and their advisors — I asked how much it cost them to run the Reichstag. I said I was sure they knew how much it cost to heat their own homes, but could they tell

The rebuilt Reichstag's environmental strategy takes cues from the old building, in particular its original natural ventilation system. 12: Fresh air is drawn into the building through a void above the west portico and down through surviving ducts. 13: A detail of the fresh air intake filters. 14: A view into the air distribution void located beneath the chamber at lower-ground level; grilles in the ceiling of this space lead to the chamber air plenum above. 15: The air plenum beneath the chamber seating. 16: The chamber floor under construction, showing the extent of the plenum.

me how much they spent on their parliamentary home. And of course nobody knew. In fact it was costing in the region of 2.5 million Deutschmarks a year to run the air-conditioning, the heating, the catering services and so on, which shocked them. I argued that, as representatives of the body that set standards of energy conservation and pollution control for the nation, they had a responsibility to provide in the Reichstag a model for others to follow. But we were also able to show that we could reduce running costs dramatically; so if they did not do it for moral reasons, then they should definitely do it for Deutschmarks. The investment, we calculated, will pay for itself in twelve years.

Working very closely with our energy and services consultants, Norbert Kaiser and Michael Kuehn, we developed a radical new solution. Down in the basement of the Reichstag building are the remarkably compact combined heat and power generators, which burn not coal or mineral oil but refined vegetable oil – or 'bio-diesel' – a wholly renewable natural fuel. When burned in a cogenerator to produce electricity, vegetable oil is remarkably clean and efficient compared to traditional sources of energy production.

Refined vegetable oil – typically derived from rape or sunflower seeds – can be considered as a form of solar energy because the sun's energy is stored in the plants (the biomass). Furthermore, carbon dioxide emissions are considerably reduced in the long term as the growing plant

17

18

19

20

absorbs almost as much carbon dioxide in its lifetime as is released in its combustion. In the Reichstag's installation it has allowed a 94 per cent reduction in carbon dioxide emissions. By burning vegetable oil, heating and cooling the building will, we estimate, produce a mere 440 tonnes of carbon dioxide per annum. If the Reichstag were to burn natural gas, that figure would be in the region of 1450 tonnes of carbon dioxide per annum – more than three times the amount, so the reduction is really quite remarkable.

At the time of the Reichstag competition we had been encouraged to regard the interior of the building as entirely disposable. In our first proposals not even the original plan around the two internal courtyards was retained. But the principle of a naturally lit parliamentary chamber at the core of the building was carried through into the second scheme. We stressed the ecological theme in our second-stage presentation, in June 1993, and we found a highly receptive audience, particularly in MPs such as Peter Conradi and Hermann Scheer who were extremely interested in ecological issues.

There was a clear ecological dimension in each of the four options we offered in the crucial second stage of the competition. In each case we produced a projection of running costs alongside capital cost and an estimate of carbon dioxide emissions. Our preferred scheme – which we eventually pursued – was the most radical, offering an entirely new chamber, the complete reconstruction of the upper floors and the idea of public access to a new roof level. Importantly it was also the most economical in respect of long-term running costs. The significance of our proposals was underlined by the fact

Elements in the ventilation strategy for the plenary chamber. 17, 18: The chamber floor is constructed from fine steel mesh which is covered with a specially woven carpet; fresh air rises naturally through the floor and the carpet performs as a filter. 19, 20: Warm, stale air rises naturally to the chamber ceiling and is drawn out via a grille in the apex of the cone, just below soffit level. Exhaust air is expelled from a vent at the head of the cone and dissipated at roof level through the open top of the cupola; here, the maintenance hatchway is shown in the open position.

that we were awarded a grant under the European Commission's renewable energy programme to develop the Reichstag's environmental design further. This project became known as 'The Solar Reichstag'.

The Reichstag lies adjacent to the Tiergarten, a green 'lung' in the city, which means that the air there is relatively clean, although Berlin is still heavily polluted. Applying traditional air-conditioning technology to a building like the Reichstag would simply exacerbate the cycle of energy wastage and pollution in the city. The 1960s rebuilding had done just that, closing off the interiors to fresh air and light so that the Reichstag depended almost entirely on mechanical services. And so we proposed to 'open up' the building once again. The quest for optimum daylighting in the chamber is linked inextricably with the issue of its natural ventilation. The cupola and the cone offer the key to the solution in both cases.

Back in the 1890s, Paul Wallot and the American engineer David Grove had capitalised on the Reichstag's generous supply – by big city standards – of fresh air. The Reichstag's original services installation was considered progressive for its time. Its ventilation system relied on natural up-draughts and flues, concealed within the fabric of the building, which cooled the parliamentary chamber in hot weather. Not that environmental issues were to the fore in the 1890s: in winter the Reichstag was heated by coal-fired boilers which burned tonnes of the noxious, sulphur-producing, brown coal that East Berliners relied upon until recently.

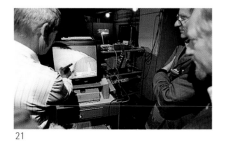

21

22

23

24

Grove's great air ducts have survived and once again they play a vital role. Indeed, without them our natural ventilation strategy would not work. Fresh air is drawn in through a duct on the west side of the building, above the portico, and is taken down into a huge plenum below the chamber. From there, it rises as low-velocity ventilation through the perforated mesh in the floor and is filtered through the loose-weave carpet. It spreads out in the room very slowly and rises gently as it heats up. This provides maximum comfort for the occupants and minimises draughts and noise.

As the warm air rises to the ceiling it is drawn into the cone at chamber ceiling level and exhausted through a wide nozzle at the top of the cone. This system works naturally, encouraged by the 'flue' effect generated by the cone and the cupola. The lantern opening is fitted with a wind spoiler to encourage air flow across the top of the cupola and facilitate the extraction process; it also protects visitors on the viewing platform from adverse prevailing winds.

Within the cone mechanical fans assist this process when required – in Grove's day, incidentally, the system was entirely mechanical. Power to drive these fans, and the shading device in the cupola, is generated by 100 solar panel modules with photovoltaic cells, located on the south-facing section of the roof. These panels provide a peak output of approximately 40kW. Heat exchangers make it possible to recover and utilise a proportion of the heat from the extract air before it is expelled

The pattern of air movement through the chamber, and the stack effect on which it relies, were modelled and tested extensively during the design process. 21-23: Wind tunnel tests are carried out in April 1996 using a precisely detailed model. The aerofoil spoiler mounted on top of the cupola was developed as a result of this process to direct air movement and reinforce the natural up-draught through the chamber. 24: Smoke tests are conducted in the chamber in April 1999 to check the effectiveness of its ventilation systems.

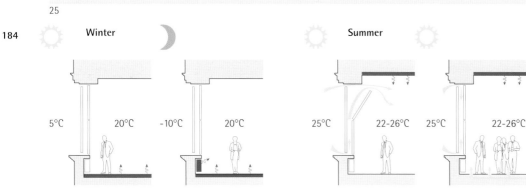

25

Winter

Summer

5°C   20°C   -10°C   20°C   25°C   22-26°C   25°C   22-26°C

26   27   28   29

through the top of the cupola. Air pressure within the chamber can be monitored and the rate of air extraction adjusted accordingly to ensure that a comfortable environment is maintained at all times.

Alongside its environmental legislation, Germany has pioneered the cause of better working conditions. Access to daylight and natural ventilation are written into law: deep-plan office floors, with desks far from an opening window, are ruled out. There is every indication, of course, that better working conditions make for better work. And the freedom to choose to open or close a window provides a considerable psychological benefit. The configuration of the typical contemporary German office space makes full air-conditioning unnecessary, allowing other – low-energy – solutions to be employed. For example, in the Commerzbank Headquarters tower, we were able to use natural ventilation and chilled ceilings – a relatively new system – to cool the office interiors.

Most of the technology I have described falls within the category of 'passive' energy saving, making better use of natural resources. Yet a parliament house is inevitably a high energy user. Sessions may take place at all hours, and on cold winter nights in Berlin heating will certainly be needed. Power is also required for lighting and electronic data systems. 'Green' power in no way means spartan conditions: Members of Parliament may set a good example, but they are entitled to the same standards of comfort as other workers. Our goal was to provide the best possible working environment in every respect.

The plenary chamber is naturally ventilated. 25: Fresh air is distributed via a plenum below the chamber; it rises naturally through the mesh of the floor. Stale air is extracted through louvres at the apex of the cone; a spoiler at the top of the dome encourages air flow; a fan within the cone aids extraction when required. Heat is recovered from the waste air via a heat exchanger. 26, 27: In meeting rooms and offices heating is provided via an underfloor system. 28, 29: Cooling is provided by chilled ceilings; ventilation can be controlled by opening windows, or by mechanical means when necessary.

Aerial view of the Reichstag. 30: Although the building occupies a city centre site its proximity to the green expanse of the Tiergarten — one of the 'lungs' of the city — ensures a constant supply of relatively unpolluted fresh air, which is fundamental to its environmental strategy.

31

32

33

34

35

Outside of the chamber, ventilation is handled using a variety of methods. The most obvious way to get fresh air into a building is to open the windows. People like opening windows and they are in tune with the German belief in user control. The drawback, of course, is noise, while windows without curtains or blinds let in hot sunlight in summer, making conditions intolerable. Moreover, there were stringent security requirements which made it impossible to restore the Reichstag's historical window arrangements. The original window openings have therefore been fitted with a new system of 'intelligent windows', a sophisticated assembly with two glazed layers. The inner, thermally separated, glazing panels are designed to open and to be operated either manually or automatically. The outer layer is laminated with a protective coating and fitted with ventilation joints to admit air from outside. The void between houses a solar shading device. The double layer also gives a high degree of security so that the inner windows can remain open whenever required, especially for night-time cooling.

Due to the constantly varying number of people using the building at any given time, we adopted a flexible energy conservation strategy. This relies on the building's inherent thermal mass to provide a comfortable base temperature from which active heating or cooling can provide 'topping up' when required. This method reduces heat load peaks by approximately 30 per cent over conventional methods and leads to substantial energy savings.

The Reichstag's power plant burns refined vegetable oil derived from rape or sunflower seeds. 31: The Reichstag's vegetable oil-burning combined heat and power generator. 32: A field of rape, a sight seen commonly across Europe. 33: The absorption cooling plant; powered by heat energy, it produces chilled water for summer cooling. 34: Detail of the chamber ventilation plant. 35: The boiler which generates hot water for heating.

⚬⚬	Combined Heat and Power Plant
☰	Absorption Cooling Plant
▲	Heat Pump
⬤	Electrical Power
▦	Heating
🚛	Refined Vegetable Oil

The Reichstag relies extensively on daylight, solar energy and natural ventilation and makes pioneering use of renewable bio-fuel. 36: The mirrored cone reflects daylight into the chamber; the sun-shade blocks solar heat and glare while admitting some sunlight. Refined vegetable oil, burned in a cogenerator to produce heat and power, is clean and efficient compared to fossil fuels. The surplus energy, in the form of hot water, drives an absorption cooling plant to produce chilled water. Excess hot and cold water can be stored in aquifers, respectively 300 and 60 metres below ground.

36

Other passive devices are used to maximise natural light and ensure a comfortable temperature within the building. Mechanical installations are provided purely as a back-up to the building's normal systems. The environmental systems have to take account of the very different thermal properties of the various elements in the building; for example, the spaces contained within the heavy masonry walls of the historical structure perform very differently from those rooms on the new third floor. In the faction rooms — and in committee rooms and other spaces where a high occupancy might be expected — we have used chilled ceilings which continuously cool the building in the summer, to ensure comfortable conditions at all times. Only in extreme conditions — for example, if a committee room is suddenly packed for a meeting — will air-conditioning cut in to cope with the additional heat load.

Rather than wasting surplus energy, the Reichstag stores and recycles it, using underground seasonal energy reservoirs. Surplus heat is discharged as warm water down one of two boreholes into a natural aquifer located more than 300 metres below ground — a depth equivalent to the height of the Eiffel Tower or ten times the height of the Reichstag to the top of its cupola. That sounds staggering, but is actually quite modest by the standards of the oil industry which routinely drills down 3000 metres or more from rigs in the North Sea. In winter, stored warm water is pumped back up into the building, via the second borehole, to provide supplementary heating via a network of under-floor pipes. Cold water

188   Natural   Mechanical

37

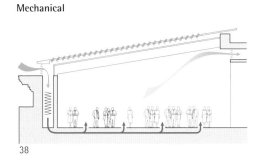

38

39

can be similarly pumped from a shallower aquifer, no more than 60 metres below ground. Moreover, using an absorption cooling plant, surplus heat energy from the cogenerator can be harnessed to chill the water required to supply the chilled ceilings.

There is a satisfying economy about the Reichstag's environmental programme which is absolutely integrated with the architecture of the building. Burning 'bio-diesel' is an environmentally friendly process, with relatively little impact on the atmosphere. The plants from which the oil seed comes are a renewable resource. The daylight and natural air supply systems in the building cost nothing to run. The services are kept to a minimum, with none of the intrusive ducting and plant installations which so disfigured the Reichstag in the 1960s. The beneficiaries are, firstly, the historical character of the building, freed from these intrusions, and secondly, the building's users.

All of this makes sense in both ecological and comfort terms. We have done away with the homogenised overheated or overchilled interiors with which we are all familiar but which few of us find comfortable. Instead the Reichstag uses precious natural resources, recycling rather than wasting, to produce a stimulating environment in all seasons. The outside temperature may be as hot as the Mediterranean or as cold as the Steppes, but the temperature inside the building will vary by no more than a few degrees. It is an object lesson in sustainability.

37: The faction rooms at third-floor level rely extensively on daylight and natural ventilation. 38: On hot summer days, or when the rooms are fully occupied, mechanical systems of ventilation and cooling can be employed. 39: A view into one of the faction rooms; solar gain is eliminated by the glazing system which incorporates 'egg-crate' baffles that admit only north light. 40: Photovoltaic cells line the south-facing portion of the roof; they convert sunlight into electrical power to drive the sun-shade within the cupola.

Testing the Acoustics

Rudi Meisel

As the building was prepared for hand-over to Parliament, a one-day acoustic test was conducted in the chamber, on 25 February 1999. For the occasion 1100 members of the Bundeswehr stood in as MPs to simulate a parliamentary session. Project architect Mark Braun took the rostrum to explain the exercise. The atmosphere was very relaxed. Officers performed as members of the government and read aloud from chosen texts to simulate political speeches; these reinforced the light-hearted theme – accounts of holidays in California and the hippies of Woodstock.

Mythos

Ordinary people are caught up in the lives of great buildings, like dust on the shoes of historical giants.

Reichstag

The Reichstag is one such building, and this is the story of a few of those

people whose lives have been touched by it.

Frederick Baker

The Reichstag is not the emblem of a single person, a city, or a party, but is dedicated to a *Volk — Dem Deutschen Volke*, 'To the German People'. For those people whose lives have been shaped or scarred by the Reichstag, the building has taken on a mythical quality: 'Mythos Reichstag'. They remember the Reichstag as maternity ward, as battleground, as photographic location, or as a looming backdrop to rock concerts, popular gatherings, and even football matches. Their stories go deep to the heart of why rebuilding the Reichstag was a challenge that goes beyond the realm of architecture and into the realm of emotional engineering. Every stone, every wall and every window has a story that is not just a matter of architecture but a clue to who the Germans are, who they have been, and how they see themselves in the future.

Yevgeny Khaldei's famous photograph of the Red Flag being raised on the roof of the Reichstag. The picture was staged as a victory photograph for Stalin on 2 May 1945, two days after Mikhail Petrowitsch Minin first hoisted the Red Flag above the Reichstag's portico.

History is literally etched deep into the Reichstag's fabric. The Kaiser belatedly allowed the building to bear its now famous inscription *Dem Deutschen Volke*, in the middle of World War I, as a sort of medal for the nation. World War II wrote its own inscription, this time not in the bronze of captured French cannon, but in the stone-stinging bite of bullets and the shrapnel of the 'Stalin Organ'; victorious Soviet voices are frozen in the chaos of the Cyrillic graffiti that still covers parts of the Parliament's walls.

Violence is also integral to the Reichstag's mythic quality. The building has been a battleground since the night of 27 February 1933 when flames licked the seats of the parliament-arians and Hitler seized the opportunity to publicly abandon democracy and introduce a state of emergency. It was this measure that marked Hitler's first move against his enemies inside Germany. Clouds of doubt still hang over the identity of the Reichstag's arsonists, a situation that has further enhanced the building's mythical status. A Dutch 'vagrant', Martinus van der Lubbe, was arrested and tried for the crime, but the fire marks the point at which the Reichstag really took its place on the international stage.

With its debating chamber destroyed, the Reichstag was abandoned. The Nazis had no interest in a building that symbolised the old order. When its repair was undertaken, it was to facilitate its use as a humble library serving an enormous, new general assembly hall proposed by Albert Speer — Hitler's architect — in his rebuilding of Berlin as 'Germania'.

194

1

2

3

4

German reunification, and the subsequent rebuilding of the Reichstag, has placed the building at centre stage once again. It is ironic that, when visiting the Reichstag building site, many old Berliners were taken back to the past. The construction work that heralded a new age paradox-ically gave the building back a flavour of the intense and frenzied activity of the war years.

One such Berliner is Mariele van der Wyst, now a 55-year-old housewife. At first sight her birth certificate is like that of any one of the thousands of Germans born under Nazi rule: brown paper, eagle, swastika. Only on closer inspection does one notice the small detail that makes it so spe-cial: the line that reads 'place of birth' has the entry *Im Reichstagsgebäude* (in the Reichstag building). This makes Mariele one of only two people known to have been born in the Reichstag. It is strangely typical of the building's twisted history that it should go one better than other parliaments: the Reichstag is a place where not just laws, but people, have been born.

Deep in the cellars of the building she recalled: 'I was always very proud to tell people that I was born in the Reichstag.' It was the first time as an adult that she had penetrated the walls that had protected her mother in labour. It was a quiet Sunday — a stark contrast to the cacophony of the nightly air raids her mother knew. Mariele was born on 15 September 1944 as Berlin was beginning to break under the strain of impending defeat: her certificate was not filled out until four months later.

In the autumn of 1940, as the first air raids struck Berlin, the authorities ordered that a makeshift maternity ward should be set up in the Reichstag's cellars. 1: Mariele van der Wyst, one of only two people on record to have been born in the Reichstag. 2: Mariele's birth certificate, giving her place of birth as *Im Reichstagsgebäude*. 3, 4: The cellars of the Reichstag, where Mariele was born, photo-graphed shortly after the end of the war.

Surrounded by the brightly coloured pipes of the newly installed heating system, Mariele reflected: 'Women from all over Berlin came here when they were close to giving birth because it was one of the safest places in the city. My mother had to make the journey from far-off Lichtenberg in East Berlin. If the baby came at night the women were allowed to stay for a bit, but if it didn't then they had to go back home in the morning and return the next night. It was a maternity shelter not a proper full-time ward.' The doctors and nurses came from the old Huguenot hospital, the *Charité*, which is still located close to the Reichstag on the opposite bank of the Spree. Research by the historian Gerhard Hahn shows that in the autumn of 1940 the city authorities ordered part of the hospital's obstetrics unit to be transferred to the Reichstag's cellars to be safe from air raids.

For most of the war, the Nazi regime continued to ignore the Reichstag. On the rare occasions that they met, the National Socialist deputies gathered at the Kroll Opera House, their temporary home from 1933. The real centre of power was Hitler's Chancellery, where the Nazi high command was based. Anti-aircraft guns were installed in the Reichstag's corner towers in 1941 to deflect the first bombing raids, and the windows were bricked up, but apart from its role as a maternity ward, the building's main function for most of the war was as a military medical archive. However, as the Allies began their encirclement of Germany, and Berlin readied itself for the advance, the Reichstag became increasingly

5

6

7

8

important as a stronghold. When the general order to prepare for the 'defence of the imperial capital' was issued on 9 March 1945, concrete bunkers were constructed on the building's flanks.

At the time, Klemens Köhler was busy in the Reichstag filling out some of the fourteen million files on the men wounded or killed at the ever-encroaching front. Himself wounded, he was put to work in the military medical archive from 1942 until the bitter end in May 1945 as part of the company of wounded soldiers, doctors and civilians who recorded military casualties within hours of their occurrence.

Klemens' story combines the conviction of one who has related it many times with a keen eye for the perversity of war: 'I remember that in the archive we stacked up the boxes to form a protective wall. We left slits to shoot through. It was crazy, each box had 100 medical records. Lying there I was being protected by pages full of doctors' descriptions of the suffering of thousands of men.' His memory of the fighting in the darkness of the Reichstag is based on a series of strong images: a hungry dog scavenging in no-man's-land; the blood of dead Germans and Russians staining the stairs where the parliamentarians used to enter the plenary chamber. After his surrender he remembers: 'I was pushed up against a wall and a machine gun was put to my chest. A Russian asked "Where is Hitler, where is Goebbels?" I replied that they were in the Chancellery. All the Reichstag housed was the military medical archive.' They believed him and so he survived to join the ranks of the prisoners of war.

During World War II the Reichstag also housed a military medical archive, which recorded casualties at the front. Its fourteen million files served as a shield for the archivists when the Red Army stormed the building on 30 April 1945. 5, 6: Klemens Köhler, a German soldier who worked in the Reichstag's medical archive, photographed after he was wounded in 1942. 7, 8: In these photographs, staged for propaganda purposes after the Russian victory, Soviet tanks approach fortress Reichstag.

Klemens explained why they had fought for the Reichstag even though it had no military significance. The answer had two letters – the SS: 'I had seen the men that the SS hanged from the bridges with the signs "I was too cowardly to defend women and children". There was the crazy idea that we would be rescued by General Wenck's army breaking through from Potsdam.'

Another young soldier – age fifteen to be precise – saw things very differently. Ernst Bittcher actually believed in General Wenck's rescue mission. He was one of the force of inexperienced teenaged boys and tired old men scraped together in the last month of the war in a last-ditch attempt to defend the capital. Today he is a professor and builds church organs, but in those days he was the brainwashed child of a believing Nazi, never countenancing defeat, even while the walls of the Reichstag that protected him 'shook with the unbelievable blast of the Russian artillery'.

Inside the Reichstag cellars he remembered: 'I wandered through the deserted rooms of one tower and stumbled upon the models of Speer's Germania. Being interested in architecture I went into the room and I remember that the dome of the Germania congress hall was so large that ducking under the model I could put my head right into it and look around! Under one of the models I found a small bronze sculpture of a young girl's head made by Arno Breker, Hitler's favourite sculptor. I stuck it in my rucksack as a souvenir.

9

10

11

12

'The Reichstag was of no particular significance to us. It was just a big building with solid walls. We had been brought up as believing Nazis, and so thought that it was just a relic of a previous era.' The old men to his left and right nod in agreement. Dr Oskar de la Chevalerie and Dr Reinhard Pohl were also anti-aircraft gunners in their mid-teens, sheltering in the Reichstag in April 1945 as the Red Army pounded the city. They point out the window on the ground floor that was the only way in or out of the building – the exit to hell or the entrance to safety depending on whether they were leaving or entering fortress Reichstag.

The Soviet advance towards Berlin began on 16 April. By 24 April the Russians had closed a ring around the city. The next day the Soviet and US armies made contact at Leipzig. On the night of 28 April, under desperate fire from German troops in the Kroll Opera House, the Soviet infantry crossed the Moltke Bridge and entered the city centre. By the next morning they had taken the Swiss Embassy, from where they could target their guns on the Reichstag and watch the approach road. Next they captured the Opera House, the last point in the defence of the Reichstag, and brought 90 heavy guns up to the front of their target.

At noon on 30 April, they launched their attack. First, a volley of heavy artillery strafed the already battered shell, blasting holes in the bricked-up windows; then, small teams of

Soviet soldiers stormed the building. Two hours later the Soviet flag was waved from a window on the second floor, but hand-to-hand combat raged on inside the building for two days until the last German troops in the basement finally surrendered. During these two days of fighting it is estimated that 2200 Soviet soldiers and 2500 German soldiers died.

As he scanned the scene of cranes and portacabins that filled the Reichstag's Königsplatz construction site Ernst remembered: 'We were all hiding in the cellars of the Reichstag when some SS officers found us and shouted at us, "You cowardly pigs". I was ordered to take bread and butter across the battlefield to the troops in the Kroll Opera House who were stopping the Russian tanks from crossing the Moltke Bridge. The next time I was sent with more than just sandwiches – a whole load of anti-tank munitions! I saw the troops pick off the Russian tanks as they tried to come over the bridge. It was senseless, because the war was already lost'.

The absurdity of the situation can be seen in the fact that on the night of 30 April when the Russians entered the building and Klemens was hiding behind the medical records of wounded soldiers, Ernst was sent across the Tiergarten Park to the Zoobunker to collect iron crosses. 'There were SS men trying to rip off their insignia, and women dressing as men to avoid being raped. Walking back, the sky was like a New Year's Eve night, full of fireworks. I came back to the Reichstag and saw it burning'.

13

14

15

16

Worse still, Ernst's world had collapsed. He had just heard that Hitler had 'died for Germany, fighting Bolshevism to his last breath'. He knew it was over: 'There was no organised defence, there were just odds and sods – sailors, parachutists and Hitler Youth air raid helpers like ourselves. The next day was 1 May and I remember other soldiers saying, "The Russians are on the roof"'.

Oskar de la Chevalerie recalled: 'I remember hearing balalaika music coming from the roof. The Russians occupied the top of the building and we were in the bottom. The front line ran across the middle of the Reichstag'. Dr Reinhard Pohl was on the first floor. His experience differs considerably from Klemens Köhler's: 'I never saw any Russians in the building. They must have been well hidden'. On 1 May he and his comrades were playing cards or chess. 'We had the order to flush the Russians out of the building, but we had no real weapons – just a few hand grenades'. The discrepancy in these two histories can be put down to the size of the Reichstag: Köhler was on the north side close to the Red Army's lines, the young soldiers were on the quieter, south-west side.

Where they agree is on the role of the SS. Reinhard Pohl: 'Sometimes I went down to the cellars to sleep, but the SS men would come and kick us out and get us into action. I don't know what we were supposed to be doing there'. It is another strange twist that the SS men so keen to defend this bastion dedicated 'To the German People', were in fact Belgians, members of the Walloon Division. But by

The Reichstag held a symbolic significance for the Red Army that far outweighed its strategic importance. Not only was it associated with the vilification of Communists after the fire in 1933, but it was the nominal home of the Nazi Government. Victory over Germany would not be complete until the Reichstag had been captured. 13, 14: Russian soldiers celebrate the raising of the Red Flag on the Reichstag's roof. 15: A despondent German soldier sits amid the ruins. 16: A reconstruction of the storming of the Reichstag, filmed by the Soviet authorities to perpetuate the myth of glorious victory.

the morning of 2 May the SS had gone and survivors in the cellars surrendered: 'The Russians treated us well, better than a football team that has just lost. They said to us, "Go home to Mutti".'

To a man they question the heroic presentation of the battle for the Reichstag portrayed in countless Russian films and museum dioramas. As Reinhard Pohl put it: 'The Reichstag was picturesque, a representative building, a facade, but it had no meaning for Hitler and his regime. For the Russians it was like a medieval castle. It was a symbolic action. There was no glorious victory to be gained. The battle for Berlin had already been decided.'

Mikhail Petrowitsch Minin is one of the Russian soldiers who stormed the Reichstag on 30 April. When Mikhail returned to the Reichstag in April 1999, wearing full uniform, his many medals jangling on his chest, the security guards looked as if they had seen a ghost. It was 54 years since his last visit. 'I didn't come in this way last time', he noted wryly, 'I came through the main entrance.' At the west door he remembered: 'We rammed it in. It's a medieval method, but a reliable one. Zaikitov was at the fat end of the log and Simienko the skinny end. Others also grabbed hold and we smashed down the door. We broke the mechanism and my comrades and I flooded in.'

Stalin was reported to have given the order to raise a flag on the Reichstag by 1 May in the name of the Red Army. Minin remembered: 'I had the banner under my shirt but had nothing

198

17

18

19

20

with which to fix it. On the way up to the roof I spotted a length of conduit for electric wires. I realised that it would make a great flag-pole. I grabbed it and it came away. When I got out onto the roof it was dark. But with the help of my comrades I found a crown on a statue. The crown had a hole in it. We erected the flag at 10.50pm local time.' And that is where the Red Flag was first placed.

Yet rather than receiving a hero's welcome, on returning to his unit, Minin hit a wall of silence. General Schatilov had already told Stalin that his, not Minin's, division had raised the Red Flag on the Reichstag. Against the word of a general, the truth and an ordinary soldier had no chance. Two model soldiers, Kantariya and Yegorov, one of them a Georgian like Stalin, were picked to take the glory. They were lauded, awarded medals and given cars, while Minin was stonewalled. Schatilov's flag still hangs like a holy relic in the Central Army Museum in Moscow. As so often in the history of the Reichstag, myth is more powerful than reality.

Yevgeny Khaldei took the photograph that Stalin used to perpetuate the myth, ensuring that the raising of the flag above the Reichstag's portico became one of the most famous images of the century. When we met, Khaldei was wearing his war medals and had his trusted Leica round his neck. He was delighted to be able to travel back in time.

Khaldei's photograph has deep roots. As he explained, it went back to an old woman he photographed in front of a panorama of ruined Murmansk: 'She was just an ordinary woman

Stalin is reported to have given the order to raise the Red Flag on the roof of the Reichstag by 1 May 1945. The goal was achieved at 10.50pm the night before. The act was restaged two days later so that it could be photographed. Two model soldiers, one of them a Georgian like Stalin, were falsely credited with the deed. 17: Mikhail Petrowitsch Minin, the soldier who really raised the Red Flag. 18: Minin with his former adversaries, Reinhard Pohl and Ernst Bittcher, before the new Reichstag in 1999. 19: Yevgeny Khaldei, the man who took the photograph. 20: Khaldei's photograph, taken on 2 May.

who had collected everything that was left of her home. When I photographed her as she was walking along, she stopped, put down her case and looked at me and said, "Why aren't you ashamed of photographing our Russian misery?" I was embarrassed at such a question. I said, "But it's history!" And she said, "Well you could be photographing our pilots bombing Berlin – that would be a good thing!" That rather threw me. I hadn't expected a simple old woman to express her thoughts like that. I replied, "Well if I'm lucky enough to be in Berlin when it happens, I shall certainly photograph it."' So off he went with the Red Army, Berlin-bound: 'My mood was the same as that of all the soldiers – that we had to take Berlin. Take Berlin and raise our flag over the Reichstag.'

While Reinhard Pohl was being told to go home to Mutti, Khaldei was moving fast. Stalin needed a victory photograph. Khaldei had run out of flags, and had been up all night quickly making another out of red tablecloths: 'It was 2 May, early in the morning, near the Brandenburg Gate. I was going to the Reichstag, not walking but running. I was in a great hurry to get there. It was raining and there was fog. I went to the Reichstag and I took out a flag and unfurled it. There were soldiers there and they said, "Come on, let's take it up to the roof." We couldn't get onto the cupola because the building was on fire. I stood there on the roof with the flag but there was no flag-pole. There was, however, a sculpture and I said, "Give me that pole from there."' He went over and took the big pole and affixed the flag to it. 'I could see that

21

22

23

compositionally everything was fine: you could see the Brandenburg Gate, and Berlin in flames, in other words it was all there. I went through two rolls of film. I had an intense feeling of victory. Despite what we had been through in Russia and what I had been through myself with my family – the Germans killed my father and my three sisters – all the same I had this sense of victory. Well that's something everyone accepts: that the raising of a flag means victory. Wherever I went through the whole war, I raised the flag and photographed it: Crimea, Sebastopol, Belgrade, Budapest and Vienna. They gave me 100 roubles for the photograph. Of course Stalin saw it. It was published in all the magazines and papers.' Not before the image had been doctored, however. One of the Russian soldiers was found to be wearing two watches – the spoils of looting – and one watch had to be touched out.

This photograph is the ultimate moment of 'Mythos Reichstag'. The Soviet troops could not read the German inscription *Dem Deutschen Volke*, but they could read the architecture. For them the Reichstag said 'Germany' loud and clear. They all knew about the Reichstag fire, the first domino in a chain of violence that allowed Hitler to unleash the war, the end of which was captured symbolically in Khaldei's photograph. The myth was maintained in dioramas of the building in Russian museums, with red lightbulbs inside simulating what was hailed as a heroic battle, and also recalling the infamous fire.

The end of the war was, however, not the end of the fighting for the Reichstag. In the aftermath of the conflict, the Allies divided Germany into four occupation zones and the

In the immediate aftermath of war, Berlin's Russian conquerors took control of the city. The legend of the heroic triumph over the Reichstag became a high point in Russian history. 21: Russian traffic signs quickly appeared throughout the city. 22: The story of the glorious victory over Berlin was promulgated with models and dioramas of the Reichstag in Russian museums. 23: The empty shell of the Reichstag was abandoned and its remaining interiors stripped to provide a valuable source of firewood. 24 (overleaf): Russian troops celebrate victory.

shell of the building became the incongruous backdrop to vegetable allotments for starving Berliners. Although located inside the Soviet occupation zone, Berlin became an island city, shared amongst the four Allied powers. However, when Stalin began to establish Communist regimes in Eastern Europe, closing the Iron Curtain, the Western Allies united against him. The resulting Cold War split Europe and divided Berlin. The Reichstag was, once again, on the front line.

Ernst Reuter was the mayor of the three western sectors of Berlin during the blockade in 1948, when Stalin tried to starve West Berliners into joining his realm. Ernst Bittcher was amongst the hundreds of thousands who gathered in front of the Reichstag on 9 September to hear Reuter make his famous appeal: 'People of the world, look upon this city'. What they were looking at was the Reichstag. It *was* 'this city'. Perhaps the Red Army had not been so wrong. The beaten and battered hulk was a fitting symbol of post-war Germany's position. Even as a ruin it focused the will of the people to resist Soviet pressure. The empty shell that Bittcher had been taught to deride by his Nazi teachers was filled with new meaning by the speech of one man. From a totem of Russian victory it became a beacon of Western values.

Through the biggest airlift in history, lasting eleven months, Stalin's blockade of Berlin was foiled, but the city remained divided. The breach was sealed with concrete and barbed wire in 1961 when the East German Government built the Wall on the eastern flank of the Reichstag, to stem the

26

27

28

29

flow of East Germans to the West. As year by year the number of crosses commemorating failed attempts to escape across the Wall increased, so did the Reichstag's symbolic power. It was history in a snapshot: from Kaiser Wilhelm to the Wall. The Reichstag became an essential destination for all jet-setting, Berlin-in-an-afternoon, politicians and dignitaries. Mariele, the Reichstag baby, grew up being photographed in front of it. She recalls proudly, 'No visitor was allowed to leave the city without seeing the place of my birth'. It was both a symbol of a divided Germany and an optimistic reminder of the commitment to reunification.

Ernst Bittcher had his own unique response to the Cold War. In 1969 the East Germans erected an enormous TV tower in the centre of Berlin. While Honecker's architects came up with a tower that looks like a pickled onion skewered on a medieval lance, Ernst's proposed riposte was for an enlarged Eiffel Tower to be built on the roof of the Reichstag, dwarfing the TV tower. 'It was meant as a symbol of freedom for all the East Germans to see', he says, although he admits the idea was absurd.

During the 1950s debate grew about the future of the Reichstag. With the creation of two German states in 1949, the Federal Republic of Germany in the West and the German Democratic Republic in the East, the seat of government of West Germany moved to Bonn. After Paul Baumgarten's refurbishment of 1961-71 the building housed only occasional meetings. Its main function was as home to a permanent exhibition of modern German history and as backdrop for public events.

After the war the Reichstag continued to be the backdrop to events both humble and momentous. 25, 27: The Platz der Republik and Tiergarten were given over to allotments to feed the city's starving population. 26: Even as late as 1957, when work on restoring the Reichstag began, the Platz der Republik was still being used as pastoral land. 28, 29: In September 1948, when the Soviets imposed a blockade to force West Berlin into the Eastern Bloc, over 300,000 Berliners gathered outside the Reichstag to hear Mayor Ernst Reuter appeal to the world for help.

By far the most spectacular event to be staged in front of the Reichstag took place on 7 and 8 July 1984, orchestrated by the Austrian multimedia artist André Heller. The show he delivered was epic. Eleven tonnes of fireworks exploded to the music of Handel, Stravinksy and Pink Floyd. Ten giant flame pictures started with the creation of the universe and ended with a gigantic model of the multi-armed Indian god Shiva, emerging to Handel's Hallelujah Chorus. As usual with the Reichstag, reminders of the war were not far away. The RAF had to clear 8.5 tonnes of unexploded wartime bombs before the show could begin. For the Vienna-born Heller it was the Cold War that was more on his mind. In describing Berlin as the 'secret capital of fantasy' he made it clear that the show's audience also included the Berliners on the eastern side of the Wall.

The vast crowds that Heller attracted outnumbered the audiences for more famous names such as Michael Jackson, Phil Collins and Pink Floyd who were to follow in his wake. Heller's coorganiser, Peter Schwenkow, recalls that when the mayor of West Berlin asked Pink Floyd to play at a different location, fearing complaints at the rock legends' deafening display, Pink Floyd said: 'We play the Reichstag or we don't play Berlin.' They understood how potent a symbol the Reichstag had become.

During the 1980s all Bernd Caillioux wanted to do at the Reichstag was play football. Between the rock concerts, the area in front of the building was given over to parkland and football

204

30   31   32   3

pitches. Bernd is a writer. He came to Berlin to chase the muse and ended up chasing a leather ball: 'The most frustrating thing about playing in front of the Reichstag was that we lost so many balls. If an over-ambitious shot landed in the Spree, you could not go after it, because the river was the frontier with East Berlin.'

Watching Bernd and his friends chase and chide each other around the pitch is an abiding memory of the strange spirit of West Berlin: the Reichstag's monolithic facade juxtaposed with the jumble of muddy legs, washed-out tracksuits and the banal prattle of park football. This prattle was typically conducted in several languages because Bernd's team contained hardly a single German; they were so diverse that they had an Iraqi Arab and a Ukrainian Jew playing in the same team.

The spirit of this prosaic football team is in many ways suggestive of the Reichstag's rekindled role as a democratic arena, open to everyone. The cupola, with its ramps and public viewing platform, is the ultimate symbol of the building's new-found accessibility. The Reichstag has become significant not just for the handful of ordinary people whose lives are enmeshed in its past, but for *all* ordinary people throughout Europe. Its mythical status may have grown from its crystallisation of twentieth-century history, but when the chamber was inaugurated on 19 April 1999, illuminating the cupola, all of Berlin was able to see that the Bundestag was sitting, signalling the building's new status as a beacon of optimism for future democracy and unity.

During the 1960s the Reichstag was refurbished as an assembly hall, but in 1971 the Soviet Union vetoed any formal sessions of the Bundestag in the building. Stripped of its intended role, the Reichstag became most prominent as a backdrop for public events. 30: The David Bowie concert in 1987. 31: The Michael Jackson concert in 1988. 32: The Pink Floyd concert in 1990. 33: When the rock stars went away, the space in front of the Reichstag was given over to local football teams.

The Eagle Flies

Rudi Meisel

On 15 December 1998 the newly fabricated eagle was delivered. At 8.5 metres in width and weighing 2.5 tonnes, it was manufactured in three sections which were assembled on site and hoisted into position above the Speaker's chair. Two days later, the eagle was unveiled by Bundestag President Wolfgang Thierse. From the front the eagle follows the profile of Ludwig Gies' Bonn eagle. However, Gies' two-dimensional bird has been translated by Norman Foster into three dimensions to allow it to hover in space. In the process it has been given a new 'back' which Norman Foster was persuaded to sign.

Chapter 4

Architecture

The Reichstag's walls both record the past and celebrate the present. The incorporation of contemporary

and

art works and the use of colour are vital ingredients in this continuing narrative. The Reichstag

Art

is a museum of memories, but it is also an extraordinary gallery of art.

Norman Foster

208   The history of the Reichstag is the history of Berlin in microcosm. Collective memories are embedded in the building's fabric. Within its walls is a record of both the most tragic and the most uplifting aspects of Germany's history and culture over the last 100 years. The integrity of that record is important for present and future generations. It relies on preserving surviving layers from the past and articulating their relationship with the present. For the most part, the clarity of these distinctions is achieved by changes of materials, textures and forms and the sharply incised detail that has been established between the old work and the new. But the new work is itself multi-layered and identifiably locked into the history and culture of its own times, the age of reunification and European integration. As this chapter describes, contemporary layers in this palimpsest include the distinctive use of colour and the integration of specially commissioned art works.

Seen at night, Gerhard Richter's gleaming glass 'Flag' glows behind the Reichstag's western portico. Together with the inscription beneath the pediment it forms another symbolic layer in the building's rededication to the German people.

In Paul Wallot's original Reichstag, stained glass, art works, wooden and stone carvings, and textiles were used to celebrate the newly achieved unity of Imperial Germany. Wallot's interiors were almost totally lost during World War II and its aftermath, while an act of civic vandalism in the 1960s brutally swept away almost all the historical fabric that had survived the bombardment. The new interiors created at this time were highly austere, as if a self-denying ordinance had been imposed to exclude any element of pleasure. We were determined to create something very different.

My first instinct was that a parliament building should have a certain 'gravitas'. This led us towards a limited palette of natural materials and quiet colours. In the past we have used colour accents as a visual aid to navigating large, complex buildings. We began at the Reichstag by devising a colour strategy along these lines, applying muted colours only to the doors and doorframes. Working with four basic colours — yellow, olive green, burgundy and dark blue — we proposed to use each colour specifically to identify a different floor level and groups of related activities: blue on the main parliamentary level, green on the mezzanine (tribune) level, yellow on the ground floor — a more extrovert shade was selected for this floor which is given over to building management and services installations — and so on. These colours were chosen as a counterpoint to a neutral background of greys and off-whites suggested by the stone, concrete, wood and plaster of the new interiors.

210

1

2

3

4

Early in the final year of the project, however, it became clear that there was a general desire among MPs for a bolder, more expressive, use of colour. This was voiced in different ways during various discussions. For example, in the chamber the Committee had rejected a chair of our design in favour of the Vitra chair originally used in Bonn. They also wanted to use the same blue. I opposed that on the grounds that the Bonn chamber had its own identity and so too should that in Berlin. That argument was accepted and for a long time the seating was established as a neutral grey, right up to the presentation of a full-size mock-up. However, in the background we were beginning to detect murmurs about the need for brighter, stronger colours — not just in the chamber — along the lines of: 'We would like a warmer, more "clubby" club room'; or perhaps: 'Can we have more joyful colours?'

To my utter surprise, the consensus for our neutral approach was destabilised by the passionate intervention of Chancellor Helmut Kohl during the only formal presentation we made to him on the project. He wanted to know why, in his experience, official buildings always had such a sad character, such 'tristesse'. He thought that our strategy was far too cautious: 'The architectural profession is obsessed with greys', he said. 'If I had my way, exposed concrete would be banned'. He was adamant that younger generations of people would expect to see bright, friendly, colourful interiors. He thought the building should express joy; it should have spirit.

The bold use of colour in the Reichstag resulted from a dialogue with Members of Parliament and in particular former Chancellor Helmut Kohl. 1, 2: Norman Foster and Danish graphic artist Per Arnoldi present colour proposals to the Building Committee in March 1998. 3: The chamber seating is upholstered in a colour known as 'Reichstag blue'. 4: Detail of a warm yellow door at ground-floor level. 5: The Foster team meets Chancellor Kohl on 14 January 1998, a moment recorded by Magnum photographer Dennis Stock.

Too often, perhaps, as architects, we are hypnotised by white, silver and grey; but here was a famously conservative politician lecturing us on the timidity of our approach. Initially I was taken aback, but I reflected and decided that he might be right. We had perhaps been too deferential, too concerned with 'good taste'. I saw that the notion of using distinctive colours for contained spaces, with specific uses, was very much in tune with our philosophy of expressing each layer of intervention within the building. In the Reichstag's large public rooms the walls are panelled up to door height, both to accommodate service runs — for cabling and the like — and to differentiate them from the retained nineteenth-century work, which is plastered. We began to explore ways in which more dynamic colours might be applied to the panelling in nineteen such rooms.

I invited Per Arnoldi, a distinguished graphic artist based in Copenhagen, to join the design team. Per and I have worked together on many projects in the past — including the Commerzbank in Frankfurt, and more recently the Biomedical Sciences Building for Imperial College in London — with an exceptional degree of shared success. For the Reichstag we devised a family of twelve strong colours, running through the spectrum: one room might be a deep French blue, another sunflower yellow, or a brilliant red and so on. We presented these ideas to the Building Committee on a freezing March morning in 1998, on site at the Reichstag. Colours inevitably carry political overtones and I was afraid that

5

we might become mired in an endless debate about which were acceptable. But Per was tremendous. Together with his combination of passion and logic, the fact that he was able to address the Committee in German proved critical. At the end of his presentation, everyone applauded! We had our approval.

Out of this came the proposal that the seating in the chamber should be purple — known as 'Reichstag blue' — although the benches in the tribunes are still upholstered in grey. Inevitably perhaps, once the building was completed and MPs were able to judge the overall effect for themselves, dissenting voices began to be heard. One such critic was Franziska Eichstädt-Bohlig, a Green Party member of the Building Committee. She had been antagonistic in the early days of the project, but was very generous in her praise towards the end, with only one reservation. She was quoted in the *Berliner Zeitung* on the day of the building's inauguration: 'The tension between the modern and the historical is inspired,' she said, 'but the choice of colours is so gaudy. The chairs should have been more grey.'

The effect is occasionally startling and some rooms are more successful than others — the Pompeiian red in the roof-level restaurant is particularly effective — but overall I think that colour helps significantly to moderate the monumental character of the building. The only areas of the building where colour does not feature are the entrance lobbies and principal public spaces on the first floor. The plenary chamber is also exceptional in that it is the one major public space in the building where no art

10

212

6

7

8

9

works are installed; here the counterpoint to the palette of stone, muted greys and white is the colour accent of the seating. The only symbolic object in that space is the great eagle that hangs behind the podium.

The story of the design of that eagle would fill a book by itself. Since 1952 a design by the German sculptor Ludwig Gies has formed the backdrop to the Bundestag's deliberations. With the move from Bonn to Berlin, however, there was a feeling that the time was right to replace Gies' plump and rather severe eagle — known affectionately as the 'fat hen' — with one that would perhaps reflect some of the 'lightness' of the new Reichstag and the optimism that accompanied reunification.

In April 1996 I was asked to put forward ideas for a new eagle and it was made clear to me that this was a personal assignment. The following month I presented my first proposals to a meeting of the Building Committee in Bonn. During the few weeks leading up to the first presentation I studied eagles, read about them, and tried to learn as much about them as possible. They are so appealing and majestic that one starts to understand why they have assumed such emblematic significance in the history of societies around the world. Their profile is distinctive whether resting, in flight, or swooping on prey.

Over the centuries there have been literally hundreds of German eagles, the earliest dating from 800 AD. I catalogued them all. I was impressed by the extraordinary variety of mood and character they conveyed: the equivalent of the full range of human nature. I listed the varying attributes of

The eagle in the chamber was a personal commission. 6, 7: The first design, a phoenix-like bird suggestive of the Reichstag's rebirth. 8: Sketching options on site. 9: Exploring variations. 10: Development drawings by Norman Foster. 11: The eagle seen through the east portico. 12: Design sketches by Norman Foster. 13: The eagle is viewed from two sides; it must have a front and a back without appearing two-headed. 14: Options are tested in the London studio. 15, 16: The eagle viewed from the chamber (15) and from behind in the east lobby. 17, 18: A full-size mock-up in the chamber.

11

Trendelkamp
Nr. Munster
15-6-98
Mark B/ Rudi M.

12

13

14

15

16

17

18

some of these historical eagles. Each of them projected the ambitions and aspirations of their times. Given these insights, what values should the 'new generation' eagle project? Should it be static or in flight? Should it be massive and swollen or lean and lithe? The first priority was to make it 'eagle-like'. That may sound obvious, but many of the historical examples were closer to crows, swans, doves or turkeys. I decided that symbolically it should be dynamic, rising like a phoenix from the ashes to symbolise the Reichstag's rebirth.

The physical circumstances of the eagle in the new Reichstag are very different from those in previous German Parliament buildings. In those situations the eagle was essentially two-dimensional and mounted on a wall, to be viewed only from the front. In the Reichstag it is suspended in mid-air in front of a glass screen, and is visible both from the front, within the chamber, and from behind in the east entrance lobby. It is therefore seen 'in the round' and has to work sculpturally in three dimensions. Traditionally the German eagle looks to the right. When suspended in space, however, it is correct if viewed from the front, but seen from the back the head points in the wrong direction. My answer to this dilemma was to place two eagles back-to-back. I had to avoid any suggestion of its being double-headed in the Imperial Russian manner, but I also saw that an eagle facing both to the East and the West could be symbolic of the act of reunification.

I sketched many variations. I investigated different materials, including perforated metal, and explored the use of distinctive colours — just as colour was becoming a powerful ingredi-

19

20

21

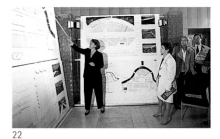

22

ent in our new interiors. In the London studio I progressed through a series of large-scale mock-ups, which were hung in front of the long riverside window. By September 1996 I had arrived at an image which responded to criticism that the first solution had been too lean and angular.

However, it soon became clear that the eagle was awakening political emotions. These began to affect the design: some were anxious that it should not be perceived as too aggressive; others wanted the talons and beak to be more prominent. Others questioned why the Gies eagle could not simply be retained. There were even those who questioned whether there should be an eagle at all. In an atmosphere of political uncertainty there was a growing sentiment that Parliament should take something familiar with it from Bonn to Berlin. Ultimately the political consensus was for a further redesign, retaining some of the character of the Gies original. I finally produced a distinctive new eagle but that provoked the intervention of the heir to the Gies estate. He made no secret of his preference for the original eagle and tried to block the new proposal on the grounds that it was a modification of the Gies design. Given the opportunity, we could undoubtedly have demonstrated that these objections were baseless, but time was against us. With a general election looming, MPs were focused on more pressing issues and political energy simply ran out. The decision was made to retain the Gies eagle. It was frustrating, but in their place I would probably have come to the same conclusion.

The Reichstag, together with the new Parliament buildings in Berlin, is one of the largest public art projects in Germany. The selection of artists was made in consultation with the Bundestag's standing Art Committee and its advisors. 19: Peter Conradi, a member of both the Art Committee and the Building Committee. 20: The Art Committee in session in Berlin. 21: Former Bundestag President Rita Süssmuth, Chairman of the Art Committee until 1998. 22: Landscape proposals for the Reichstag and the wider group of buildings in the Spreebogen area are discussed by the Art Committee.

23

24

25

26

The eagle that hangs in the chamber today is therefore faithful to Gies' 'fat hen' when viewed from the front, but it has been enlarged, made three-dimensional and given a new back view. Naturally, after two and a half years of conceiving and detailing eagles it is disappointing not to have been able to realise a new design. But I remind myself that the 'headline' has always been the Reichstag; the eagle was a fascinating project in itself, but in the context of the total it was the fine print. However, the translation of the original two-dimensional bird, pinned on a wall, into a three-dimensional eagle hovering in space is a creative act in itself. I have to say that I am not displeased by the final transformation, although perhaps the London *Times* of 10 February 1999 should be allowed to have the last word. Commenting on the advent of the twin eagles — plump at the front and thin at the back — it said:

Cynics say [it] fairly represents the transition from Helmut Kohl, the previous Chancellor, to his successor Gerhard Schröder — a bird that still likes its dinner but is willing to forego second helpings — a pragmatic weight-watching kind of eagle.

They might also observe that from the back the eagle appears to be winking; but I could not possibly comment on that.

The artists chosen for the Reichstag are predominantly German, but the four Allied Powers who occupied Berlin after World War II are also represented. The American artist Jenny Holzer has installed a piece in the north entrance lobby. 23: Holzer's installation features an integral digital light system that quotes from famous German political speeches. 24: Jenny Holzer. 25, 26: Jenny Holzer and Norman Foster oversee the art work's installation in April 1999.

27

The Reichstag and the new complex of government buildings in the Spreebogen area is Germany's most significant public art project. In the matter of public art commissioning, as in so much else, Germany has taken the lead. The *Kunst-am-Bau* legislation provides that two per cent of the cost of a public building must be allocated for art works. At the Reichstag, the figure went beyond this statutory provision to three per cent which — given the scale of the project and the fact that some politicians had begun to call for the abolition of the *Kunst-am-Bau* law as economic belts were tightened — represented an extraordinary investment in culture.

The Bundestag has, in fact, assembled an impressive art collection over the years in Bonn and many items from this collection have come to Berlin, some to the Reichstag. But the essence of the new art programme has been to commission major works which relate to the spaces within the building. In line with this philosophy we developed a strategy for locating art works, identifying key spaces and vistas where art works might be placed, much as you might identify '*rond-points*' and markers in squares and avenues in an urban context.

The Bundestag has a standing Art Committee, which advises on its collection. With the decision to move to Berlin, its remit was expanded to encompass all the new government buildings. The Committee comprises twenty politicians together with two art advisors for each of the new

27: The French artist Christian Boltanski has installed an art work in the lobby of the entrance from the Jakob Kaiser House, comprising approximately 7500 metal boxes; each box represents an MP who has sat in the democratic German Parliament, while a single black box signifies the dark period of Nazi dictatorship from 1933 to 1945.

Berlin buildings. The advisors on the Reichstag were Professor Dr Götz Adriani, Director of the Tübingen Museum, and Dr Karin Stempel, a consultant curator. The Committee's secretary Dr Kaernbach was supportive of our approach, as was Rita Süssmuth who, as President of the Bundestag, took the chair (this role is presently filled by the new President, Wolfgang Thierse). She was prepared to back innovative and contentious works of art: as in so much else she was able to get to the heart of the issue, arguing the case that the state had a clear cultural role alongside its constitutional and social responsibilities. The Art Committee had to confront many questions. Are sufficient German artists represented or are there too few international artists? Have artists from East and West been treated equally? What role should the political art of the past play in the new building? Are established artists too dominant? Would young artists lack the experience to command both space and architecture?

   Under the Committee's supervision twenty artists were commissioned to create works for the Reichstag, all of them site-specific. The key theme was to celebrate contemporary art and culture. The majority of works are by eminent living German artists, but the four Allied Powers which occupied Berlin after 1945 are also represented: by Christian Boltanski from France, Jenny Holzer from the United States, and Grisha Bruskin from Russia. Interestingly, the Committee decided — a pleasant surprise — that I was the artist already representing Britain.

28

29

30

31

   Most of the works occupy the more formal spaces, such as entrance halls or large reception and protocol rooms. Some artists — particularly the non-Germans — have made direct reference to the Reichstag's chequered history and role: for example, Jenny Holzer's 15 metre-high column in the north entrance lobby has an integral digital light system which quotes German political speeches; these illustrate the history of Parliament, as well as being canonic in themselves. Using all four sides of the column she is able to convey different voices simultaneously. These texts run vertically from floor to ceiling 24 hours a day on a cycle that takes twenty days to complete. Every time there is a round of applause on the archival recordings Holzer lets the transcript jump and drop a little so that anyone travelling in the lift, looking out through the glass on to the column, would think that the cables had been cut. The piece is a very powerful reminder of the ephemerality of human speech — and the fragility of democracy.

   In the same spirit, Christian Boltanski, who is well-known for illuminating the lost lives of those who perished in the Holocaust, and whose work focuses on memory, has created one of the most haunting objects in the building. His installation, deliberately hidden away at the entrance from the Jakob Kaiser House beneath the east entrance lobby, is an 'archive' of approximately 7500 metal boxes, one for every MP who has sat in the democratic Parliament of Germany. Each box bears the name of an individual and the date of his or her election to Parliament. Together they form a linear space approximately

28: A multi-panelled work by Grisha Bruskin, which hangs in the first-floor club room; it depicts historical Russian characters from Peter the Great to the soldier who raised the Red Flag above the Reichstag in 1945. 29, 30: Katharina Sieverding oversees the rehanging in the first-floor members' lobby of her memorial to members of the Reichstag murdered or persecuted by the Nazis. 31: A panorama of German history by Bernhard Heisig, an East German artist, which hangs in the cafeteria on the first floor.

4 metres high, 10 metres long and 1.5 metres wide. In the middle of one wall a single black box represents the period between 1933 and 1945 when democracy was crushed by Nazi dictatorship. Boltanski set out not to create a monument, but rather a place where the truth is stored for those who seek it. Alongside this symbolic archive is a collection of historical documents containing Acts of Parliament and biographical material relating to parliamentarians who famously held office. This collection will be accessible to the public.

A memorial to those members of the Reichstag who were persecuted by the Nazis has remained in the Reichstag. First installed in the building in the early 1990s, it is a large-scale piece by Katharina Sieverding which symbolises reconstruction as well as destruction.

Grisha Bruskin's Jewish background brought him into conflict with the Soviet system; his work was proscribed and he went into exile. In his multi-panelled work, hung in the first-floor club room, he explores the complex relationship between Russia and Germany and between different versions of Soviet authoritarianism, as represented by figures from Peter the Great to heroes of World War II and beyond. Notably there is a depiction of the Soviet soldier who hoisted the Red Flag over the Reichstag in 1945, an almost mythical figure whose image has become iconic in the history of the building.

Artists have been free to work on any scale and on any theme. Through careful collaboration a remarkable collection has taken shape. As the list of commissions was finalised, my

218

32

33

34

35

colleague Mark Braun and I collaborated closely with many of the chosen artists, not only on the practical aspects of their contributions – discussing how they would be installed and displayed in the building, even how they would be made – but in refining their proposals in tune with the context. The Reichstag's west entrance lobby, the place where public and politicians meet, posed perhaps the greatest challenge. Accordingly, two giants of German contemporary art and founders of the German Pop Art movement, Sigmar Polke and Gerhard Richter, were chosen to create works that would confront each other across this symbolically charged space. Mark and I visited many of the artists in their studios – including Richter and Polke – looked at models, sketched and exchanged ideas.

We met Richter in his studio in Cologne, against the backdrop of some of his tremendous seascape paintings. Born in the East but long resident in the West, Richter is one of the great abstract artists of the post-war era. He has a strong architectural sense and has produced a powerful response to the foyer as a civic space. His 22 metre-high elongated 'Flag' in the German colours – black, red and gold – has a verticality which emphasises the upward thrust of the space. The flag is deliberately fragile, made of glass, with a mirrored surface that encourages reflection in both senses of the word.

Richter first conceived the flag in canvas and it was originally banded vertically. The idea of using coloured glass came through our collaboration. I was impressed by his dedication to

The west entrance lobby is given to works by two giants of the German Pop Art movement; Gerhard Richter and Sigmar Polke. 36: Richter's installation takes the form of a German flag, fabricated from glass, using sheets in the largest size manufactured. 32, 33: Norman Foster and Mark Braun visit Richter in his studio in Cologne in July 1998. 34: In its early incarnations the flag was banded vertically. A series of options was explored using a scale model of the space, before the final form was decided. 35: Norman Foster studies the model.

the idea of integration, to creating a work that related to its context and was not self-referential or philosophically preoccupied. When it came to fabricating the flag, we were able to give him technical advice, helping to source the largest sheets of glass available which, in turn, resulted in a changed geometry.

The Reichstag is a far remove from the typical context of the gallery or museum. Richter, like many of the artists at the Reichstag, was, I think, apprehensive about the impact of the space in which his work was to hang, needing reassurance and support — it was a conversation with the German President which finally persuaded him that the German flag was not taboo.

We met Polke in his studio in Cologne. Polke is very dapper, very precise, but he is wonderfully unpretentious, full of humour, and open to ideas. He has an amazing collection of ethnic musical instruments on which he gave an impromptu recital. Polke is famously preoccupied with popular consumer culture and his work is full of witty juxtapositions. For our meeting he had prepared concepts based on graphic themes that he had explored in the past, using his trademark 'Polke dots'. He showed us these together with another idea he had worked up which referred ironically to advertising billboards.

He seemed sure of the first, but not the second which, he said, had not been done before. He asked what I thought. 'There is no doubt about it', I said, 'You have to do the second'. His reaction was fantastic. I have never seen anything like it. He went wild, hopping backwards around the stu-

37

38

39

40

dio, mad with enthusiasm, and saying that he had been waiting for someone to tell him just that. He had not been able to make up his mind, but I had confirmed his instincts. It was a wonderful moment.

He talked about possible materials and suggested prismatic plastic, so that the effect of the work would change constantly as the viewer moved around the space, giving it an almost holographic effect. Later, through our contacts in the advertising company J C Decaux — for whom we have designed a range of street furniture — and other sources, we were able to direct him towards people with the technical expertise to carry it out. The work's knowing reference to advertising media fits with our notion of the lobby as the 'piazza' — an outdoor room — within the Reichstag's 'city' of spaces. The collaboration of these two great artists has produced an intriguing dialogue and a powerful interplay between art and architecture. They represent a thoughtful riposte to the all too frequently cosmetic concept of public art which I characterised a long time ago as 'putting lipstick on the gorilla'.

The process of linking artist to location was a highly sensitive matter, but some simply seemed right for a particular space. Günther Uecker, for example, an artist with a deeply spiritual vision, was commissioned to execute the multi-faith chapel on the first floor. He was the first of the Reichstag artists I met and I was struck by his work. He is best known for his distinctive use of nails. Some of his pieces are constructed, others are impressed in paper, but they always have a poetic charge.

Sigmar Polke, whose installation faces that of Gerhard Richter in the west lobby, is famous for his trademark 'Polke dots'. In the Reichstag, however, he chose to pursue a new direction using techniques associated with the advertising industry.
37: Sigmar Polke. 38: Norman Foster and Mark Braun meet Polke in his studio in Cologne in October 1998. 39: Polke's art work is installed on site.
40: Meeting the press at the official unveiling.

41

Uecker's chapel is on the first floor, directly to the south of the plenary chamber. It is a space with a meditative ambience appropriate for its use as a place of worship by followers of different religions and its intimacy invites quiet contemplation. This was the first time that Uecker had worked at such a scale, but his concept for the space was so powerful that we worked with him to realise it: a screen wall was introduced in front of the windows to modify the quality and direction of light; we removed the door and frame to make entry less formal; we rendered the walls and floored the room in granite, introducing a step at the mid-point to define an area around a simple stone altar of Uecker's design. Although small, this little chapel is one of the most remarkable and affecting spaces in the building.

Gotthard Graubner is another artist with whom we developed a creative dialogue. His work almost defies categorisation, falling between conventional definitions of painting and sculpture. He creates objects that are almost organic. His 'cushion' paintings are large, colourful and three-dimensional. We met in his studio near Neuss, an extraordinary complex of artists' studios and galleries in a landscaped setting on the outskirts of Cologne. We talked at length about the way he might address the large second-floor protocol room that he had been assigned. As our collaboration progressed he moved from proposing a triptych to a single painting, which was more appropriate to the space. It also became apparent that the vivid yellow we had specified for the room was too strong a counterpoint, even for work

41: Sigmar Polke's installation comprises a series of five illuminated boxes with a viewing surface of prismatic plastic which encourages the images to 'move' as the eye travels across them. The panels incorporate references to iconic figures from Germany's democratic past, including Bismarck and Konrad Adenauer.

as powerful as Graubner's; he needed a far more neutral backdrop. Together we decided that the yellow should be replaced with a neutral grey. Even though the panelling had been made and was on its way to being installed, the change was made relatively easily and inexpensively, which illustrates an interesting point: the panels are demountable, and the colour finish is only a thin layer of paint, so in principle any colour in any room can be changed in the future if another one is considered more appropriate.

One of the problems thrown up by the commissioning process was that some works were not agreed by the Art Committee until very late in the day. By that time the Reichstag's tight construction programme had already forced us to finalise colour schemes in the major spaces. In certain rooms, not knowing what the art works would be, our first choice had been to provide neutral backgrounds in order to avoid a 'shotgun marriage' between art and colour. But, as I have described, we were persuaded to adopt a more assertive colour scheme under pressure from our client. With the benefit of hindsight one might have chosen differently. We did not know, for example, until almost the last minute, whether Anselm Kiefer would contribute a work. By the time his participation was confirmed the first-floor corner meeting room he had been allocated was painted apple green. Reactions to the combination vary from enthusiastic support to the more equivocal feelings of others, like myself, who find the combination too strong. I would have preferred a more complementary colour, but the panels can always be repainted.

222

43

45

42

44

Art in the context of the Reichstag has generally been offered as something to be questioned and discussed. But sometimes art has to be accepted at face value. The work of Georg Baselitz, for example, deliberately goes against the grain. In the 1970s he achieved a degree of notoriety with his 'upside-down' paintings. His two canvases acquired for the south entrance lobby typically occupy the ground between the abstract and the figurative, their subject matter alluding to two historical woodcuts by Caspar David Friedrich. I first saw these two pieces hanging alone in Baselitz's studio where they commanded the space and I think they sit together very comfortably now.

I suppose my natural sympathy is towards art that is at home in the context of our architecture, with its vocabulary of light and space. Generally, I think that the most successful installations in the Reichstag are those in the context of public spaces – such as Richter's, Polke's and Boltanski's – where the colour schemes are neutral and we had an early introduction to the artist; or those where the artist was defined from the outset – such as Uecker or Graubner – and was able to influence the design of the setting. In other situations, where the art works – such as those by Baselitz or Holzer – enter a simple dialogue with an essentially neutral space, the result is equally happy.

In some instances the real potential of spaces within the building has only been fully realised with the installation of art works. Rupprecht Geiger's colourful treatment of one of the

Günther Uecker's multi-faith chapel on the first floor represents perhaps the most complete interaction between art and architecture in the Reichstag. In collaboration with Uecker the room's general arrangement and finishes were specified to reinforce his overall vision. 42-45: Norman Foster discusses the development of the space with Uecker in the artist's studio in Düsseldorf in February 1998. 46: The room was modified by introducing a wall to screen the existing window, while a step in the floor defines an area in front of the altar.

47

224

48

49

50

second-floor tower rooms is a good example of how art can bring a space alive. Its bands of red and yellow pigment throw a warming light across the room. It is an amazingly youthful and vigorous work by an artist now in his nineties. But the building also has the strength to welcome work of a very different kind, such as the panorama of German history which Bernhard Heisig has produced for the small cafeteria on the first floor, which has conscious echoes of the Socialist Realist art that predominated in the old GDR.

　　　　　The massive dignity of Ulrich Rückriem's stone reliefs in the south courtyard offers another example of the way in which art can help an understanding of a building. Rückriem's two pieces are formed from polished granite slabs that have been shattered and reassembled. They carry an echo of the building itself which has twice experienced the upheaval of destruction and renewal.

　　　　　It is difficult to imagine a greater contrast than that between the austere grandeur of Rückriem's sculpture and the delicacy of Stefan Schröder's 'Das Feld' – 'The Field' – of yellow ceramic flowers, which I hoped would eventually occupy one of the roof-level courtyards. It was the last art-work to be commissioned and I was closely involved in its selection. Schröder is a young artist, born in 1966. It was important for me to be able to include a work by a member of this generation alongside the estab-lished masters. Schröder's piece also has great resonance in terms of the environmental aspect of our work in the Reichstag, reminding us that the building is powered by vegetable oil, from rape and sunflower seeds.

Gotthard Graubner's cushion painting in the second-floor protocol room occupies the ambiguous ground between sculpture and painting. 47: As the dialogue with Graubner unfolded it became clear that the planned colour scheme for the room — a vivid yellow — would have overpowered his work; consequently the yellow was replaced with a neutral grey. 48- 50: Norman Foster and Mark Braun meet Gotthard Graubner in his studio near Neuss in July 1998.

The Reichstag has works by two prominent German artists linked to the Neo-Expressionist movement: Georg Baselitz and Anselm Kiefer. 51, 52: Norman and Elena Foster and Mark Braun meet Georg Baselitz in his studio in October 1998. 53: Baselitz's two canvases in the south entrance lobby are hung 'upside-down' to challenge conventional perceptions. 54: Installing Kiefer's canvas — 'Only with wind, with time and with sound' — which occupies a first-floor committee room. 55: The painting's fractured surface expresses the scars left on Germany through its history.

53

51

52

55

54

It is wonderfully optimistic, very much in tune with the spirit that we have tried to engender in the building. Unfortunately, at the time of writing, it looks as if it will not be installed.

The artists commissioned for the Reichstag, or whose works — generally small-scale drawings or watercolours — were acquired to hang there, were of every generation, the oldest born well before World War I. Alongside direct commissions, the art budget allowed for the purchase of works by some of the most eminent artists of Germany's recent past. These include pieces by Joseph Beuys and the German-Jewish artist Otto Freundlich, whose sculpture 'The New Man' was depicted on the poster advertising the Nazis' 'Degenerate Art' exhibition of 1937. He died tragically in the Lublin-Maidenek concentration camp in Poland in 1943.

Beuys' bronze object '*Tisch mit Aggregat*' — 'Table with Aggregate' — was already controversial. It had been put on temporary display in the Bundestag in Bonn. Admired by some, it had been crudely vilified by others. For Rita Süssmuth, however, Beuys' philosophy, 'aims right at the heart of our existence … it strengthens our will to shape our world responsibly in freedom and maturity'. She actively promoted its move to Berlin, and with the help of Professor Adriani, Beuys' table came to the Reichstag on permanent loan. It was Rita Süssmuth again, as President of the Bundestag, who was so instrumental in bringing Christo and Jean-Claude's 'Wrapped Reichstag' to fruition after more than twenty

226

57

56

58

59

years of political indecision. She had antagonised many in her party by lending her support to a project they had misguidedly tried to block. I was particularly pleased, therefore, when one of Christo's collages of this visionary project was acquired to hang in the roof-level public restaurant. It is a powerful reminder of what was surely one of the most remarkable events in the life of the building.

For me, seeing the 'Wrapped Reichstag' in its sparkling silver shroud and witnessing the extraordinary festival that sprang up spontaneously around it was a magical and moving experience, and one of the high points of the Reichstag project. Just like the crowds that now wind daily through the Reichstag's cupola, the people that thronged around the building then were amazing. Everybody seemed to be there — families and couples, politicians and intellectuals, acrobats and artists, old and young, rich and poor — in a wonderfully varied and good-humoured mix. The whole of Berlin appeared to be *en fête*, picnicking, dancing or just absorbing the atmosphere.

I remember especially, on the last day of that event — 6 July 1995 — walking through the Reichstag with my wife Elena and Christo and Jeanne-Claude, seeing the silvery light filtering through the fabric and saying 'goodbye' to the old building's past. Early the following morning the wrapping came down and the demolition men moved in. The transition from art work to building site was as sudden as that. The Reichstag had shed its chrysalis and was about to be reborn.

56: A detail of Stefan Schröder's 'The Field', intended for one of the third-floor courtyards. 57: A vigorously colourful piece by Rupprecht Geiger which hangs in a second-floor committee room. 58: Joseph Beuys' 'Table with Aggregate' came to the Reichstag from the Bundestag's collection. 59, 60: Two stone reliefs by Ulrich Rückriem occupy the southern courtyard. 61 (overleaf): A collage from the 'Wrapped Reichstag' series by Christo and Jeanne-Claude hangs in the roof-level restaurant, a reminder of one of the most poignant moments in the building's history.

Opening Ceremony

Rudi Meisel

In a ceremony on the steps of the Reichstag on the morning of 19 April 1999, Norman Foster presented Bundestag President Wolfgang Thierse with a symbolic key, thus officially handing over the building to Parliament. At noon the inaugural session of the Bundestag began. Speaking in that first session, Chancellor Gerhard Schröder said: '... the politics of understanding and good neighbourliness ... as well as the aura of life lived in freedom, have all helped to make possible the Berlin Republic in a United Germany ... We are going forward to the centre of Europe.'

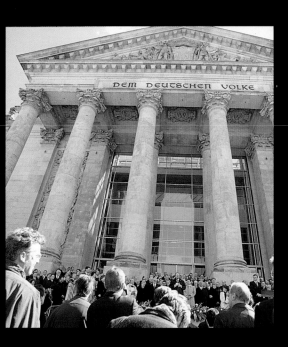

The
Reichstag:
Metamorphosis

The Reichstag is synonymous with German democracy's turbulent history, from Wilhelm II's resistance

to democratisation in the 1890s to Hitler's dictatorship between the wars. The building's

transformation signifies the new vigour of democracy in a reunified Germany.

Wilhelm Vossenkuhl

232 Recently, intellectuals have pondered 'the end of history'. Although it may be wrong in general terms, this idea is not wholly beside the point when examined on a more specific level. Some histories have ended. The demise of the Cold War, for example, was welcomed in the late 1980s, and nationalism, we hope — at least inside Europe — has no future. Although it was conceived as a symbol of democracy, the Reichstag was, until 1989, tainted by nationalism and the tensions of the Cold War. It was devastated twice, both at the beginning and at the end of the darkest period in German history, in 1933 and 1945 respectively. Only after German reunification did contemporary Germans gradually begin to realise that the building was more than the epitome of the disasters of German history. It stands now for the hope that the two Germanies, East and West, will really merge and that Berlin will be just one among many European capitals.

On 9 November 1989 the East German Government suddenly announced the opening of the border between East and West Germany. Berliners rushed to breach the barrier that had divided them for 28 years. The Reichstag, situated hard by the Wall, lost its status as a symbol of separation and became instead the place where reunification would be realised.

The national formation of Germany was belated compared to that of Britain, France or the USA. Only after the Franco-Prussian War did Germany become a nation state, with Berlin as its capital. That is why, in 1871, Germany had no parliamentary building to hand. For two decades after its constitution, the Reichstag met in a temporary venue at the former Royal Prussian Porcelain Manufactory. In the summer of 1884 Kaiser Wilhelm I laid the foundation stone of the new Reichstag building and a decade later, in December 1894, Kaiser Wilhelm II laid the keystone. From then on the name of the building and its political function were synonymous.

The first all-German Parliament was a political lightweight. As a legislative body, it lacked the authority to challenge the Kaiser, or the Chancellor and his ministers. It had a long way to go to gain political influence and to become a truly democratic body. Bismarck, in his almost pathological fear of social democracy, shrewdly ensured that Members of Parliament received no salary, thus excluding all but the well-to-do from Parliament. Little wonder that out of a total of 382 MPs in 1871, 11 were princes, 34 were counts and 103 were either barons or knights. On top of this approximately 100 MPs were either members of the administration or belonged to the military.

When the Reichstag took up its work in Wallot's new building in the 1890s, that picture had already changed. The majority of MPs wanted a 'monumental house of parliament' and

234

1

2

3

4

they got it. Yet, its monumentalism had no coherent architectural style. Elements from a variety of historical periods and origins — Gothic, Germanic, Romanesque, Baroque, French and Spanish — were mixed to express rather noisily, as it were, imperial power and national dignity. Nobody seemed to expect an architectural expression of the building's democratic function. A small amount of daylight made its way into the plenary chamber through a glazed dome, which brought with it an element of vertical transparency — but not the horizontal kind more appropriate for democratically-constituted political bodies.

By the turn of the century the Reichstag had transmuted into what was, for its time, a truly progressive democratic parliament. Due to the growing influence of the Social Democratic and Liberal parties, social policy gained in momentum. The groundwork of German social security — the system of social insurance — was founded. The political fight for social justice and equality was headed by politicians such as Bebel, Liebknecht, Lasker, Windthorst, Erzberger and von Ballestrem, from a variety of centre, liberal and left parties. These pioneers were followed by enlightened parliamentarians such as Nauman, Ebert, Basserman, Scheidemann and Stresemann.

In the process, the number of nobles in the Reichstag had shrunk — from 148 in 1871 to 49 by 1912 — while the number of middle and working-class representatives of trade unions and corporations had steadily grown. However, the progress of democracy facilitated by the Reichstag was

Democracy was not fully established in Germany until the country was unified in 1871. As a result there was no existing parliament building and a new one had to be created. The progress of democracy was soon obstructed, first by the forced resignation of Bismarck in 1890 and then by the outbreak of World War I. 1: The foundation stone of the Reichstag is laid by Kaiser Wilhelm I in 1884. 2: Kaiser Wilhelm II lays the keystone in 1894. 3: The statue of Bismarck, erected in front of the Reichstag in 1901. 4: The Reichstag takes the decision to mobilise troops on the Western Front, 4 August 1914.

continually inhibited and often reversed by Wilhelm II. Determined to be both respected and obeyed, he was fiercely resistant to the increasing democratisation of German society. In 1890, he forced Bismarck – easily the most influential political figure in Germany in the second half of the nineteenth century – to resign, thereby concentrating political power in his own hands.

Bismarck had been no partisan of democracy. There are few mentions of the Reichstag in the three volumes of his memoirs, *Thoughts and Recollections*, and not a single one concerning its building. But Wilhelm was openly hostile towards the Reichstag. It is telling that he would not allow the democratic dedication *Dem Deutschen Volke* – 'To the German People' – to be inscribed above the main entrance. This was remedied belatedly in 1916, in the middle of World War I, when the Reichstag – too late as it turned out – began to ponder political reform.

Not inappropriately, the end of the Wilhelmine monarchy was proclaimed from a Reichstag balcony on 9 November 1918 by Philipp Scheidemann. The last Chancellor of the Reich, Prince Max von Baden, announced Wilhelm II's resignation before the monarch was really prepared to do so. Within a few days there were political convulsions in Berlin. Friedrich Ebert, the Social Democrat leader, proposed general elections for a new constitutional assembly. Two months later, in January 1919, radicals on the Left staged an unsuccessful armed revolt and the newly constituted National Assembly fled to Weimar.

5

6

7

8

For years the Republic was jeopardised. Radicals from the Right murdered Matthias Erzberger, the Minister of Finance, in 1921, and Walter Rathenau, the Foreign Secretary, a year later. The Weimar Republic only achieved normality in 1923 when Friedrich Ebert was elected President and Gustav Stresemann became Chancellor. Both died prematurely, Ebert in 1925 and Stresemann in 1929.

Ebert's successor, Paul von Hindenburg, having seen a series of appointed chancellors fail, reluctantly called on Adolf Hitler to become Chancellor in January 1933. Shortly after, on the night of 27 February, the burning of the Reichstag ushered in the end of democracy – and humanity – in Germany. Approximately 200 MPs were thrown into jail or, even worse, into concentration camps, where more than 30 were killed and six were driven to commit suicide. Another 100 MPs chose to emigrate. Of these, four fell victim to the Stalinist terror in the Soviet Union. Only 30 of the surviving members of the Reichstag became members of the Bundestag after the war.

The Cold War brought with it the blockade of Berlin which isolated the three western sectors – under the control of France, Britain and the United States – until it was broken in May 1949. During this period, even as a ruin, the Reichstag focused the will of the people to resist Soviet pressure. On 9 September 1948 more than 300,000 Berliners gathered in front of the Reichstag where Ernst Reuter, the newly elected mayor, addressed them.

World War I sparked an upturn in the fortunes of German democracy. 5: The Kaiser finally allowed the dedication 'To the German People' to be inscribed on the Reichstag in 1916. 6: At the end of the war the Kaiser abdicated and the Social Democrats declared a republic, but extremism was a constant threat. 7: A demonstration against the Spartacus League, 1918. 8: Troops defend the Reichstag against the right-wing Kapp Putsch of 1919.

In those days nobody knew what might happen to the Reichstag building. As early as January 1946 Hans Scharoun, the Berlin City Architect, judged that enough had survived 'the storms of destruction' to enable its complete restoration. Others, such as the former President of the Reichstag in the Weimar Republic, Paul Löbe, thought it should be kept as a ruin. In the early 1950s a public debate started to generate proposals for its future. Finally, in 1957 Ludwig Gerstenmaier, then President of the Bundestag in Bonn, proposed to renovate the Reichstag on the grounds that it was one of the few national symbols to have survived the war. The renovation that he instigated was completed in 1971.

After nearly 40 years, parliamentary work could start again in the Reichstag but it did so only in a restricted way. Meanwhile, the Berlin Wall was erected within feet of the building and the Soviets tried to obstruct all political activities in the city which might support the claim that West Berlin was part of the Federal Republic of Germany. The last plenary meeting of the Bundestag in Berlin before the fall of the Wall was in April 1965. Even then it was not held in the Reichstag.

By the mid-1960s, the symbolic value of the Reichstag had reached its final dimension. It was a historical reminder of German national unity — which might again be achieved in a democratic state based on the political self-determination of all Germans — and a symbol of freedom and Western democracy. For Willy Brandt, mayor of West Berlin from 1957 to 1966, the Reichstag was more than

238

10

11

12

a historical symbol: it stood for the political commitment to achieve these goals, a commitment that was reiterated every year during the annual May Day celebrations in front of the Reichstag. From 1971 a permanent exhibition staged in the building — 'Questions on German History' — offered an account of German history since 1800, and hundreds of thousands of visitors from West Germany came to see the Reichstag.

Then, in 1989, something happened that seemed to be beyond all hope — the political and economic breakdown of East Germany and of Soviet rule in Eastern Europe. Suddenly it became possible to transform the symbolic value of the Reichstag into political reality. On 4 October 1990, the day after reunification was formally announced, Chancellor Kohl addressed the assembled members of the Bundestag from the podium in the Reichstag chamber.

Shortly before the physical process of reconstruction began, in 1995, millions of people saw the Reichstag enveloped in Christo's silver shroud, which responded spectacularly to light and motion during day and night. Inadvertently Christo created the cocoon to start a final metamorphosis through which the Reichstag became the home of the Bundestag. It needed an artist to give appropriate expression to the most improbable and unimaginable political change in recent history.

Of course, the metamorphosis of the Reichstag into the Bundestag presupposed a fundamental change in design and a new architectural language, a demanding, fascinating and

Even as an empty hulk, the Reichstag remained in the minds of Berliners. 9 (previous): When the Soviet Union imposed a blockade in 1949, Berliners gathered at the Reichstag to protest. In 1957 work began on making the building safe and a decision was made to renovate it as an assembly building.
10: Bundestag President Ludwig Gerstenmaier, the main advocate of renovation, inspects the Reichstag in 1957.
11: Mayor Willy Brandt in 1959 at the May Day celebrations, held annually at the Reichstag. The facade is under repair.
12: The decision to renovate the Reichstag is announced.

responsible task that could be mastered neither by nostalgia nor by historicism. Within the limits of its historical fabric and appearance the Reichstag was to be converted into an open and accessible democratic arena.

It was generally accepted that spectators and the media should share natural light and air with the politicians in the plenary chamber and in the lobbies. The shape and altitude of the dome, therefore, had to follow its function – to collect daylight and fresh air – and not the other way around. The new was not to be integrated into the old. Rather, the direction of fit was to be reversed: the old was to be integrated into the new. This strategy is most obvious from an environmental perspective, where a radical new system of energy generation and conservation has been fully integrated with the surviving fabric. Moreover, the Reichstag is designed to be a centre of public interest and identification. It manifests German history and the democratic future of a reunited people. The publicly accessible 'lighthouse' on top of the Reichstag is indeed symbolic of modern German democracy.

In early debates about the new Reichstag, Norman Foster's philosophy of democratic transparency and openness was attacked. It was argued that democracy could never find manifestation in a building, not even in a prominent one like a parliament building. As a general statement, this is neither true nor false. On the one hand, bricks and mortar in themselves have no normative meaning, idea or value. Even if a building looks like a temple it might be something different – a cinema or a casino, for exam-

13

14

15

ple. On the other hand, if builders and architects had never tried, say, to praise God using bricks and mortar, cathedrals would not exist. Obviously, values and ideas can be expressed in the design of buildings.

Democracy, admittedly, is no god and therefore should not be deified. But it still needs praise and recognition. In its historical form the Reichstag was not exactly a convincing visual expression of democratic values such as dignity, freedom and equality. If anything, it promoted national values above all. Democratic values came second. It was an agreed premise in the process of redesigning the Reichstag to keep the shell and not to get rid of all the symbols of its old-fashioned architectural language. However, what initially seemed to be an obstacle to free architectural expression turned out to be a source of inspiration for mastering all the historical and political difficulties of design and function. The new Reichstag found an architectural language of its own. In reality it is even lighter and more luminous than it first seemed from the architect's model.

First and foremost, the new Reichstag is indeed an architectural expression of the German democracy which defined its principles in Bonn after the war, long before it eventually found its real and full domain in Berlin. This democracy was finally tested by reunification, a task which for years existed only in theory and in propaganda. The challenge was to bridge a tremendous and unexpected gulf between East and West Germany. None of these crucial concerns could have been expressed by a *new*

With West German parliamentary activity in Berlin barred by the Soviet Union under the Quadripartite Agreement, after its restoration in the 1960s the Reichstag played a symbolic rather than a practical role in the democratic government of Germany. 13: A sign appealing for 'Freedom and Peace for the Whole World', one of many which appeared on the Reichstag during May Day celebrations in the 1960s.
14, 15: Views of the permanent exhibition, 'Questions on German History', housed in the Reichstag from 1971.

parliamentary building. It would have been irresponsible towards the origins of German democracy, and towards its extinction by the Nazis, to even think of a new Bundestag replacing the Reichstag. The old Wilhelmine shell was necessary to enable the new Reichstag symbolically to capture and resolve the tensions between past and present German democracy, and the divergent cultures of East and West Germany.

Nietzsche, in an essay about 'The Uses and Abuses of History' coined the idea of a 'critical history'. He wholeheartedly denied a monumentalist or antiquarian way of understanding the past. 'Any past', Nietzsche declared, 'is worth being condemned'. He could not have known how true this was for a period in German history to begin shortly after his own demise. The notion of 'critical history' sheds an interesting light on the task of redesigning the Reichstag. It indicates that a critical understanding of the past presupposes the strength and independence to determine the future. Inadvertently, Norman Foster has realised Nietzsche's notion. When antiquarian and monumentalist arguments were used to support historicist versions of the Reichstag he demonstrated that he was more concerned with German democracy than German history, by looking to the future of the Reichstag rather than to its past.

It may be looked upon as the cunning of reason that no German was given architectural responsibility for the new Reichstag. Due to the historical, political and architectural complexity of the task it might have been impossible to find within Germany the emotional and intellectual inde-

240

16

17

18

19

pendence required. But it is hard to tell which took more courage, to ask a non-German to undertake the most prominent architectural job in the country, or to accept the commission. With such a risky business it was definitely an example of independence, vigour and openness on both sides. Germany obviously had to go a long way to arrive at a position where national feelings would not be injured by the very fact that a British architect won the competition for its most prominent national building. Although this notable fact will not count in international political transactions it says more — and in a more reliable way — about Germany's integration within Europe than many ritual incantations to the same effect.

The Reichstag represents the European stage of modern German politics. Future generations of visitors will find that a British architect built the dome from which they enjoy an exciting view above the city and an intriguing glance into the plenary chamber. This is good news both for German visitors and for those coming from abroad. We will be able to judge the success of this message when eventually it is accepted as matter-of-fact, void of excitement.

The new Reichstag is, of course, neither a museum nor a gallery. The political battles to be conducted inside will resemble those we already know from Bonn or elsewhere. But unlike the Bonn Parliament building, the Reichstag will visually confront all political agents and spectators with a reminder that democracy is a fragile good, easily lost.

In 1989 a tide of reform swept across Eastern Europe and one by one, Communist regimes collapsed. The fall of the Wall on 9 November laid the ground for the Reichstag's restoration as the seat of German democracy. 16: Berliners face border guards across the Wall, 9 November 1989. 17: The morning after, the confrontational mood is relaxed. 18: Holes in the Wall by the eastern flank of the Reichstag. 19: The first meeting of Parliament in the Reichstag since 1933, held on 4 October 1990. 20: Crowds gather outside the Reichstag to celebrate the reunification of Germany on 3 October 1990.

Public Open Days

Rudi Meisel

Following the opening ceremony, the Reichstag's doors were thrown open to the public from 21 to 25 April 1999. On the first day 24,000 people stood patiently in line. An astonishing total of 150,000 visitors was recorded in the five-day period. Most climbed the ramps up to the viewing platform on foot, but some very young ones made the trip in buggies and others in wheelchairs. The atmosphere on the roof terrace was celebratory, like the Christo event but more so. Within the cupola, hushed voices carried across the space as they might in the whispering gallery of a cathedral dome.

Looking back on the Reichstag project, a little more than a month after its opening, I was reminded by a colleague that parliament buildings have a tradition of being protracted undertakings, victims perhaps of 'too many cooks'. In the mid-nineteenth century it took Barry and Pugin 30 years to complete that most iconic of parliaments, the Palace of Westminster. At the end of the century it took Paul Wallot twelve arduous years from 1882 – the year he won the competition – to complete the Reichstag; he retired early to academic life, exhausted by political wrangling and regal intervention. After World War II, following years of indecision, it took Paul Baumgarten a decade from 1961 to 1971 to rebuild the Reichstag. And, more recently, Günter Behnisch toiled for twenty years to realise the Bundestag building in Bonn, only to see it voted into obsolescence in 1991, a year before its completion.

    I am happy to say that we broke that mould. Our experience was very different. We were fortunate to have had a very professional client body, in the form of the Bundestag's Building Committee. We also had tremendous support from successive Bundestag presidents: Rita Süssmuth until 1998 and latterly Wolfgang Thierse. Working within a historical shell was always going to take longer than doing a new building, but far from being a protracted process, for us the time-scale was incredibly short. From winning the competition in June 1993, it took a little under six years to design and rebuild the Reichstag, and less than four of those years were spent on site.

244

Postscript

Norman Foster

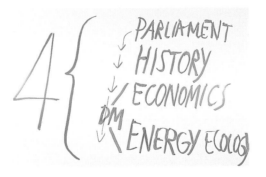

    There is a real sense of achievement, shared by all those involved in the project – architects, engineers, contractors and craftspeople – in having brought the new Reichstag to fruition in such a short period to finish exactly on schedule. That achievement was the result of excellent teamwork, and of swift and effective decision-making; not just by us, but by our clients, the politicians.

    I remember when I first presented our scheme to the competition jury, writing on a large sheet of paper the key considerations of the project as I saw them; they were: 'Parliament', 'History', 'Economics', and 'Energy and Ecology'. By 'Parliament' I meant an understanding of the institution and its inner workings; but I also included a commitment to public access and transparency in its new home. That goes hand-in-hand with a belief in the social context: a conviction that buildings are generated first and foremost by people and their needs, which are both spiritual and material. By 'Economics' I meant not just, 'how much will this building cost to build?' but also, 'how can we reduce running costs and ensure value for money in the long term?' That leads naturally to 'Energy and Ecology', by which I meant a firm commitment to adopting natural methods of environment control and investing in alternative sources of energy production in order to reduce our reliance on fossil fuels.

    Those were the aims of the project and with the encouragement of our client we were able to explore them to the full. Within that agenda, the Reichstag has given us the opportunity to stretch the boundaries of two issues which I believe are particularly significant in the future growth of cities: the role of public space and the quest for a more ecologically responsible architecture. It is in these two areas that I believe the Reichstag truly raises the threshold of expectations and offers a model for a coming generation of public buildings, whether they be new structures or historical buildings given a new lease of life.

We could not have opened up the Reichstag to the public in the way that we have without the support of the politicians. They could have said 'no' to us at any point and it is a tribute to their open-minded approach that they chose instead to embrace the idea wholeheartedly. This reinforces another, crucial, point which is that as architects we can only move forward with enlightened political support. The decision to award the 1999 Royal Gold Medal for Architecture to the city of Barcelona shows just how deeply that relationship is coming to be understood. The renaissance of Barcelona has its roots in new public architecture, infrastructure and civic space; and those roots have been nourished by a succession of mayors. They have believed in the power of the built environment to improve the quality of urban life; a view which is increasingly being shared by city administrations across Europe.

As growing numbers of people around the world spend their lives working and dwelling in cities, the public realm becomes ever more important. Imagine how different our cities could be if their civic buildings opened themselves up as the Reichstag has done and embraced the public in a more friendly and constructive way. We have to fulfil utilitarian needs and respect privacy and security, but we also need to celebrate the public domain, creating inspirational routes and accessible spaces for everyone to enjoy.

In ecological terms, the Reichstag has shown how public buildings can challenge the status quo: big buildings do not have to be big consumers of energy or big polluters. In environmental terms the Reichstag represents a significant step forward. The strategy we have adopted will help to slow the rate at which the Earth's precious natural resources are eroded, and reduce environmentally damaging carbon dioxide emissions.

Although that first step is minuscule in terms of the journey yet remaining, imagine the impact that those strategies could have if they were applied more widely around the world. If every new building – public or private – were to follow this lead, the energy equation could be stood on its head. Rather than consuming energy, these buildings would be net providers; rather than emitting carbon dioxide, they would be broadly neutral. The savings in resources and running costs would be immense.

In these two important respects the Reichstag is focused on a new century. But the Reichstag is also a building with a history; and within that, our interventions represent only the most recent episode. When I spoke of 'History', contained within my definition was an understanding of not just how the new should meet the old, but of how the building's scars record its troubled past; and how these, once revealed, could be preserved as a 'living museum' for future generations. The Russian graffiti are a vital part of the Reichstag's troubled story.

At the time of writing, however, voices on the political Right are being raised in favour of eradicating this record. Wolfgang Zeitlmann of Bavaria's Christian Social Union has gone so far as to suggest that these graffiti are morally offensive, something better painted over and forgotten. I can think of no more compelling reason for retaining them than the fact that – more than half a century after the event – they still have the power to inspire such an emotion. It is important that we remember the tragedies and traumas of the past, and that we stand ready to draw lessons from history, even as we look forward eagerly to the future.

245

Reichstag chronology

The history of the Reichstag is almost the history of Germany itself, so closely has this deeply symbolic building been associated with events at the heart of German national life. The following chronology is therefore not narrowly confined to dates specific to the building itself, but is contextualised by key dates in German history and events that have impacted on the German Parliament — as both the Reichstag and the Bundestag — which have affected the life of the building more generally.

18 January 1871 Following the defeat of France in the Franco-Prussian War, King Wilhelm of Prussia declares himself emperor of a unified Germany in the Hall of Mirrors at Versailles.

1871–72 An architectural competition is held for a building to house the Reichstag, the new Imperial Parliament. Ludwig Bohnstedt wins first prize and George Gilbert Scott second. The scheme founders when Count Raczynski, owner of the proposed site on the Königsplatz beside the River Spree, refuses to relinquish his property until after his death. The Reichstag meets in its temporary home at the converted Royal Prussian Porcelain Manufactory on the Leipzigerstrasse.

1882 After years of wrangling following Count Racynski's death in 1874, the site for the Reichstag building is acquired and a second competition is held. The Frankfurt-based

28 July 1914 The assassination of Archduke Franz Ferdinand of Austria-Hungary by a Serb nationalist sparks the outbreak of World War I. The network of alliances that binds the European powers brings Germany and Austria-Hungary into conflict with Russia, France and Britain.

December 1916 The inscription *Dem Deutschen Volke* ('To the German People'), designed by architect Peter Behrens, is unveiled on the Reichstag's west portico. The letters are cast from bronze cannon captured from Napoleonic troops at the Battle of Leipzig in 1813. The *Spandauer Zeitung* newspaper for Sunday 23 December announces: 'A Christmas present for the German people'.

9 November 1918 With Germany facing imminent defeat in World War I, Kaiser Wilhelm II abdicates and emigrates to the Netherlands. Social Democrat leader Philipp Scheidemann declares a German Republic from a Reichstag balcony: 'The old and the rotten have broken down. Long live the new! Long live the German Republic!'

6 January 1919 The Reichstag is attacked by Communists supporting the Spartacus Uprising. The building is occupied and defended by troops loyal to the new Social Democratic leadership.

6 February 1919 Political unrest and street fighting in Berlin force Parliament to abandon the Reichstag building and meet in provincial Weimar, where a new constitution is later passed.

248

1930

1946

1961

architect Paul Wallot wins. He later writes: 'The building is primarily intended for practical use and the design reflects this. At the same time, it had to fulfil ideals of what is great or elevating. As a rule, grand and monumental interiors are not comfortable; a compromise had to be found, therefore, between two conflicting but equally justified demands'.

9 June 1884 The Reichstag's foundation stone is laid by Wilhelm I and construction of the new building begins.

1889 Following interference from Kaiser Wilhelm I and the Building Commission, Paul Wallot submits a new design for the Reichstag's dome, constructed from steel and glass in place of the original stone.

5 December 1894 Kaiser Wilhelm II performs the topping-out ceremony at the Reichstag. He privately dubs it the 'Imperial ape house' (*Reichsaffenhaus*). Architect Ludwig Hoffmann, Wallot's contemporary, describes the building as 'a first-class hearse'. The building has a volume of 400,000 cubic metres and a net usable area of 12,000 square metres with a parliamentary chamber capable of seating 400 MPs.

1900 The Reichstag's interior decoration is completed and the final art works are installed.

1901 The Bismarck memorial, designed by Reinhold Begas, is erected in the Königsplatz in front of the Reichstag.

1912 Already too small by the time of its inauguration, the Reichstag is extended by enlarging the roof structure to provide an additional floor of offices.

30 September 1919 Parliament resumes assembly in the Reichstag but one week later the SPD chairman, Hugo Haase, is fatally wounded by a gunman in front of the building.

13 March 1920 The Conservative Freikorps leader Wolfgang Kapp stages a putsch and seizes the capital. The Reichstag is briefly occupied. Berliners organise a general strike and the putsch fails.

24 June 1922 Jewish Foreign Minister Walter Rathenau is assassinated by right-wing extremists, infuriated by the left-wing minister's negotiations with the Soviet Government at the Treaty of Rapallo.

1927 A competition is launched for the enlargement of the Reichstag. The brief is unsatisfactory and there is no result.

1929 A second competition is held to extend the Reichstag but economic and political crises prevent its implementation.

14 September 1930 In national elections the Nazis win 107 Reichstag seats, becoming Germany's second largest political party.

31 July 1932 Following President Paul von Hindenburg's dissolution of the failing government, the Nazis win 230 Reichstag seats in new national elections, becoming the largest political party in Germany.

30 August 1932 Hermann Göring, former leader of the Nazi SA, becomes President of the Reichstag.

30 January 1933 Nazi Leader Adolf Hitler becomes Chancellor of Germany at the invitation of President Paul von Hindenburg.

27 February 1933 The Reichstag chamber is mysteriously destroyed by fire. A Dutch 'vagrant', Martinus van der Lubbe, is arrested in the building and charged with arson. The crime is used as a pretext to arrest many leading Communists accused of conspiring in the plot. The deputies henceforth meet in the nearby Kroll Opera House.

1933–39 The Reichstag building's dome is reglazed and the building partially restored. It is used for propaganda purposes, including two exhibitions, 'The Eternal Jew' and 'The Bolshevik Terror'.

1937–41 Under Adolf Hitler's patronage, Albert Speer creates plans for rebuilding Berlin as 'Germania'. The Reichstag is to be refurbished as a parliamentary library within a new government quarter, featuring a huge new assembly hall, the *Grosse Halle*, capable of holding 180,000 people.

1 September 1939 Outbreak of World War II.

Autumn 1940 Following heavy bombing raids on Berlin, the city authorities order a maternity shelter to be created in the Reichstag.

1941 The Reichstag's corner towers are equipped as anti-aircraft positions. Towards the end of the year, the library and archive are emptied, making way for the building's transformation into a military medical archive.

9 September 1948 West Berlin Mayor Ernst Reuter addresses over 300,000 citizens gathered in front of the Reichstag to demonstrate against the blockade. He declares: 'We cannot be bartered, we cannot be negotiated, we cannot be sold ... People of the world, look upon this city!'

12 May 1949 The Berlin blockade is lifted.

23 May 1949 The western zones of Germany are formed into an independent democratic state, the Federal Republic of Germany, and the capital moves to Bonn. Berlin remains divided between the four occupying powers with its eastern sector serving as capital of Soviet Germany.

7 October 1949 The Soviet zone of Germany becomes the German Democratic Republic.

22 November 1954 Having been declared unsafe, the steel frame of the ruined Reichstag dome is successfully demolished; cold weather had thwarted an earlier attempt on 23 October.

1955–57 The Bundestag regularly debates the question of rebuilding the Reichstag and founds the *Bundesbaudirektion* (BBD) to deal with the issue.

6 February 1957 The Bundestag votes to spend DM2.5 million on making safe and conserving the Reichstag. Work begins immediately on clearing rubble, conserving the facade, lowering the four corner towers and placing a temporary roof over the void left by the loss of the dome.

1979

1995

1999

4 April 1942 The great bronze chandelier from the Reichstag's octagonal entrance hall is sent to Hamburg to be melted down for armaments.

9 March 1945 As Allied armies close in on Berlin, concrete emplacements are built around the Reichstag as part of the preparations for the defence of the *Zitadelle*, the very heart of the city.

30 April 1945 Soviet troops launch an attack on the Reichstag, blasting holes in its bricked-up openings with heavy artillery, before occupying the building. The Red Flag is raised above the east portico at 10.50pm, achieving Stalin's command that a flag should be raised on the Reichstag in the name of the Red Army by 1 May.

2 May 1945 Russian Colonel-General Chuikov accepts the surrender of Berlin from General Weidling.

8 May 1945 VE Day. Field Marshal Keitel signs Germany's final act of capitulation.

3 July 1945 Germany is divided into American, French, Soviet and British occupation zones. Berlin becomes an 'island city' located in the Soviet zone in the east, but administered by the four Allies. The Allied Government meets in Berlin but not in the Reichstag.

24 June 1948 Following the collapse of the four-power administration of Germany, the Soviet Union cuts the electricity supply and all road and rail connections to West Berlin in an attempt to force it to join the Communist Bloc. Air is the only remaining supply route and the largest airlift in history in launched.

1957 The Federal Government decides that Berlin should be the German capital after reunification. A competition, 'Capital Berlin', is launched for the rebuilding of the Spreebogen as a government district. Bundestag President Ludwig Gerstenmaier leads the movement for the Reichstag's restoration as a temporary seat of the West German Bundestag, saying: 'We are not rich enough in traditional buildings to consider not rebuilding this ruin ... One must also have the courage not to brush aside painful memories ... [but] I am not for domes and towers and old hoo-ha'.

1960 The Minister for Current Affairs announces a limited competition in which ten architects are asked to submit proposals for the restoration of the Reichstag.

January 1961 Paul Baumgarten is commissioned to refurbish the Reichstag.

13 August 1961 The Berlin Wall is erected, blocking movement from Communist East Berlin to the West. The Reichstag is located beside the Wall in West Berlin, in the British military sector, but 39 metres of its east facade is technically in the Soviet military sector.

21 March 1971 The rebuilt Reichstag is opened exactly 100 years after the establishment of the Imperial Parliament. It has a completely new assembly hall, 650 seats for MPs, and a reception hall for 1500. Additional floor levels increase the net usable area to 17,000 square metres. A permanent exhibition, *Fragen an die deutsche Geschichte* ('Questions on German History') opens at the same time. The Reichstag is also used for other special exhibitions, ceremonial events and congresses.

3 September 1971 Under the Quadripartite Agreement on Berlin, the Soviet Union vetoes meetings of the Bundestag in Berlin. Ties between the Federal Republic of Germany and West Berlin are recognised but West Berlin remains a separate entity, under Allied control .

1972 The Bulgarian artist Christo makes his first collage for 'Wrapped Reichstag, Project for Berlin'.

7-8 July 1984 Austrian multimedia artist André Heller stages a spectacular music and firework show outside the Reichstag, intended to be seen by East Berliners.

19 June 1988 Michael Jackson performs to massive crowds in front of the Reichstag, yards from the Berlin Wall.

9 November 1989 With East German refugees flooding to the West via Hungary and Czechoslovakia, and continuing mass protests within the GDR, Gunter Schabowski, East Berlin's Party Chief, makes a surprise announcement at his weekly press conference: that East Germans are allowed to cross directly into West Germany with immediate effect. The Berlin Wall is demolished after 28 years. Celebrations take place in front of the Reichstag. The Polish Solidarity paper *Gazeta Wyborcza* writes: 'In Berlin, the heart of Europe has triumphed in the dispute between freedom and barbed wire'.

18 March 1990 The first free elections to the East German Chamber of Deputies are held.

31 August 1990 The Unification Treaty between the Federal Republic of Germany and

26 June 1992 Competition documents are dispatched. The brief calls for 33,039 square metres of space — almost twice the amount provided by the existing Reichstag. Parliament sets summer 2000 as the target date for its move to Berlin.

23 October 1992 Eighty entries are submitted to the Reichstag competition.

30 October 1992 The Bundestag moves into Günter Behnisch's new Parliament building in Bonn, but is forced to return temporarily to its old home in the Waterworks building due to problems with the new building's acoustics.

7-8 January 1993 First session of the Reichstag competition jury.

27-29 January 1993 A second session of the Reichstag jury awards joint first prize to Pi de Bruijn, Santiago Calatrava and Norman Foster. Foster receives 75 per cent of the vote, but requires a unanimous vote to win outright, hence the decision to award a joint first prize.

19 February 1993 The results of the Reichstag competition are officially announced. On the same day Berlin-based architects Axel Schultes and Charlotte Frank are declared winners of the Spreebogen masterplan competition.

12-13 March 1993 A second colloquium takes place in the Reichstag chamber in order to test public and political opinion.

25 March 1993 The Council of Elders decides that there should be a second stage to the Reichstag competition.

250

1898

1940

1945

the GDR is finalised, stating: 'The capital of Germany shall be Berlin. The seat of Parliament and government shall be decided after the establishment of German unity'.

3 October 1990 Germany is formally reunified.

20 December 1990 The united German Parliament opens the Twelfth Legislative Period of the Bundestag in the Reichstag building.

20 June 1991 The German Parliament narrowly votes for Berlin as the future seat of government with 338 for and 320 against. Dr Wolfgang Schäuble of the CDU Party says: 'The symbol of unity and freedom, of democracy and the rule of law was always, like no other city, Berlin'.

30 October 1991 The Council of Elders votes to restore the Reichstag as the seat of the united German Parliament.

14-15 February 1992 First Reichstag colloquium.

22 April 1992 The *Bundesbaudirektion* (BBD) announces a competition for the conversion of the Reichstag building. It is open to all German architects; in addition, fourteen international architects are invited: Pi de Bruijn (the Netherlands), Santiago Calatrava (Switzerland), Dissing & Weitling (Denmark), Norman Foster (UK), Coop Himmelblau (Austria), Hans Hollein (Austria), Helmut Jahn (USA), Juha Leiviska (Finland), Fumihiko Maki (Japan), José Rafael Moneo (Spain), Jean Nouvel (France), I M Pei (USA), Aldo Rossi (Italy), Jiri Suchomel (CSFR).

29 April 1993 The three competition winners are briefed by the Building Committee in Bonn, chaired by Dr Dietmar Kansy. They are asked to revise their schemes to suit a new brief with the total area reduced from 33,039 square metres to 9-12,000 square metres.

21 June 1993 The Building Committee meets to judge the three revised proposals. Foster receives sixteen of the eighteen votes cast, de Bruijn receives two and Calatrava none.

1 July 1993 The Council of Elders declares Foster the winner.

September 1993 The Bundestag moves back into the Behnisch Parliament building in Bonn after the initial acoustics problems are resolved.

9 September 1993 Foster is asked to produce a 'dome study'. He refuses outright to contemplate reconstructing the historical dome in replica, but includes an analysis and costing for the reconstruction for comparative purposes.

10 September 1993 Parliament founds the *Bundesbaugesellschaft Berlin* (BBB), an independently run development company, 50 per cent government owned, to act as client on its behalf for the construction and management of the new buildings in the Spreebogen area.

14 January 1994 The German Government allocates DM20 billion to move Parliament, government and the civil service to Berlin.

4 February 1994 A cost limit of DM600 million is established for the conversion of the Reichstag. Cost savings are required to meet the budget.

25 February 1994 The Bundestag approves proposals by Christo and Jeanne-Claude to wrap the Reichstag. It is the first time in history that the existence of a future work of art is debated and voted on in a parliament. The voting is 292 in favour, 223 against, with 9 abstentions. Speaking for the group Alliance 90/Greens, Konrad Weiss says: 'We ourselves will become part of Christo's work of art ... There is no disgrace in the wrapping. It is an expression of reverence and creates an opportunity for contemplation of the essential ... Through the wrapping, we will be reminded of what has passed in this building — the creation, downfall and rebirth of democracy'.

26 April 1994 Legislation is finalised concerning the future governmental roles of Berlin and Bonn. Eleven ministries will go to Berlin and five will remain in Bonn.

28 April 1994 The Building Committee meets at the Reichstag. Conservative MP Oscar Schneider produces an engineering study by Berlin architect Georg Kohlmeier, claiming that rebuilding the historical dome is technically feasible. The Building Committee asks Foster to produce a 'modern dome'.

16 June 1994 Foster presents two alternatives for a structure rising above the roof: a glazed, drum-like form known as the 'lighthouse' and a cupola with a truncated top.

2 February 1995 At the suggestion of the Building Committee, Foster presents a cupola design fully rounded at the top, alongside an earlier option for a cupola with a flat top.

9 March 1995 The Bundestag votes in favour of Foster's 'rounded-up' dome.

June 1997 Construction of the cupola begins.

16 July 1997 Their Majesties the King and Queen of Spain visit the Reichstag. The King presents two copies of the Spanish constitution, one historical (1812) and one post-Franco (1978), to Bundestag President Rita Süssmuth.

18 September 1997 A traditional 'topping-out' ceremony is held. The building is opened to the public for two days and receives 60,000 visitors.

14 January 1998 The eagle and a mock-up of the chamber including furniture is presented to Chancellor Kohl. He requests the introduction of bright colour into the building.

6 March 1998 Danish graphic artist Per Arnoldi joins Norman Foster to present proposals for the use of colour in the Reichstag's principal rooms.

June 1998 The Building Committee decides to retain the eagle designed by Ludwig Gies for the Reichstag chamber. It is modified by Norman Foster to suit new spatial conditions and for the first time is viewed from two sides, front and back.

27 September 1998 In German Federal elections the SPD wins a majority and forms a Red-Green coalition. Gerhard Schröder becomes Chancellor.

10 November 1998 In his inaugural speech, Chancellor Gerhard Schröder says: 'For many, Berlin sounds too Prussian and too authoritarian, too centralist ... [but] we are taking a lively and stable democracy to Berlin ... at the centre of Germany and the centre of Europe'.

1979

1995

1999

16 June 1995 Christo and Jeanne-Claude begin final preparations for 'Wrapped Reichstag'. A lightweight steel structure is erected around the building, and a team of riggers cloaks the building with silver polypropylene fabric secured with blue ropes.

23 June-6 July 1995 'Wrapped Reichstag' sparks a two-week popular festival in Berlin.

7 July 1995 Christo's fabric is removed and demolition of the Reichstag's 1960s structure begins.

October 1995 The chamber and central area of the building are finally demolished. With 240 workers on site, 45,000 tonnes of demolition material are removed over four months, in 35 truckloads per day. Altogether one-third of the existing fabric of the Reichstag is removed, including all its technical installations.

13 March 1996 With demolition complete, the shell and core contractor begins construction of the steel and concrete primary structure.

April 1996 At a Building Committee meeting Norman Foster is given a personal commission to design the eagle for the new Reichstag chamber.

December 1996 Meetings of the Parliamentary Art Committee are established to begin commissioning artists for the Reichstag.

May 1997 General steel and concrete works are completed. Contractors' drawings are submitted for checking, verification and adjustment. More than 25 separate trade contractors are now at work in the Reichstag.

17 December 1998 New Bundestag President Wolfgang Thierse unveils the eagle.

25 February 1999 To test lighting and acoustics, 1100 soldiers from the Bundeswehr visit the chamber to simulate a live parliamentary session.

19 April 1999 The official handover of the Reichstag building to Parliament. Norman Foster presents a symbolic key to Bundestag President Wolfgang Thierse. The first session of the house begins at 12.00 noon. Chancellor Gerhard Schröder says: 'The move to Berlin is not a break in the continuity of German history ... The success of the Bonn democracy, the politics of understanding and good neighbourliness, a firm anchorage in Europe and the Atlantic Alliance, as well as the aura of life lived in freedom, have all helped make possible the Berlin Republic in a unified Germany ... We are going forward to the centre of Europe'. Former Chancellor Helmut Kohl says: 'For me it's a day of great joy. I have worked all my life for this'.

21-25 April 1999 Public open days; over 150,000 people visit the Reichstag.

26 April 1999 The Reichstag's roof terrace and restaurant are opened to the public.

23 May 1999 Social Democrat Johannes Rau is elected Federal President and promises to be the leader 'of all Germans and all those living and working in Germany'.

24 May 1999 The 50th anniversary of the Federal Republic is celebrated in the Reichstag.

1 September 1999 Administrative staff officially begin working in the Reichstag.

8 September 1999 The Bundestag commences regular plenary sessions in the Reichstag.

Credits

The team in Foster and Partners' Berlin studio spell out a greeting for Norman Foster's sixtieth birthday on 1 June 1995. Opposite: The Reichstag team gathered in front of the Reichstag as Christo's 'wraps' come off on 7 July 1995.

252

Foster and Partners project team
Norman Foster, David Nelson, Mark Braun, Stefan Behling, Christian Hallmann, Ulrich Hamann, Dieter Müller, Ingo Pott, Mark Sutcliffe

Christofer Allerkamp, Claudia Ayaz, Nick Baker, John Ball, Tanya von Barnau, Alexander Barry, Stephan Baumgart, Simon Beames, Serge Belet, Susanne Bellinghausen, Nicola Bielski, Toby Blunt, Etienne Borgos, Giuseppe Boscherini, Simon Bowden, Arthur Branthwaite, George Brennan, Caroline Brown, Kevin Carrucan, Hing Chan, Kei-Lu Cheong, Rachel Clark, Charles Collett, Mark-Andrew Costello, Brian Thomas Ditchburn, Ilona Dohn, Ivo Dolezalek, Robert Dörr, John Drew, Constance Edwards, Benjamin Ellwanger, Matteo Fantoni, Henri Louis Ferretti, Anja Flesch, Mark Ford, Kevin Galvin, Susanne Geiger, Xenia Genth, Martin Geyer, Russell Gilchrist, Frank Glaesener, Ulrich Goertz, Helen Goodland, Niall

Greenan, Nigel Greenhill, Tanya Griffiths, Daniela Grijakovic, Adelheid Gross, Pedro Haberbosch, Brandon Haw, Andreas Hell, Oliver Hempel, Anne Hengst, Wendelin Hinsch, Robert Hoh, Alison Holroyd, Wiliam Hunt, Ken Hutt, Martin Hyams, Thomas Ibach, Helmut Jacoby, Nadi Jahangiri, Michael Jakob, Adrienne Johnson, Rebecca Jones, Ralph Klabunde, Dirk Koslowski, Carsten Krohn, Madeline Lee, Ian Lomas, Ellen van Loon, Andrea Ludwig, Valérie Lutton-Laub, Alan Marten-Wilkinson, Giles Martin, David McDowell, Emma McHugh, Michelle Meier, Rudi Meisel, Olaf Menk, Andreas Mertens, Jons Messedat, Julia Mooney, Max Neal, Uwe Nienstedt, Matthew Parker, Sunil Parmar, Robin Partington, Simon Peckham, Nikki Pipe, Andrea Platena, Tony Price, Adam Pritchard, Dagmar Quentin, Michael Richter, Tilman Richter von Senfft, Jan Roth, Matthias Rudolph, Sans Ruiz Montserrat, Gudrun Sack, John de Salvo,

Peer Schärer, Robert Schmid, Paul Scott, Wei Y Seah, Rupert Sherwood, Ken Shuttleworth, John Small, Paul Sommer, Kinna Stallard, Kai Strehl, Henning Stummel, Bernd Treide, Huw Turner, Ruggero Venelli, Juan Vieira, Wilhelm Vossenkuhl, Ken Wai, Robert Watson, Antoine Weygand, Rolf Wiethege, John Michael Zeuner

Client
Federal Republic of Germany represented by Bundes-baugesellschaft Berlin mbH

Consultants
Acoustics Müller BBM GmbH, IKP Professor Dr Georg Plenge
Catering Facilities LZ Plan-Team
Cladding Consultants Emmer Pfenninger Partner AG
Conservation Consultants Acanthus
Fire Protection Professor W Klingsch
Lifts, Materials, Handling Technology Jappsen & Stangier
Lighting Claude and Danielle Engle

Mechanical, Electrical and Environmental Services Planungsgemeinschaft Technik GmbH, Amstein & Walthert, Fischer – Energie and Haustechnik, Kaiser Bautechnik, Kuehn Bauer and Partner, Planungsgruppe Karnasch-Hackstein, Hock & Kaletta
Project Management ARGE Projektsteuerung Reichstag, Professor Weiß & Partner und Weidleplan
Quantity Surveyors Davis Langdon & Everest
Quantity Surveyor, Site Supervision Büro Am Lützowplatz
Structural Engineer Leonhardt Andrä and Partner, Ove Arup & Partners, Schlaich Bergermann & Partner
Visual Communication Buro für Gestaltung

Suppliers and Subcontractors
Acoustic Blinds Clauss Markisen GmbH
Alarm Systems BOSCH TELECOM Leipzig GmbH, Telenorma VN Berlin

Asbestos Removal ARGE Reichstag Berlin-Asbest, E Schütze GmbH, HAKAP-Berlin GmbH
Carpets Anker Teppichfabrik, Gebrüder Scholler GmbH + Co KG
Chairs Howe A/S, Tecno SA, Gebrüder Thonet GmbH, Walter Knoll, Vitra GmbH
Core and Shell ARGE Hochbau Reichstag, Ed. Züblin AG, Dechant Bau GmbH, Löhn Hochbau
Demolition ARGE Rückbau Reichstag, Ingenieur-und Tiefbau GmbH
Door Handles Valli & Valli Fusital
Dome Construction and Cladding ARGE Reichstagskuppel, Waagner-Biro GmbH Wien
Electrical Systems Elektro-Anlagenbau Wismar GmbH
Facades and Windows ARGE Götz GmbH/Dillingen, Waagner-Biro GmbH München/Wien
Fireproofing Svt Brandschutz GmbH, Total Walther
Fit-Out – Ceilings, Render, Dry Walls Klaus Rogge GmbH, Spezialtiefbau
Fit-Out – Chamber Lindner AG
Fit-Out – Counters Ostfriesische

Möbelwerkstätten
Fit-Out – Wall Panels, Doors, Built-in Elements Vereinigte Holzbaubetriebe, W Pfalzer und H Voyt
Furniture Artemide, Cassina SpA, Fritz Hausen A/S, Knoll International, Tecno SA, Wilkhahm GmbH & Co
Glass Panels BGT Bischoff Glastechnik GmbH & Co KG
Glass Walls and Internal Doors Magnus Müller GmbH & Co KG
Kitchen Equipment ARGE Elektrolux Professional GmbH, Therma Großküchen GmbH ARGE (Großküchentechnische Einrichtungen), Therma Großküchen

Lifts Fujitec, Deutschland GmbH
Lighting – Dome BEGA, Gantenbrink Leuchten GmbH
Lighting – Interiors ERCO Leuchten GmbH
Locks and Keys Weckbacher GmbH
Maintenance and Cleaning Systems Greifzug GmbH
M+E – Heat Storage Drilling and Planning BLM Gesellschaft für Bohrlochphysik und geoökologische Messungen mbH, E+M, Bohr-und Brunnenbau GmbH
Metal Ceilings Gefatec GmbH, Haver & Boecker
Metalwork Kirchgässner E-Technik GmbH, Trube & Kings,

Metallbau mbH
Model Maker Atelier 36 GbR, Foster and Partners model shop
PA Systems, Telephones Siemens AG
Painting and Coating Eisenschutz Otto Buchloh, Brandenburg GmbH
PV Cells Engotec GmbH
Raised Floors and Screed Fa Burkhardt GmbH & Co
Restoration – Internal Stone Facades Ellwart Steinrestaurierung
Roof Cladding Dachdecker GmbH, Schulze & Sohn
Room Control Panels Weidmüller GmbH + Co
Signage Schilder Gerlach GmbH

Stone Cladding – Walls and Floors Kiefer-Reul-Teich Naturstein
Stone Reconstruction FX Rauch KG, Naturstein am Bau
Tiling Rabe Fliesen-und Marmor-Centrum
Ventilation, Air Conditioning, Sprinkler Systems, Plumbing, Heating ARGE Reichstagsgebäudetechnik, Nickel/WLG/K-U-Z, Heinrich Nickel GmbH
Xenon Lights – Dome MP Pesch

Book Production Credits
Editorial: David Jenkins, Philippa Baker, Gerard Forde, Kenneth Powell, Christine Davis, Amiyo Ruhnke

Design: Mark Vernon-Jones
Picture Research: Sophie Hartley, Katy Harris, Elizabeth Walker, Ingo Pott, Jan Roth
Research: Kate Stirling, Sarah Wedderburn
Drawings: Andrew Birds, Richard Portchmouth, Michael Russum, Ted Neilan, John Hewitt, Michail Blösser
Translation: Caroline Gutbrod, Marika Monnier
History Consultants: Dr P Lemburg, Wolfram Schwachulla, Professor Dr Wilhelm Vossenkuhl
Photographers: Rudi Meisel, Richard Bryant, Dennis Gilbert, Michael Westmoreland, Nigel Young

Index

Page numbers in *italic* refer to the illustrations.

Picture Credits

l = left, m = middle, r = right, t = top, b = bottom
Thanks are due to the following for permission to reproduce copyright photographs and drawings:

Drawings and Diagrams
AKG London: 38 (1)
Courtesy of The Architectural Archives, University of Pennsylvania: 166 (2)
Berliner Morgenpost: 86 (83)
Klaus Böhle, *Die Welt*: 141 (40)
British Architectural Library, RIBA, London: 38 (2), 169 (14), 173 (30)
DACS: 173 (31)
Das Neue Berlin, Martin Wagner (ed.), Deutsche Bauzeitung, 1929, courtesy of Kunstbibliothek Berlin: 46 (24-26)
Das Reichstagsgebäude in Berlin, Cosmos Verlag, Leipzig 1897, reprinted Büscher-Repro, Bielefeld, 1987: 38 (3), 39 (5, 6), 42 (14), 43 (18), 180 (9, 10)
Fondation le Corbusier © FLC/ADAGP, Paris and DACS, London: 166 (3), 171 (24)
Norman Foster: 24 (28), 26 (32, 35, 36), 27 (39, 41, 43), 29 (51), 32 (57, 58), 33 (60), 73 (39, 44), 74 (45, 47), 75 (51, 52), 78 (64), 85 (78, 80), 132 (1, 2), 133 (4, 6), 136 (14, 18), 137 (22, 27, 30), 139 (37), 153 (70), 158 (88), 212 (10), 213 (12, 13), 244
Foster and Partners: 18 (12), 26 (33, 37), 28 (45, 48), 29 (50), 30 (54), 33 (61), 50/51 (37), 51 (40), 62 (1, 5), 63 (6, 9), 66 (20), 68 (26-29), 69 (30, 31), 70 (32-35), 87 (85-89), 90 (91-95), 91 (96-101), 92 (102-107), 93 (108, 109), 96/97 (112), 100 (118, 119), 100/101 (121), 101 (120), 106 (127-129), 106/107 (130), 135 (10, 11), 148 (63, 64) 148/149 (65),

149 (66), 154 (73-78), 156 (82), 157 (84), 166 (1), 178 (2, 3), 179 (5-8), 184 (25-29), 187 (36), 188 (37, 38)
Hachfield, *Neues Deutschland*: 141 (42)
Helmut Jacoby: 32 (56)
David Nelson: 134 (7, 8)
Schoenfled, *Hamburger Abendblatt*: 86 (82)
Klaus Stuttman, *Leipziger Volkszeitung*: 141 (41)

Photographs
AKG London: 44 (19), 45 (20), 47 (29, 30), 48 (33, 34), 52 (42, 43), 118 (1), 121 (13, 14), 124 (29), 169 (16), 199 (21), 200/201 (24), 203 (27, 29), 234 (4), 235 (8), 250 (l, m)
AKG London/Gert Schütz: 56 (58), 238 (10)
Courtesy of The Architectural Archives, University of Pennsylvania: 167 (6), 168 (10)
Archivbeständen der BBB, Deutscher Bundestag Berlin: 123 (26), 194 (3)
Berlin – Bilder der dreißiger Jahre, Berlin, Verlag Jürgen Schacht, 1995: 234 (3)
Berlinische Galerie: 120 (7), 121 (10, 11, 15)
Bildarchiv Foto, Marburg: 172 (28), 173 (29)
Bildarchiv Preußischer Kulturbesitz, Berlin: 45 (22), 47 (28), 48 (31), 51 (39), 52 (41), 55 (52), 118 (2, 3), 121 (12, 16, 17), 124 (28), 195 (7, 8), 234 (1, 2), 236/237 (9)
Richard Bryant: 22 (22), 83 (75), 98 (113), 105 (125), 108 (131), 109 (134), 111 (136, 137), 112 (138), 113 (140), 131, 153 (71), 210 (3), 216 (27), 217 (28), 223 (46), 226 (58), 227 (60)
Bundesarchiv, Koblenz: 42 (13), 43 (16), 240 (19)
Das Reichstagsgebäude in Berlin, Cosmos Verlag, Leipzig 1897, reprinted Büscher-Repro, Bielefeld, 1987: 40 (7-10), 41 (11), 118 (4), 120 (6),

120 (9), 172 (25)
Richard Davies: 22 (23), 26 (38), 27 (40, 42, 44), 28 (46, 47), 136 (17, 20), 137 (25, 26, 28), 138 (33-35), 139 (36), 251 (l)
Deutscher Bundestag Berlin, M Krajewsky: 81 (70), 82 (73), 194 (4)
Deutsches Historisches Museum -GmbH, Berlin: 54 (45)
Fondation le Corbusier © FLC/ADAGP, Paris and DACS, London: 166 (4), 168 (9), 172 (26)
Norman Foster: 16 (3), 17 (8)
Foster and Partners: 20 (19, 20), 25 (27, 29, 30), 61, 62 (2-4), 63 (7, 8), 86 (84), 88/89 (90), 135 (9)
Hulton Getty: 37
Dennis Gilbert: 6, 18 (9-11), 19 (14, 16), 80 (66), 85 (79), 94 (110), 94/95 (111), 102/103 (122), 104 (123), 105 (126), 110 (135), 112 (139), 152 (68), 153 (72), 157 (85), 178 (4), 210 (4), 213 (16), 215 (23), 219 (36), 225 (53), 228/229
John Gollings, Melbourne, courtesy Mitchell/Giurgola Thorp Architects, Canberra: 167 (5), 168 (11)
Reinhard Görner: 221 (41), Lucien Hervé, FLC/ADAGP, Paris and DACS, London: 170 (19)
Image Bank/Antony Edwards: 186 (32)
Imperial War Museum, London: 53 (44)
Christian Kandzia, courtesy Behnisch & Partner Architects, Stuttgart: 169 (15)
Ken Kirkwood: 16 (4), 17 (5)
Gerlind Klemens: 194 (1, 2), 196 (9, 10, 12), 198 (17, 18)
Klemens Köhler: 195 (5, 6)
Ian Lambot: 17 (6), 19 (15), 178 (1)
Landesbildstelle, Berlin: 39 (4), 42 (12, 15), 49 (36), 54 (46-51), 55 (53-56), 56 (60, 61), 66 (19), 67 (21-25), 81 (69), 98 (115), 123 (20-22), 196 (11), 233, 248 (l, m)
Lehnartz-Fotografie, Berlin: 123

(24), 124 (27), 239 (14), 240 (16-18), 246/247
G Löwendahl, Stockholm City Museum: 167 (7)
Magnum Photos Ltd: 250 (r)
Magnum Photos Ltd/ Erich Lessing: 238 (11)
Magnum Photos Ltd/David Seymour: 202 (25)
Magnum Photos Ltd/Dennis Stock: 211 (5)
Rudi Meisel: 7, 8, 12, 16 (1, 2), 22 (24, 25), 23 (26), 25 (31), 58/59, 64 (10-13), 64 (14-17), 72 (36, 37), 73 (38, 40-43), 74 (46, 48), 75 (49, 51), 76 (53-56), 77 (57-60), 114/115, 126 (32-35), 127 (36-39), 128/129, 139 (38), 140 (39), 142 (43-46), 143 (47-50), 144 (51-56), 145 (57-61), 146/147 (62), 150/151 (67), 156/157 (83), 162/163, 165, 169 (17), 173 (32), 174/175, 181 (16), 183 (21-24), 186 (33-35), 190/191, 206/207, 210 (1, 2), 212 (6, 8, 9), 213 (14, 17, 18), 214 (19-22), 215 (24-26), 217 (29, 31), 218 (32-35), 220 (37-40), 222 (42-45), 224 (48-50), 225 (51, 52), 225 (54, 55), 226 (56-59), 230/231, 242/243
Tom Miller: 26 (34), 30 (52, 53), 31 (55), 32 (59), 33 (62), 133 (5), 212 (7)
Novosti, London: 117, 120 (8), 193, 197 (13-16), 198 (19, 20), 199 (22)
Oltmann Reuter: 249 (r)
South American Pictures/Tony Morrison: 167 (8)
Courtesy of Albert Speer & Partner Architects, Frankfurt-am-Main: 50 (38)
Stiftung Archiv der Akademie der Künste/Sammlung Baukunst/Orgel-Köhne: 82 (72)
Tim Street-Porter: 17 (7)
Süddeutscher Verlag Bilderdienst: 235 (5)
Ullstein Bilderdienst: 43 (17), 45 (21, 23), 47 (27), 48 (32, 35), 55 (57), 56 (59), 66 (18), 119

(5), 122 (18), 123 (19, 23, 25), 124 (30), 125, (31), 199 (23), 203 (26, 28), 204 (30, 31, 32), 205 (33), 235 (6, 7), 238 (12), 239 (13), 241 (20), 249 (l)
Ullstein/Peter Georgi: 248 (r)
Ullstein/Günter Peters: 20 (17)
Ullstein/Günter Schneider: 20 (18), 21 (21)
Ullstein/Stephan Schraps: 239 (15)
Wolfgang Volz: 252 (l, r)
Maurice Weiss/Ostkreuz: 251 (r)
Antonia Weiße, Berlin; copyright Bundesamt für Bauwesen und Raumordnung, Berlin: 57 (62-64)
Michael Westmoreland: 152/153 (69)
Reimer Wulf, Elmshorn, Germany: 185 (30)
Jans-Joachim Wuthenow: 81 (67), 98 (116), 105 (124), 108 (133)
Nigel Young, Foster and Partners: 4, 15, 19 (13) 29 (49), 78 (61-63), 79 (65), 81 (68), 82 (71), 83 (74, 76), 84 (77), 85 (81), 98/99 (114), 99 (117), 108 (132), 132 (3), 136 (12, 13, 15, 16, 19, 21), 137 (23, 24, 29, 31, 32), 155 (79), 155 (80, 81), 158 (86, 87), 159 (89), 160/161 (90), 168 (12), 169 (13), 170 (20), 171 (21-23), 172 (27), 177, 180 (12), 181 (13-15), 182 (17-20), 186 (31), 188 (39), 189 (40), 209, 213 (11, 15), 217 (30), 224 (47)
Christo and Jeanne-Claude: Wrapped Reichstag, Berlin 1971-95:
Wolfgang Volz: 34 (bl), 249 (m), 251 (m). With special permission of Wolfgang Volz - Rudi Meisel: 10/11, 34/35, 25; Lehnartz-Fotografie, Berlin: 246/247

Every effort has been made to contact copyright holders and the publishers apologise for any omissions which they will be pleased to rectify at the earliest opportunity.